Satan Unmasked

Foreword by Tom Skinner

262 - Rapture
266 - Overcoming death

Earl Paulk

Copyright 1984
K Dimension Publishers
Atlanta, Georgia

Printed in the United States of America
Library of Congress Catalog Card Number: 84-82492
ISBN 0-917595-03-3

DEDICATION

To my father, Pastor Earl Paulk, Sr., who fought all opposition to speak the truth. Thank you for fearlessly living the words you proclaimed. Your example fixed my heart toward seeking the Kingdom of God and your life demonstrated the reality of the Gospel from my earliest memories.

To my mother, Addie Mae Tomberlin Paulk, who carefully cultivated the seeds of Kingdom life in her children. Thank you for firm gentleness, laughter, faith and love that pressed me toward faithfulness to God and instilled in me the responsibility to the calling of God on my life.

May the fruit of my life be worthy of such treasures from the Lord as you have given to me. I love you.

ACKNOWLEDGEMENTS

I want to thank the Publications Department of Chapel Hill Harvester Church for their daily efforts and faithfulness to the Lord in making this book possible.

I especially thank Tricia Weeks for diligent oversight and direction in rewriting and editing these manuscripts.

I sincerely appreciate the contributions of members of our Editorial Staff: Chris Oborne, Gail Smith and Gayle Blackwood; Assistant Editors: Beth Bonner, Joy Owens and LaDonna Paulk.

For all the technical aspects of producing this book, I thank Don Ross and Todd Cole for graphics, Wayne Henderson for word processing, and Donna Eubanks and Gail Smith for typesetting.

Finally, I am grateful for faithful volunteers who give their time and skills to the Lord in assisting in the Publications Department.

May the seeds of these words bear much fruit to the glory of Christ's Kingdom.

INTRODUCTION

Discernment is the mark of spiritual maturity and the time has come for the Church to grow up. Satan is hiding today behind the subtle mask of various scriptural interpretations. Conflicting interpretations of God's Word preached in pulpits around the world leave people confused as to the central message of the Church. Deception thwarts and defeats the influence of believers in the eyes of the world. Christians focus on their differences more than the message which has the revolutionary power to change the world and alter the hopeless downward spiral of social order. The Kingdom of God is born in revelation and not in interpretation.

When Christians reject revelation from God given by the Holy Spirit through the mouths of anointed apostles and prophets, they back away from the truth that God is speaking to this generation. What kind of faith do Christians demonstrate daily? Too many Christians choose a limited gospel message of good feelings, comfort and God's permissive will. Traditions, denominational doctrines and old religious patterns are comfortable and safe. Few believers press their lifestyles into actual Kingdom obedience and spiritual confrontations. Who willingly chooses combat and change? Who willingly gives away securities, social applause, approval and possessions for a greater cause requiring self-sacrifice?

God's soldiers in the world today are those who have ears to hear God's commands. They have a foretaste of the Kingdom of God in their mouths. Kingdom fulfillment is their meat and drink. They are moved to action by God's revealed Word which they willingly demonstrate. They listen for specific spiritual direction from the Holy Spirit and are easily prompted to do God's will. They are the heroes of a mighty war. They are the Overcomers who will unmask Satan.

Satan Unmasked is written to those who have ears to hear what the Spirit is saying to the Church in this generation. This book is written with one central goal: to mature the Church through spiritual discernment so that Jesus Christ can come again to find a mature Bride. The content of this book demands spiritual maturity in the reader. Revelation, fresh insights into God's Word, is the spiritual food for a mature Christian. The Church's maturity is essential to the most long-awaited event in the history of the Church and all creation — the return of Jesus Christ. Interpretation of revelation is served to the Church by called evangelists, pastors and teachers who break down God's Word so that even "little ones" can understand and apply Kingdom revelation to their lives.

Let no man deceive you by any means; for that Day will not come unless the falling away comes first, and the man of sin is revealed, the son of perdition, who opposes and exalts himself above all that is called God or that is worshiped, so that he sits as God in the temple of God, showing himself that he is God. (II Thessalonians 2:3-4)

The Church is responsible to take Satan off the throne and put Christ on the throne in worldly kingdoms. This is accomplished through a demonstration of God's alternatives which offer the world a choice between kingdoms of darkness and light. Our demonstration of Kingdom principles is more than a witness to the world. Our most vital witness is to powers and principalities of the air. That heavenly witness generates the tremendous warfare that we experience on earth.

Satan deceives Christians with spiritual mixture and issues which delay Kingdom demonstration. Satan's strategy is to discount the work of God in the Church and to examine constantly the human elements of ministry. Influences of humanism, grace without repentance, inaction instead of discipleship, and a concentration on the faults and failures of God's servants totally opposes God's purposes for His Church. Satan expertly attempts to destroy the unity of believers. No wonder that the world as well as Christians themselves are confused about the message they proclaim. No wonder the Church speaks with so many conflicting voices.

In spiritual battles we can no longer rely on any strength of the flesh. We must engage in heavenly warfare by inviting heavenly forces to join with us. War rages in the heavenlies and human life is a constant struggle. Before we can understand our roles in the conflict of both the dimensions of time and absolute timelessness in the spiritual realm, we must identify the forces in this all-encompassing battle. We must understand our choices and the eternal importance and consequences of those choices. Although all people participate in this battle regardless of their conscious recognition of it, only God's people can affect the outcome of the warfare intended to defeat the Saints in this generation.

Human beings are much more than insignificant pawns in some cruel, supernatural contest. Though few Christians actually live in the realization of their historical importance and potential, men and women who trust in Jesus Christ and are empowered by His Spirit have the opportunity of finalizing the victory in this ancient war.

The two battlegrounds of our warfare are the flesh and the spirit. Flesh warfare lasts a lifetime. Flesh warfare is usually obvious sins and the Church has concentrated on disciplines of the flesh for centuries with consistent standards of moral behavior. Spiritual deception is much less of a problem in warfare of the flesh than in spiritual warfare.

Warfare of the spirit is much more subtle. Spiritual sins begin with critical spirits which move quickly into manifestations of unbelief which affect Christians' lifestyles. Unbelief leads to spiritual deception which may or may not include rebellion against God's authority. Spiritual deception causes confusion and discouragement among God's people. Unchallenged deception can destroy the work of God in a local church. Deceived people are religious and sincere. They easily attract others to their arguments with their sincere convictions. The height of unbelief and the final degree of deception is blasphemy against the Holy Spirit. The process of critical spirits growing into sins of deception and blasphemy against God culminates Satan's devastating destruction in believers who "fall away."

Among Christians at all levels of spiritual maturity, God is looking across the earth for people He can trust. A new apostolic and prophetic authority will speak such clear words from God that God's people will clearly recognize Satan's strategies in warfare. Only spiritual discernment and prophetic insights can unmask Satan. Revelation gives direction from God. Revelation uncovers paths which seem "spiritual" when the end of those paths are self-serving instead of serving God and the coming of His Kingdom to earth.

As I have already stated, the Kingdom of God is born in revelation and not in interpretation. Neither our warfare nor our weapons are carnal. Warfare that establishes God's Kingdom on earth is that witness to powers and principalities in the spiritual realm. Heavenly beings are carefully noting the choices of God's people. The greatest warfare is waged against those who have committed their lives to fully following the Lord.

God's chosen people say and do the same things that Jesus's ministry demonstrated. We expose and overcome Satan just as Jesus did (I John 3:8). In spirits of meekness and humility, God's powerful warriors will be "wise as serpents and harmless as doves" in the final warfare of history. The meek shall inherit the earth!

Satan Unmasked is divided into three parts. I believe that this division will lead you, the reader, into an understanding that will give direction, purpose and power in your spiritual calling. Part one challenges the "status quo" of contemporary Christian thinking. God began to show me how much spiritual mixture has become acceptable to God's people throughout Church history. I discuss worldly kingdoms and the alternatives that the Church must offer the world in contrast to Satan's distortions, mixture and substitutions.

Part two sets the Church in order. I believe that God has given insights "for such a time as this" to give His people confidence and authority in warfare. Deception in the Church has left believers becoming gods unto themselves. Church leadership struggles without God's direction and power and the people of God are in confusion. How do we find God's "sure Word" for this hour? God designates those callings and ministries to speak His Word to the Church and His sheep know His voice.

The theme of part three is "in the fullness of time." Without a vision of Kingdom reality, we will never overcome the enemy. Maintaining revolutionary zeal and consistent, daily righteousness, peace and joy in the Holy Spirit insures spiritual endurance to the end of the age. Endurance depends on our vision. The realization of "Christ in us" is the volatile issue which signals the culmination of human history. Our daily faith and choices are the hope of creation. Part three presses the Bride of Christ toward maturity and readiness to welcome the Bridegroom.

Open the eyes of your heart to understanding. Ask God to confirm His truth in you. Blessed are those who hear and do that which God speaks by the Holy Spirit. We have the opportunity throughout all eternity to testify as those who are more than conquerors!

FOREWORD

By Tom Skinner

Earl Paulk is a twentieth century prophet. His book, **Satan Unmasked**, is a long overdue book for both believers and non-believers. Jesus taught His disciples to pray, "Our Father, who art in heaven, hallowed be Thy name. Your kingdom come, Your will be done on earth the way it is in heaven." Obviously in the mind of Jesus, there was something going on in heaven that He wanted to happen on earth. Heaven, for the sake of definition, is that sphere of influence where God is in control. What makes heaven "heaven," is that in heaven, Jesus is Lord. Everything is happening precisely the way God wants it to happen. So in heaven there is no war, there is no poverty, there is no violence, there is no oppression, there is no conflict, there are no broken relationships—all of these things are the works of the devil, and he has no influence in heaven.

That is obviously not true about earth, because on earth there is war, violence, hatred, conflict, oppression, poverty and hunger. Jesus is saying to the Church that we are to pray, ". . . that the Kingdom will come on earth the way it is in heaven." The Church is to be the live expression on earth of what is happening in heaven, so that anytime anyone wants to know what is going on in heaven, all they have to do is check with the people of God. The Church must become the presence of the Kingdom of God, the expression of the values of the Kingdom and the personification of the Lordship of Jesus on earth.

What makes it very difficult for this understanding to prevail in the Body of Christ today are several myths among the people of God that Bishop Paulk unveils.

— We should accept Jesus as our personal Savior then twiddle our thumbs waiting for the Kingdom to come. This has made the people of God very passive.

— The prevailing attitude that Satan himself fosters that he is the rightful owner of this world. The argument of this book, **Satan Unmasked,** is that when Christ was nailed to the cross, He rendered a fatal blow to Satan and that the people of God are to arrive on the territory that Satan claims is his and proclaim repentance because the Kingdom of heaven has arrived. In other words, if we believe that the kingdoms of this world are going to become the Kingdom of our Lord and of must begin that process now by taking the territory and modeling what it will look like.

— The false view is that the Kingdom is something in the distance and that we must allow evil to prevail in the world until that sudden moment when Christ will appear and rectify everything. Thus Satan has cleverly put up "No Trespassing" signs. Wherever he has a "No Trespassing" sign, the people of God have said, "That is off limits because Satan is in control." Yet Jesus tells us to occupy until He comes. The word "occupy" is a military word for occupational force. An occupational force is a group of soldiers who slip behind the enemy's line, grab a piece of his territory, and claim it and hold it until the invasion comes.

There is an invasion coming. The kingdoms of this world are going to become the Kingdom of our Lord and of His Christ. He is going to reign forever and ever. But until that time, God's people take territory and occupy. The very fact that Paul tells us in Ephesians 6 "... to put on the whole armor of God that we may be able to stand against the insanity of the devil" is testimony enough that we will be engaged in a warfare. We are not to be passive people twiddling our thumbs waiting for the Kingdom to come.

— The sudden imminent return of Jesus Christ has made God's people put off their warfare because they expect that at any moment, Christ should return. Many people ask me, "Tom Skinner, don't you believe the Lord is on His way?" "No, I do not believe the Lord is on His way because it doesn't take Him that long to get here." I don't know about your Scripture, but mine says something like "the twinkling of an eye." Jesus says, "Occupy till I come." God's people must stop being obsessed with when Christ is coming, because it is none of our business. Our job is to occupy, and it's God's business to take care of when He will come. We must therefore occupy the business world, the economic community, the sports arena, the arts, the entertainment community, the educational system, and the world of politics . . . in other words, God's people must move into every phase of the world and occupy and take territory. We must let our nets down, put on the whole armor of God, and stand firm on this territory that we may model on earth what is happening in heaven.

Bishop Paulk's book is long overdue. I trust that you will find, as I have found, this exciting reading and that it will turn your mind to become part of God's occupational force to identify the enemy and his works and destroy the works of the devil now with our two feet planted on the earth. We are God's people on earth on our way to heaven.

Tom Skinner is President of Tom Skinner Associates in New York City where he has lived all his life. He is a widely-acclaimed author of four books and speaker on Leadership Development in the areas of education, sports, politics, business and entertainment. He was formerly the chaplain of the Washington Redskins, and occasional chaplain to the New York Giants and New York Jets. He has conducted leadership development seminars for five east coast professional baseball teams.

*Tom Skinner is listed in **Who's Who In Black America** and serves on the board of directors of numerous businesses and nonprofit organizations. He spends his life in dedication to raising up a generation of qualified Christian leadership in American society.*

TABLE OF CONTENTS

Stormin' The Gates Of Hell
by Reba Rambo and Dony McGuire

(Verse 1)
We've got the eye of the tiger
We're spotting that liar
And ripping off his clever disguise.
We've got the strength of a lion
The forces of Zion
Are cutting every foe down to size.

(Bridge)
We are an army united
A people excited
The Spirit is a flame on our tongue.
The Light is pushing back darkness
A night that was starless
Shines like the Son.

(Chorus)
We're stormin' the gates of hell
And Heaven will prevail.
We're stormin' the gates of hell
And Heaven will prevail.
We have met the enemy
He's alive but he sure ain't well
We attack him day and night
We're stormin' the gates of hell.
We're stormin' the gates of hell.

(Verse 2)
We've got the wings of an eagle
We're swift and we're regal
We sweep down and capture our prey.
We've got the teeth of a grizzly
And it ain't no mystery
Cause we devour demons all day.

Repeat Bridge
Repeat Chorus

Part 1

"And then shall that Wicked be revealed, whom the Lord shall consume with the Spirit of His mouth, and shall destroy with the brightness of His coming."

II Thessalonians 2:8

1

COME AND DINE

This book is written for Christians who are hungry for meat. A spiritually mature army cannot wage war against a powerful enemy on a diet of spiritual milk. The army of the Lord must be ready to move as God says, "Move!" They must understand where the enemy is and how to use mighty spiritual weapons to bring down the strongholds of Satan. God is serving meat in these last days to Christians who are willing to serve Him as soldiers in His army.

The mature Bride of Christ will welcome Jesus's return as King of kings and Lord of lords with a shout of victory. But God's Word clearly teaches that the coming of the Lord will not occur until the Church first experiences a falling away of those Christians who are unwilling to endure to the end. Before Christ comes again, the man of sin, the son of perdition must be revealed (II Thessalonians 2:3). To unmask Satan requires a maturity among God's people throughout the Church which until now has only been demonstrated in one man, Jesus Christ. How is this demonstration possible? One evidence of spiritual maturity is a people who hunger for spiritual meat.

Then Jesus said unto them "Children, have you any food?" They answered Him, "No." And He said to them, "Cast the net on the right side of the boat, and you will find some." So they cast, and now they were not able to draw it in for the multitude of fish. Therefore that disciple whom Jesus loved said to Peter, "It is the Lord!" Now when Simon Peter heard that it was the Lord, he put on his outer garment (for he had removed it), and plunged into the sea. But the other disciples came in the little boat (for they were not far from land, but about two hundred cubits), dragging the net with fish. Then, as soon as they had come to land, they saw a fire of coals there, and fish laid on it, and bread. Jesus said to them, "Bring some of the fish which you have just caught." Simon Peter went up and dragged the net to land, full of large fish, one hundred and fifty-three; and although there were so many, the net was not broken. Jesus said to them, "Come and eat breakfast." Yet none of the disciples dared ask Him, "Who are You?" — knowing that it was the Lord. Jesus then came, and took the bread and gave it to them, and likewise the fish. This is now the third time Jesus showed Himself to His disciples after he was raised from the dead. (John 21:5-14)

The three words, "Come and dine" (KJV), have great spiritual implications. Jesus had risen from the dead and was standing upon the shore. When the disciples came near and saw Him preparing food, His invitation to them was, "Come and dine." The invitation that the Lord makes to us today is the same — "Come and dine." We are likely to desire natural food, but Jesus is not speaking of natural food. When He said, "I have food to eat of which you do not know" (John 4:32), He was speaking of spiritual food. In the Word of the Lord, Jesus said, "Man shall not live by bread alone" (Matthew 4:4; Luke 4:4). The words that Jesus spoke must become spiritual food or sustenance to us as He invites us to "come and dine."

The knowledge of spiritual truth is often referred to as "the milk of the Word," or "the meat of the Word," but there is a significant difference between the two. After seeking the Lord about the matter, I believe that the milk of the Word is that which has been revealed to us in the Word of God. Holy men of old were moved upon by the Holy Spirit and were given revelation that comprise the written Word of God. It is milk to us because it becomes a constant, sustaining force that helps us to grow as milk helps an infant to grow.

Jesus greatly desired to tell His disciples more than they were ready to receive while He was with them. He had given them milk, but there were many other insights that He would have given them if they had been mature enough to receive them. "I still have many things to say to you, but you cannot bear them now" (John 16:12).

3

Knowledge of things to come is revealed to God's chosen servants. This knowledge is prophetic insights which become the meat of the Word. "Things yet to be revealed" are insights that Jesus referred to as the "mystery of the kingdom" (Mark 4:11). A lack of maturity is the only thing that prevents God from giving us meat. God will not give meat to us as His Church until we have reached the place where we can properly digest the food that He gives us.

We continue to live on the milk of the Word while we back away from the meat. Salvation and healing are brought to us through the milk. The love we have for one another comes through the milk. Before the Kingdom of God can be manifested upon this earth, however, we must have the meat of the Word. Maturity in the Word helps us comprehend things that God has not previously revealed to mankind.

Many people will not accept this concept because they feel that it is a new doctrine and they fear adding to the revelation of God. Yet Jesus said,

However, when He, the Spirit of truth, has come, He will guide you into all truth; for He will not speak on His own authority, but whatever He hears He will speak; and He will tell you things to come. (John 16:13)

The time has come when God desires to reveal hidden truths to His Church. Paul's letter to the Corinthian church helps us further understand what the meat of the Word really is.

It is doubtless not profitable for me to boast. I will come to

visions and revelations of the Lord: I know a man in Christ who fourteen years ago — whether in the body I do not know, or whether out of the body I do not know, God knows — such a one was caught up to the third heaven. And I know such a man — whether in the body I do not know, God knows — how he was caught up into Paradise and heard inexpressible words, which it is not lawful for a man to utter. (II Corinthians 12:1-4)

Some things must be revealed which before now would have been unlawful because man was not mature enough to understand them. When Christ talked about relationships, He said that in the Kingdom of God there would be neither marriage nor giving in marriage. Although we do not know exactly what the Kingdom relationship will be like, Jesus said that it would be like the angels' relationships are now. I believe that the hour has come when we must transcend old understandings and comprehend new dimensions of relationships, both individually and among the nations of the earth. As the Church begins to mature, God will provide that meat of maturity. I believe that provision is imminent.

There are three areas in which the Church must mature before God will reveal the meat of the Word. The first area of maturity is described in I Corinthians 3:1-8.

And I, brethren, could not speak to you as to spiritual people but as to carnal, as to babes in Christ. I fed you with milk and not with solid food; for until now you were not able to receive it, and even now you are still not able; for you are still carnal. For where there are envy, strife, and divisions among you, are you not carnal and behaving like mere men? For when one says, "I am of Paul," and another, "I am of Apollos," are you not carnal? Who then is Paul, and who is Apollos, but ministers through whom you believed, as the Lord gave to each one? I planted, Apollos watered, but God gave the increase. So then neither he who plants is anything, nor he who waters, but God who gives the increase. Now he who plants and he who waters are one, and each one will receive his own reward according to his own labor. (I Corinthians 3:1-8)

The Apostle Paul told the Corinthians that he was ready to give them meat which was hidden in the mysteries of the Word of God. Understanding could not come, however, because they were still carnal and not spiritually ready to receive understanding. Therefore, the deep truths of God were put into parable form. Mysteries of the Kingdom will be revealed to us only by the Holy Spirit and they will not be revealed until we are free from strife and have ceased to walk as carnal men. Until we reach a place where we walk as spiritual men upon the earth, God cannot trust us with meat. He cannot give us dominion or authority. Jesus gave a little authority to His disciples, and they were ready to call down fire from heaven to destroy people. God can give meat only to people who have proven that they are mature enough to be trusted with meat.

Malachi holds another secret to receiving the meat of the Word of God. The prophet spoke,

"Bring all the tithes into the storehouse, that there may be

food in My house, and prove Me now in this," says the Lord of hosts, "if I will not open for you the windows of heaven and pour out for you such blessing that there will not be room enough to receive it. And I will rebuke the devourer for your sakes, so that he will not destroy the fruit of your ground, nor shall the vine fail to bear fruit for you in the field . . . And all the nations will call you blessed, for you will be a delightful land . . ." (Malachi 3:10-12)

God said that He wanted meat in His house to bless the nations of the earth. He was not referring to natural food such as steak and potatoes. The meat from God is the mysteries of the Kingdom of God — revelation and in-depth understanding. God said that when He could give us that revelation, the nations of the earth would be blessed. God is waiting to bring meat to His house —to find an obedient people to whom He can give revelation. I believe that God is beginning to find that obedient people. The meat of revelation will soon be in the house of God like we've never known before.

The third requirement for receiving the meat of the Word of God is found in Hebrews.

For though by this time you ought to be teachers, you need someone to teach you again the first principles of the oracles of God; and you have come to need milk and not solid food. (Hebrews 5:12)

The Hebrews were not yet ready to be teachers because they still needed milk and not solid food. God is calling for the release of ministries. He is calling for teachers. He is calling for those who have passed beyond the milk stage. If someone can handle only those things which he reads (the milk of the Word), he is still a babe. Many people are frightened by this concept because they feel that the Word of God is being discounted. Unless we first have the milk of the Word, we will never be ready for the meat of the Word. The meat of the Word never disagrees with the milk of the Word. The milk of the Word, however, will not produce the Kingdom of God. Only the meat of the Word will bring Jesus Christ back to this earth.

For everyone who partakes only of milk is unskilled in the word of righteousness, for he is a babe. (Hebrews 5:13)

Righteousness is the first ingredient of the Kingdom of God which is righteousness, peace and joy in the Holy Ghost. In order to talk about the Kingdom of righteousness, we must move beyond the milk to the meat of the Word.

But solid food belongs to those who are of full age, that is, those who by reason of use have their senses exercised to discern both good and evil. (Hebrews 5:14)

We now begin to comprehend that we have reached the place God so desperately wants to bring us — to the place where He can give us the meat of the Word instead of just the milk of the Word. The Garden of Eden was a place of choice. There was the tree of the knowledge of good and evil which gives us the knowledge of worldly things: material assets, mammon and gratifications of the flesh. In that same Garden was the tree of life which represents the meat that God wants to give us.

The tree of life produces eternal life. The tree of life gives us an endless flow from the throne of God. I believe that today God has placed the tree of the knowledge of good and evil and the tree of life within the Church. God is trying to tell us that the time has come when He wants to release the meat of His Word to us so that Christ can come again and find a mature Bride.

There are three areas in which we need the meat of the word, or revelation, to help us. First, we must have meat in the areas that will help us to unmask Satan. Jesus said that in the last days, there would be deception. We must have new understanding of how to unmask Satan. Jesus Christ said, "When He, the Spirit of truth, has come, He will guide you into all truth . . ." (John 16:13). Those who choose the tree of life will, by the Spirit of God, enter great spiritual warfare.

We must have the meat of revelation to unmask Satan in doctrines that deceive even the very elect. Any doctrine or theory that delays the coming of the Lord by delaying the maturity of the Church or causes us to be looking for Christ in the wrong place must be unmasked. We must say boldly, "That's the wrong path to go down. You will never grow to full maturity if you go that way." Only the meat of the Word through revelation will unmask Satan and reveal truth.

Secondly, we must have meat in order to bring

9

maturity to the Church. Paul said, "Now we see in a mirror dimly . . ." but when we put away childish things, we will see "face to face" (I Corinthians 13:12). I believe God now wants His people to see Him face to face. He wants a mature Church that can say, "I have seen the Lord. I've been to the mountain top. I have had visions and revelations, and here is what God is saying to this generation." That is the cry of the hour. The time has come when we must see God for ourselves.

Paul said, "Put away childish things." Speaking with tongues might be a childish thing if someone spent all of his time doing it, whether in intercession or in glorifying God. If one never goes beyond that, he will continue in the milk of the Word. Deeper spiritual truths lie beyond praying in tongues. Tongues may edify us personally, but we must go beyond the need for milk only and use spiritual meat principles in order to take God's message to the world.

We need meat to tell us how to put on the whole armor of God. Armor should not be put on a wounded body, and the Church cannot put on the armor of God until her wounds are healed. We must learn how to make the earth God's footstool. Kingdom dominion will come only by revelation. We must learn by revelation how to move in the unity of faith. We must allow the Spirit of God to lead us into the meat of the Word.

Thirdly, we must have meat in order to bring the kingdoms of this world under submission to the Kingdom of God. No matter what the kingdom is — art, drama, music, finance — every kingdom of the world must be confronted by the revelation of God to such an extent that the Kingdom of God will present a clear choice.

The meat of the Word comes in four different ways. In I Corinthians 12 the Apostle Paul spoke of the spiritual gifts placed in the Church, but in Chapter 13 he said, "These gifts are great, including tongues, but if I have all the gifts of prophecy and understand mysteries and knowledge and have not love, the gifts mean nothing." "That which is perfect," which Paul describes (I Corinthians 13:10), is the Kingdom of God, the revelation of God, God coming again into the lives of mankind.

Pursue love, and desire spiritual gifts, but especially that you may prophesy. For he who speaks in a tongue does not speak to men but to God, for no one understands him; however in the spirit he speaks mysteries. But he who prophesies speaks edification, exhortation and comfort to men. He who speaks in a tongue edifies himself, but he who prophesies edifies the church. I wish you all spoke with tongues, but even more that you prophesied; for he who prophesies is greater than he who speaks with tongues, unless indeed he interprets, that the church may receive edification. But now, brethren, if I come to you speaking with tongues, what shall I profit you unless I speak to you either by revelation, by knowledge, by prophesying, or by teaching? (I Corinthians 14:1-6)

Revelation, knowledge, prophecy and teaching are the four meat principles which move beyond speaking with tongues. This scripture does not mean that we are to choose one of these principles exclusively. All of them are necessary for our edification. We need to edify ourselves and pray and intercede in the Spirit because doing so keeps us strong. But if we are going to bring God's Kingdom to pass, we must move by the combined principles of revelation, knowledge, prophecy and teaching.

First of all, how do we define revelation? I purposely did not go to *Webster's Dictionary* but to the Holy Spirit to give me understanding. Revelation unfolds the secrets of God's heart and turns men to God's intentions and purposes. Revelation tells us what God wants and seeks today.

The milk principle is found in the written Word of God but in order to press beyond that to the meat, we must allow God to speak to us about specific problems, such as governmental or social ills, prejudice, or the god of Mammon. Specific answers or solutions must come to us through the power of the Holy Spirit as He reveals the heart of God Himself. What is the heart of God toward us today? The answer comes by revelation.

The second meat principle is knowledge. Knowledge, as the Holy Spirit defined it for me, consists of those things known through personal experience — that which one knows by tasting of the heavenly manna — the knowledge that comes to us by tasting of the tree of life. Jesus said, "I have meat that you know not of." He had experienced death and had gone into hell itself. He knew what it was to be victorious. Today we have meat that enables us to say, "We know our Redeemer lives! We know who we are in Jesus Christ! We know the authority of God's Word, and we know the power of God as He speaks today!"

The third meat principle God has provided is prophecy. Paul said that tongues edify the individual, but prophecy tells of things to come.

But he who prophesies speaks edification and exhortation and comfort to men. . . Therefore tongues are for a sign, not to those who believe but to unbelievers; but prophesying is not for unbelievers but for those who believe. (I Corinthians 14:3,22)

The hour has come when God must now speak to believers by prophecy. He must speak to us concerning our belief in Him and about things to come as He prepares us for the future. God wants to speak through prophecy to His Church so that the Church will know of things to come even before events take place. Prophecy told Joseph to take Mary and the baby Jesus and flee. In the same manner prophecy gives warnings to the Church today. Spiritual warfare has entered such a dimension that we must know the dangers so that we can prepare ourselves as the true Body of Christ.

Just before the Kingdom is established on earth, Christians will experience persecution such as we have never known before. I believe the hour of persecution against the true Church is about to begin, and we need to know how to prepare ourselves, take a stand, and be ready for the battle.

The fourth meat principle is teaching or doctrine. Doctrines that become meat are the patterns of God. The ways in which God consistently moves become doctrines. The character of God becomes an undeniable doctrine that God is love and truth and that the Church is the Body of Jesus Christ. These become meat principles to us because they are doctrines.

Therefore, leaving the discussion of the elementary principles of Christ, let us go on to perfection, not laying again the foundation of repentance from dead works and of faith toward God, of the doctrine of baptisms, of laying on of hands, of resurrection of the dead, and of eternal judgment. (Hebrews 6:1-2)

For it is impossible for those who were once enlightened, and have tasted the heavenly gift, and have become partakers of the Holy Spirit, and have tasted the good word of God and the powers of the age to come, if they fall away, to renew them again to repentance, since they crucify again for themselves the Son of God, and put Him to an open shame. (Hebrews 6:4-6)

We are not to argue over doctrines that have been established, or spend time worrying about the validity of the divinity of Christ. We know that Christ is divine. We are not to worry about the resurrection. We must be established in these basic doctrines and move forward to maturity. Having tasted of the heavenly things of God, we must pursue them. As we do, God will give us new insights and new understandings.

I Corinthians 14:8 is a key verse of scripture. "For if the trumpet makes an uncertain sound, who will prepare himself for battle?" I believe that the Church is the trumpet and if the Church does not give a certain sound, how will we know to prepare for battle? The

Church as a trumpet must now prepare itself as never before to give a sure and confident sound. The Church is God's voice in the world today.

This is the day of the Word in motion, the Word demonstrated. The Word of God will move by the Spirit. The Church is the vehicle for proclaiming the Word of God. The Church provides milk like a mother's breast. The milk of the Word is always important because it brings babes to Christ and it is where we all begin to grow. However, from that milk, we must grow in our Christian walk by the four meat principles: revelation, knowledge, prophecy and doctrine. By the meat we will grow to the place where the trumpet of God — the Church of Jesus Christ — can stand with authority and say. "Thus saith the Lord God of Israel." The Lord God of the New Jerusalem, the Lord God of the Israelites is the Lord God of the redeemed people, the priesthood of God. When God speaks, the Church declares to the world what He says.

We must have as much maturity to hear the Word of the Lord as we do to speak it. God directed us to pray to hear with anointed ears that we might hear with maturity. We need the meat of the Word to bring understanding as we submit to the flow of the Holy Spirit.

As battles continue to be fought, separations will occur more often as God finds a people who desire the solid meat of the Word and who pray for the "tree of life" rather than the "knowledge of good and evil." The mature Christian does not seek to discern the things of the world. We seek to discern the things of God as we move in the Spirit to bring the Kingdom of God to pass.

Something very special happened in an insignificant town to a very insignificant little family of the smallest Israelite tribe. The prophet Micah foretold, "But you, Bethlehem Ephrathah, though you are little among the thousands of Judah, yet out of you shall come forth to Me the One to be ruler in Israel, whose goings forth have been from of old, from everlasting" (Micah 5:2).

The stable was small and the stench was bad. The animals were milling about and the hay was dirty. The manger was crude and uncomfortable, but God was somehow at work in this insignificant, unreasonable circumstance at which the world would surely laugh. Businessmen of the day probably said, "What a foolish way to try to get attention! Why, there's nothing divine there. Nobody will pay any attention to that." But hovering over that little scene was an angelic choir, praising God and singing, "Glory to God in the highest, and on earth peace, good will toward men." In that simple setting, a little baby cried, and that cry later became the prophetic voice of God.

God uses the simple things to absolutely confound the world and its systems. We are insignificant according to worldly concepts. We are just another stable on a hillside. But the angels are leaning over the balconies of heaven and saying, "You've got something special now." God is saying, "I've given you revelation and understanding. You are My trumpet."

2

WHERE SATAN DWELLS

Deception exists in the Church because of our inability to identify where Satan dwells. Until we can adequately uncover Satan's throne, we do not have the ability to war victoriously against satanic forces. The Church has usually focused on the problems of the flesh and has failed to discover the true source of Satan's ability to hinder us. The Bible clearly states that fleshly discipline alone will not overcome hindrances to the Kingdom of God. Moral behavior is not the major issue. The Kingdom of God is righteousness, peace and joy in the Holy Spirit. Satan too often emerges the victor in the arena of carnalities (problems of the flesh) because that is where he is cleverly deceitful. Paul recognized Satan's subtlety of the flesh when he wrote to the church at Corinth. In the same letter Paul commended them on their oneness with Christ, he also challenged the Corinthians to a higher walk with God by telling them, "You're carnal" (I Corinthians 3:1-4).

Carnality opens the door for the schemes or "wiles" of Satan (Ephesians 6:11) to divert and in some cases eventually destroy our witness. Satan's wiles are cunning devices he uses with expert accuracy. The power of our flesh is no real match for Satan. Our warfare against him must be waged with spiritual weapons so that we can stand against principalities, powers, rulers of the darkness of this world and spiritual wickedness in high places. Satan's schemes are often enough to discourage Christians from pressing into a demonstration of the Kingdom of God. As we identify and recognize Satan's schemes, carnalities lose their grip in our lives.

In writing to the church at Pergamos, the Holy Spirit gave John a revelation that is just as relevant to the Church today as it was in his day.

I know your works, and where you dwell, where Satan's throne is. And you hold fast to My name, and did not deny My faith even in the days in which Antipas was My faithful martyr, who was killed among you, where Satan dwells. (Revelation 2:13)

Satan pulls us into arenas of warfare that he chooses. In those areas of warfare we become bloody and defeated. We are convinced that if we can only conquer and be victorious over the flesh, the Kingdom of God will be established. Wrong! Satan will not be unmasked and defeated until we identify the kingdoms of this world, how Satan works in those kingdoms and what his underlying schemes are. We must know his weapons as well as the weapons given to us by the Spirit of God (Ephesians 6:10-18).

"For nation will rise against nation, and kingdom against kingdom. And there will be famines, pestilences, and earthquakes in various places" (Matthew 24:7). Jesus said the evidence of the establishment of His Kingdom in the last days is tremendous warfare. We cannot know how to battle until we can adequately identify the kingdoms of Satan. For instance, to use the shield of faith (Ephesians 6:10) we must identify the direction from which the evil darts come toward us. Satan is a master of camouflage. He reminds us of our faults, attacks our emotions, and tempts us through fleshly desires. Satan wants us to believe that these temptations are the issues of important battles. On the contrary, fleshly problems are not the eternal focus of the battle which will bring Christ's Kingdom to earth.

Satan subtly hides himself in the kingdoms of this world. He flamboyantly runs over us because we overlook him. Satan, the deceiver, will tell us that we are defeated when we do something wrong. He tries to convince us that the Kingdom of God will never come to earth because our flesh is weak.

The fulfillment of the final purposes of God rests in His Church. This purpose is revealed in Revelation 11:15 which says, "Then the seventh angel sounded:

'And there were loud voices in heaven, saying, The kingdoms of this world have become the kingdoms of our Lord and of His Christ, and He shall reign for ever and ever!' "

And in the days of these kings the God of heaven will set up a kingdom, which shall never be destroyed; and the kingdom shall not be left to other people; it shall break in pieces and consume all these kingdoms, and it shall stand forever. Inasmuch as you saw that the stone was cut out of the mountain without hands, and that it broke in pieces the iron, the bronze, the clay, the silver, and the gold — the great God has made known to the king what will come to pass after this. The dream is certain, and its interpretation is sure. (Daniel 2:44-45)

Daniel's dream had to do with the kingdoms of this world. Daniel, by revelation, said that a Kingdom not made with hands will come forth. This Kingdom cannot come by human wisdom, but comes only from God by His revelation and authority.

For unto us a Child is born, unto us a son is given; and the government will be upon His shoulder. And His name will be called Wonderful, Counselor, Mighty God, Everlasting Father, Prince of Peace. Of the increase of His government and peace there will be no end, upon the throne of David, and over His kingdom, to order it and establish it with judgment and justice from that time forward, even forever. The zeal of the Lord of hosts will perform this. (Isaiah 9:6-7)

God's ultimate purpose for mankind is to return us to a place where we can fellowship with Him. When He put man in the Garden, He gave him dominion. Man was God's pleasure, unencumbered and free. Man's sin defeated what God had intended and from that point of defeat, man deteriorated or fell. Built within the Garden itself and within the seed of woman was the promise of One to come Who would bruise the head of the serpent, symbolizing the kingdoms of this world. Out of that seed would come the Messiah Who would come to the throne of David and reign with the mature Church forever and ever. God will not perform total restoration except through the Church. He is telling us go back and assume the lost dominion that we had in the Garden.

Today God searches the earth for "a people who were not a people" to complete an adequate witness of His Kingdom to the powers and principalities of the air. This unique nation — unidentifiable by genealogy, geography, race or denomination — will convict the world of sin as God's voice in the earth. This "holy nation" (I Peter 2:9) is the true Church who is being transformed into the image of Christ. This "people who were not a people" will make restitution of all things (Acts 2:34) so that Christ can come again to rule on earth. But the birthing of this witness in the earth will cause great travail to God's people. Satan must first be exposed and defeated by the Church. His age-old tactics are still effective, and we must examine how he works to deceive us.

Where does Satan dwell? John said that Satan could

be found in the lust of the flesh, the lust of the eyes, and the pride of life. Mankind was placed in the Garden of Eden with authority to have dominion, to rule, reign and subdue everything. Satan could not tolerate a relationship that God had established with his own likeness.

> *Now the serpent was more cunning than any beast of the field which the Lord God had made. And he said to the woman, "Has God indeed said, 'You shall not eat of every tree of the garden'?" (Genesis 3:1)*

Since Satan was more subtle and more beautiful than any other beast, vanity is an area where he is most comfortable. Lucifer was the angel of beauty. For that reason, he can easily influence people toward beautiful, carnal things.

When Satan is uncovered, he runs elsewhere. John gave us an insight as to where we can look for Satan when he said that Satan would disguise himself. He changes himself into an angel of light. He will come to us with certain scriptures. He will use the Word of God to condemn us, though God does not condemn or accuse anyone. God's holy righteousness opens areas of our lives that should be disciplined by Him, but God will never condemn us with accusations.

We usually don't recognize an angel of light; therefore, we have difficulty exposing Satan. By discovering where Satan dwells, we can shed the light of God on him. Satan emerges in bad attitudes and negativism. All of his pessimism, jealousy, strife, envy and division come to us in beautiful sheep's clothing. Only through revelation by the Holy Spirit can Satan be revealed. He surfaces in his camouflage, and those who are deceived say, "I have found answers! I have found truth!" when all the time behind what appears to be "truth" is Satan. The Church must test "truths" to see if they are negative, causing divisions, contrary to God's character, or undermining God's authority in His Church.

We need to learn quickly that Satan's arena of battle is God's Word. Satan used the scripture (Matthew 4:11) on the Mount of Temptation to try to bring Jesus into deception. He uses the Word of God to deceive us with wrong interpretations of the scriptures. In the Garden of Eden, Satan said, "Has God indeed said, 'You shall not eat of every tree of the garden'?" The woman replied, "We may eat the fruit of the trees of the garden." This was her first mistake. She should have said to the devil, "I resist you and I will have no conversation with you." Don't ever explain anything to Satan. Paul says in Ephesians 4, "Make no place for the devil." Eve continued explaining to the serpent (Satan),

"But of the fruit of the tree which is in the midst of the garden, God has said, 'You shall not eat it, nor shall you touch it, lest you die.'" And the serpent said to the woman, "You will not surely die. For God knows that in the day you eat of it, your eyes will be opened, and you will be like God, knowing good and evil." (Genesis 3:3-5)

Adam and Eve did not die physically at that moment. However, they did die spiritually. What God told them was true, yet Satan took an element of truth and caused them to be deceived. He said, "God knows that it will make you like God."

So when the woman saw that the tree was good for food [lust of the flesh], that it was pleasant to the eyes [lust of the eyes] and a tree desirable to make one wise [pride of life], she took of its fruit and ate. She also gave to her husband with her, and he ate. Then the eyes of both of them were opened, and they knew that they were naked; and they sewed fig leaves together, and made themselves coverings. (Genesis 3:6-7)

Sin opened Adam and Eve's eyes and they realized their vulnerability and inadequacies. They saw their failures, their carnalities and their weaknesses. As long as they walked in faith and obedience to God, they weren't aware of their human qualities. They didn't know they were naked. They enjoyed life and were God's pleasure, but their lives were changed from perfection to imperfection because of their disobedience to God. Then they knew that they had sinned. Human problems quickly began and mankind has experienced them daily throughout human history.

The Kingdom of God is not just a salvation experience. Satan subtly deceives Christians by keeping them satisfied with repentance and elementary Christian beliefs. They become shortsighted concerning the lifestyle of the Kingdom. The manifest sons of God must understand demonstrating the Gospel of the Kingdom. Jesus did not say that when we have made a witness of repentance to all nations, the end will come. He said that preaching and demonstrating the Gospel of the Kingdom will usher that Kingdom into the world. A firstfruit must live out Kingdom lifestyles and recognize who he is in Christ. God's people must move with authority so that the Kingdom of God will be established.

Jesus sent seventy disciples throughout Judea to demonstrate the Kingdom of God to whoever would receive them (Luke 10:1-11). He did not send them to proclaim the message of repentance, to preach a revival, or to hold a rally. Jesus sent them to demonstrate the Kingdom by living out Kingdom principles in any home where they were received.

To attack our witness, Satan will try to use the Word of God to defeat and accuse us. Satan is extremely subtle, but he will be unmasked. Where is our love? Motivation is where we begin to uncover Satan in our lives. For instance, the love of money is the root of all evil, so falling in love with money gives Satan our allegiance.

How do we identify the lust of the flesh, the lust of the eyes and the pride of life? Lust of the flesh and the eyes does not merely refer to sexuality. Lust describes inward desires that control us. Lust can be manifest in seemingly innocent pursuits like buying property or writing a book. Lust is where self-centered desires take the place of the love of God in our lives. If Philip, for example, had not gone to the Ethiopian, he would have gone the way of the "lust of the flesh." Jonah's disobedience was that he went the way of the "lust of the flesh" when he went to Tarsus rather than to Nineveh. Satan tempted Jesus by showing Him kingdoms of this world, hoping to trap Him with the lust of the eyes. When Satan entices us into the battleground of our natural appetites, the devil knows he can usually win the victory.

The pride of life is reflected in an unwillingness to submit. Satan dwells in an "I'm going to do it my way" attitude. Have we let the devil pull us into some area where we know we are going to be defeated? Paul cried out, "Oh, wretched man that I am! The things that the flesh does not want to do, I find myself doing. The things that I should do, I never accomplish. The devil has me in this battle and I will never be able to win." Yet, Paul began to lift his eyes to another arena when he said, "Thanks be to God, I find my victory in Him."

Satan cunningly dwells in areas where he can turn fleshly desires in the wrong direction. Christians must recognize that enticement and say, "This body is the temple of the Holy Spirit, and God can use it to manifest His glory and love. I will not partake of the corruption that the world produces."

The pride of life can become one's god. God's perfection within us enables us to worship Him and support each other. When a person makes the pride of life his god, he cannot direct others to the true God. Jesus was led into the wilderness to face temptation (Matthew 4). He was hungry because He had been there for forty days without food. Satan came to Him with a cunning approach. "If You are the Son of God, command that these stones become bread." The implication was that if Jesus didn't do it, He was not the Son of God. Satan always asks questions that one can't answer with the

26

fleshly or carnal mind. Satan tempted Jesus by trying to challenge His identity.

The higher the revelation, the deeper the thorn, but the thorn is not trouble to the people of God. That thorn is a wound to Satan. He trembles when we receive revelation because he knows that through revelation, truth will come to this generation. The devil quakes and trembles and musters his forces as revelation, fresh insights into God's Word, begins to come forth. God always dispatches ministering angels with instructions to help and protect His people. God can open our eyes as He did for Elijah and his servant. We can see ten thousand angels for every demon the devil sends to torment or mislead us.

When Christ was on the cross, Satan thought he had won the final victory. Jesus knew that He could have called ten thousand angels, but He would not allow them to help Him. The angels looked on as Jesus went through the shadow of death and was put into hell. In hell itself, Jesus stripped the devil of every power he possessed and emerged victoriously over Satan.

Jesus knew the Spirit of the Word of God and He used the Word quickened by the Holy Spirit to answer Satan. "It is written, 'Man shall not live by bread alone, but by every word that proceeds from the mouth of God.'" We cannot battle the kingdoms of this world without a thorough knowledge of God's Word. Our offensive weapons are God's Word and praying in the Spirit. Through the revelation of Jesus Christ and the anointing of the Holy Spirit, God will bring His Word to us in the moments that we need to know them.

With Jesus's answer that "man cannot live by bread alone but by every word that proceeds from the mouth of God," Satan realized failure. Satan tempted Jesus again by saying, "If You are the Son of God, throw Yourself down." Satan tried to use pride to defeat Jesus. Once more Jesus said, "It is written again, 'You shall not tempt the Lord Your God.' " Jesus's purpose was not to lift Himself up in pride.

Again, the devil took Him up on an exceedingly high mountain, and showed Him all the kingdoms of the world and their glory. And he said to Him, "All these things I will give you, if you will fall down and worship me." Then Jesus said to him, "Away with you, Satan! For it is written, 'You shall worship the Lord your God, and Him only you shall serve.' " (Matthew 4:8-10)

Today Satan is at work in the systems or the kingdoms of this world. "We know that we are of God, and the whole world lies under the sway of the wicked one" (I John 5:19).

Satan works in the political, scientific and educational systems. He is at work in commerce and dominates the area of finance. He is at work in the kingdom of the arts: music, dancing and drama. He also rules in the kingdom of sports. God created these kingdoms, yet Satan rules and reigns over these areas. Families are devastated because they do not recognize the source of satanic influences in their lives. Another kingdom where Satan dwells is false religions. He deceives people with religions of the mind. He involves himself with extreme religions of prosperity, the occult, traditions, doctrines and forms of ungodliness.

Now, brethren, concerning the coming of our Lord Jesus Christ and our gathering together to Him, we ask you, not to be soon shaken in mind or troubled, either by spirit or by word or by letter, as if from us, as though the day of Christ had come. Let no one deceive you by any means; for that Day will not come unless the falling away comes first, and the man of sin is revealed, the son of perdition. (II Thessalonians 2:1-3)

God has told us to reveal the devil. God wants His people to know where Satan is at work. He wants us empowered by spiritual discernment to say, "That's good." "That's bad." "That is not of God." "That is the Spirit of the Lord." God wants His people to discern rather than judge. The sons of God are not judged by the letter of the law. They are led by the Spirit.

Maturity is determined by our ability to discern. God has said, "Until he (Satan) is revealed, the Kingdom of God cannot be born" (II Thessalonians 2:3). Until we are able to discern the differences between the kingdoms of this world and the Kingdom of God, God cannot establish His Kingdom on earth.

A prototype community of people on the earth where God's Kingdom can become a witness must first have unity. The family of God will demonstrate the Gospel of the Kingdom. One person's disobedience will keep others from entering the Kingdom.

Oil was poured upon the head of Aaron, which symbolizes Church leadership, or the pastorate. Until that oil of oneness and unity is poured out, it cannot go to the rest of the garment, or the rest of the body. God watches us and asks the question, "Are you the generation who will usher in My Kingdom, or will you hold on to your own plans, securities, dollars and talents?" God is challenging us to live like Kingdom people. We must say, "I am going to put my time toward the Word of the Lord. I am going to uncover Satan in my thoughts and my life. By discernment, I will be able to demonstrate that which is good and will witness to the authority of the King in my life."

Some Biblical fundamentalists have interpreted prophetic scripture to say that Satan would sit in the temple during a time of tribulation. Rather than speculate on some future warfare, the Church must address the question, "Where is Satan's throne now?" Many Christians ignore Satan's throne in their lives today while they look for some future Antichrist. John said that the spirit of the antichrist is already in the world (I John 4:3).

The god of this age has blinded our minds (II Corinthians 4:4). Each of us individually must be able to uncover Satan in our lives by recognizing the ways that we are controlled by the kingdoms of this world.

Establishing the Kingdom of God on earth is more important to the Church than the message that Martin Luther preached during the Reformation, or Church doctrines written by Zwingli or Calvin. The Kingdom message is a lifestyle. God has said this message fulfills His purposes for the world.

30

I studied the scripture which says, "God tempted Abraham to slay his son" (Genesis 22:1-2). The original wording says, "He proved Abraham" and that is what the actual Hebrew word means. God proved Abraham so that He would know for certain that Abraham was a man of faith. Abraham left that mountain saying, "I know in my heart I sacrificed my son to God."

My brethren, count it all joy when you fall into various trials, knowing that the testing of your faith produces patience. (James 1:2-3)

Patience means perseverance. We should consider trials as joy in our lives because Satan has entered into the battleground where we have the power to win. On that battleground, we can say to the devil, "Greater is He that is within me, and you are going to lose."

Satan will accuse a person who has a deliverance ministry of having familiar or evil spirits. Satan used that same accusation against Jesus. He always takes a truth and turns it around for his own purposes. When Jesus healed people on the Sabbath, the devil said, "You shouldn't do that on the Sabbath." The Pharisees uttered the words, but it was the devil speaking through them. He will make people feel guilty for using the Lord's day for God's purposes.

Satan deceives us by saying that love is lust, or lust is love. He distorts truth. But God establishes the five-fold ministry so that we can be perfected in maturity and unity of faith.

Satan will say, "Sickness and death bring glory to

31

God." The Bible never says that. In Hebrews 11, we read about people who were literally cut in half, brutalized, and eaten alive by wild animals. God's glory shone because these martyrs' faith remained true to God, but God was not glorified because they died in the process of demonstrating their faithfulness. The Bible says that the last enemy to be conquered is death. When we learn that death is an enemy and sickness is the result of evil, we will be able to stand up and say, "Devil, I know who you are and I know what you are doing." Until then, Satan makes us into spiritually unhappy martyrs who go around saying, "I am suffering for the cause of God." That thinking is deception and lies.

We can stand for God in spite of personal suffering. We can walk a life of faith even suffering pain because we know that God Himself does not inflict pain. God only removes the hedge from around His children to allow Satan to get them so that He can show Himself strong in their behalf. Many say that Job was a perfect man, but the Bible doesn't say that. The Bible refers to Job's righteousness to a certain degree, but the book of Job says that Job declared, "The thing I feared most has come upon me" (Job 3:25). Satan was able to get to Job because Job was afraid. Only God's perfect love casts out fear. God's people need to hold their heads up high and say to the devil, "I am a son (or daughter) of God. I belong in the Kingdom of God. I know who you are, and I know what your tricks are."

No wonder the devil wars us. He is both subtle and deceitful. Jesus warned us of Satan's character when

He said, "Satan is not only a liar, but he is the father of lies." The task of the Church is to unmask and disclose where Satan works, and where his seat of authority rests. Satan has one primary goal in his battle against the people of God. He wants to wage war against Christ and His Kingdom until the kingdoms of this world finally destroy God's plan so completely that he can establish his own antichrist kingdom on the earth. We must fight as we have never fought before as soldiers of the Lord. We uncover Satan when we begin to point out where he works.

KINGDOM OF POLITICS

Where are the kingdoms of this world in which Satan has so subtly hidden himself? First, Satan rules in worldly political systems. God approves of order; therefore, some worldly structures of power and authority are ordained of God. We often console ourselves by believing that all governments are of God. We become complacent toward evil because the scriptures tell us that all authority comes from God. While many aspects of government are good, Satan has mightily infiltrated politics. Where has the greatest deception taken place in the last few years? Where have the greatest deceivers been exposed?

Immoral actions are rampant in government places. Political systems have become thoroughly corrupted. Today in our own country we do not know the extent of our nation's involvement with other nations or the true political motives for our alliances. Kings and presidents have been assassinated and we don't know who has killed them or their reasons for doing so. The governments of this earth have become satanic, and the wickedness in high places is so great that we do not know what is or isn't of God. Certainly not all the people involved in government are evil, but the worldly system of politics is governed by Satan himself.

Israel had a theocracy and God ruled His people by prophetic revelation. When God needed to communicate, He used a prophet to speak to the people. God intervened constantly. One day the people said, "We want a king. We want a government to suit ourselves. We want to be like other nations." From that hour, satanic forces entered into their political system and became a place where Satan could hide. Government is necessary for social order. We must "render unto Caesar" and be responsible citizens. We must pay our taxes and obey laws, but beyond that point we must recognize that Satan rules and reigns in governments.

Satan took Jesus up on a mountain and showed Him not only political kingdoms and the provinces of Galilee, Judea and Samaria, but also the kingdom authority of the world. Many governments and political leaders display themselves in garbs of righteousness while they hide corrupt motives behind "church" language. Sometimes nations that are actually ruled by "religious" systems are politically corrupt.

Governments in certain parts of South America are examples of political corruption. Such political systems are where Satan is in control. John's Revelation says that the kingdoms of this world will one day become the Kingdom of God, but the ultimate Kingdom will not be established by an act of God alone. The world must witness the manifestation of the sons of God. God, through His people upon this earth, must offer alternatives to the kingdoms of this world. The Kingdom of God cannot happen any other way.

When a political system becomes proper and just before God, the fruits of its philosophy will assist in ushering in the Kingdom of God. Christian people need to be involved in government and the political work force. Before the Kingdom of God can be established on earth, politics must be subject to the Kingdom of our God. I believe that God is beginning to work in the hearts of kings, rulers and leaders in governments around the world. We will soon see a great spiritual revival among political leaders. We will see evidence of this when the current power structures turn away from paths of selfishness, greed and ambition. We accept idolatry too easily in politics, but every form of idolatry must come under the rulership of Jesus Christ.

In God's plan, those in authority become "public servants" who are sensitive to their people's needs. Kingdom people unmask Satan in politics by infiltration and influence. God is calling many Kingdom men and women today to become light and salt to the world in county, state and federal legislative offices by running for public office. They are boldly declaring truth and righteousness daily as they take a stand against the satanic influences of greed and ambition in political decision-making. They are offering positive solutions for the negative, hopeless circumstances that bring eventual destruction and death to people who are at the mercy of their governments.

In the spirit of Daniel and Joseph who held high political offices in a spiritually adverse environment, these Kingdom public servants recognize political involvement as a ministry to which they are called by God for such a time as this. They seek wisdom from God for the insoluble, social chaos that only spiritual insights can restore to godly order and harmony.

All Kingdom-minded believers are called today to exert influence against satanic political control as God's people take rightful dominion of this kingdom. Responsible Christians must vote and write letters to public officials on critical issues. They must sign petitions concerning matters that will promote peace, harmony, goodness and true freedom.

The Kingdom of God is the only true "nation under God." That nation is composed of spiritual kings and priests, the Church, speaking what the Spirit is saying. The time has come for the Church to be God's spokesman to political leaders. We have abdicated our responsibility, our privilege, far too long. We represent the King of kings, Jesus Christ, to the governments of this world. Jesus is the way, the truth and the life. Following His words often requires outspoken, radical, social action.

The result is Kingdom influence coupled with persecution, but the time to act is now. God waits for that generation who will communicate and demonstrate His alternatives. Spirit-minded people will infiltrate and influence as He directs.

KINGDOM OF SCIENCE

Scientific research complements our knowledge of creation. Knowledge is of God. Too often, however, the god of science says to us, "God had nothing to do with creation." Modern science works to explain the creation of man according to its own concepts. Science says that we are gods unto ourselves and science then becomes a religion which Satan controls. Satan works through scientific theories which leave no room for divine creativity. We see an example of Satan's control in medical science. The Bible says, ". . . lean not to ungodly counsel." The hour has come when we must begin to recognize medical advice that is not of God. We need to learn that we have not been granted power to decide whether to take or give life.

Medical science makes decisions on such matters as life and death with no regard for sacred responsibility. To abort a pregnancy or end a life apart from godly direction through spiritual authority calls for God's judgment. The kingdom of Satan says, "These decisions are matters of human choice. Medical science is god." Our dependence upon medical science when we plug someone into a life-saving machine is inhumane in some cases. I believe that as long as someone has life and breath, we must fight death as an enemy of God. However, we must not rob someone of his dignity simply because of scientific capabilities that keep the heart beating and lungs breathing.

The Bible says, "Precious in the sight of the Lord is the death of His saints," but this is not because they die by yielding to Satan's destruction. Romans 8:38 says,

"Neither death nor life, nor angels nor principalities nor powers, nor things present nor things to come . . . shall be able to separate us from the love of God." Satan may at times have permission to slay one's body as he slew John the Baptist. Satanic powers put Jesus on the cross, but Jesus said,

"And do not fear those who kill the body but cannot kill the soul. But rather fear Him who is able to destroy both soul and body in hell." (Matthew 10:28)

The doctor's oath is taken in the name of the Greek scientist-philosopher Hippocrates, who is said to be the father of medicine. Doctors take an oath to uphold a philosophy of man, not a truth of God. Any oath associated with a man's name becomes a form of idolatry.

Science creates nuclear weapons which are placed in the hands of ungodly men whose knowledge and control could destroy the world. Peter prophetically looked into the future and saw the world on fire ". . . the elements will melt with fervent heat" (II Peter 3:10). Satan desires to destroy everything that God has ever done in creation.

Many in the Church are deceived concerning the condition of our world. We are in a mighty arms race which is ruled by the kingdom of Satan. God is looking for a nation of people who will say, "The Lord God is our strength. He is our fortress. Underneath the shelter of His wings will we trust." Our strength does not lie in the arms race. Our strength lies in righteousness, peace and joy with God. God raises up His forces to fight against the evil forces around us. When we retreat, those forces becomes a kingdom controlled by Satan. The kingdom of science is a vast, influential kingdom of this world. People need to learn the knowledge science teaches, but we should also know that Satan powerfully uses scientific theories and research to undermine God's plan for His creation.

Students come to me saying, "Pastor, my professor is trying to prove by findings in archeological research that most of the Bible is a myth." Pure science never undermines God's creation or His Word. Rightly understood, the Word of God is never in opposition to pure science. Opposition surfaces in the minds of scientists who deliberately attempt to discount belief in God, the Creator. Humanistic thinking is controlled by the kingdoms of this world.

God is concerned about the life, health and welfare of His creation. Science under Kingdom dominion always reflects the character of God which is goodness and blessing for all created things. God called His creation "good" and blessed it. Under God's plan for the world, sickness was nonexistent and nature flowed in perfect balance.

The restoration of God's plan to the kingdom of science will take great maturity in Kingdom people. Christianity offers medical science and psychiatry a dimension of healing in which the Holy Spirit controls and directs the soul (emotions, intellect and will) and the body. I admire Oral Roberts for building a hospital in which the knowledge of medical science is combined with prayer and the gifts of the Spirit to bring healing to people. I believe that God will give insights and miraculous breakthroughs in medical science to Christian doctors and research scientists who know how to pray according to God's will. I believe that someone will unlock the link between emotional stress and diseases like cancer which are so devastating. God never intended for people to suffer sickness and death.

The earth reflects God's character. Destruction of the earth by pollution, greed or nuclear war is Satan's attack on God's plan. Kingdom people must support ecological efforts to preserve and protect God's creation. We need to recognize the source of pollution as one facet of a satanic attack against God's creation. God told man to subdue the earth and become its caretaker or steward, yet many Christians are oblivious to the varying disguises of satanic warfare against the earth.

Satan wants total destruction of God's creation, and nuclear arms are a viable vehicle to accomplish his evil plan. Unfortunately, the Church is divided on this issue, and God is unable to speak in one clear, resounding voice to the nations of the earth. Kingdom people with uncertain opinions concerning nuclear arms should ask themselves what God's will for creation really was and still is. Has His plan changed? Are Russian Christians who are now experiencing the fires of revival our enemies? Are Chinese Christians who kept spreading the Word of God for decades after their missionaries left or were killed our enemies? Is God able to defend His people?

The kingdom of science must come under God's control as Kingdom scientists offer positive alternatives to satanic destruction. We must focus on God's character as we test the spirit of research and discoveries in medicine and technology. Consider whether God or humanism is glorified and honored. Humanism says, "Look what we have accomplished," but only accomplishments in the Kingdom of God are eternal and able to bring true life.

KINGDOM OF EDUCATION

Another kingdom that Satan controls is the kingdom of education. The kingdom of education began in the Garden of Eden and is associated with the tree of knowledge. Knowledge acquired through books which instruct us is not to be confused with true wisdom which comes from God.

The writer of Proverbs says, "For the Lord gives wisdom" (Proverbs 2:6). We can gain all the knowledge that education offers and never understand the wisdom of God. A brilliant, well-read scholar with numerous graduate degrees may be totally ignorant of God's truth. The world and the Church clash repeatedly over issues where God's wisdom and worldly knowledge are in conflict. Much of the thinking in the Church reflects spiritual mixture because of these issues.

Many prejudices arise because Satan rules in education. Through the kingdom of education, even some churches began to say, "We will build private schools because we want to keep Christian families together." Unfortunately, the purpose of many private schools is to separate children from children of another race. Running from any situation because of prejudice prevents people from ever seeing the Kingdom of God.

Prejudice is always the fruit of a kingdom where great warfare exists. Some of the greatest controversies within communities focus on issues related to education. Racial issues, still very much alive in this kingdom, need to be uncovered and resolved. Most educational institutions are not ruled by the Kingdom of God. The time has come for the Church of the living God, as a firstfruit of the Kingdom, to demonstrate the proper atmosphere and purpose of schools by unmasking the subtle control Satan exerts over education.

We are to be a light to the world. How can Christians be witnesses if they are hidden under a bushel somewhere in schools established because of prejudices? Satan has subtly moved in and said to us, "Be sure your children get a good education," when the true motive has been separation from the world.

The kingdoms of this world have taken over education, and Satan subtly demands that people go to extremes. Some people go to great expense to see that their children attend private schools because they are afraid to put them in public schools.

God can start Kingdom fires burning in public schools. Joseph, Moses and Daniel received wisdom directly from God in societies that did not honor their beliefs. God's Church must be an extension of teaching the Kingdom of God, and we must look very carefully at the curriculum we teach our children. Nothing should be taught unless that information becomes an extension of the Kingdom of God. God is raising up teachable young people, Kingdom boys and girls, who will soon go out to establish God's Kingdom on this earth.

Kingdom curriculum must include teaching about the Holy Spirit and the gifts of God's Spirit. Satan has moved very insidiously to take control even in many church schools. Remember that some of the greatest universities in the United States began as religious institutions. Harvard, Yale and Princeton are only a few of the Ivy League schools which were founded as church-related institutions. State schools were started later because Satan had to perpetuate his own secular educational system. But what happened to those excellent church schools? They became more interested in the knowledge of this world than in the wisdom of God. In many cases they became havens for atheists and agnostic intellectuals. These "intellectuals" breed agnosticism in the name of "higher learning."

The time has come for us to stop and say, "The Holy Spirit will teach us." Christian parents can overshadow any ungodly influence in public schools by becoming actively involved in PTA, school board issues and parent support groups as they make their involvement a stronghold for God.

The Apostle Paul was an educated man who studied under the great teacher, Gamaliel. However, after Paul met Jesus on the road to Damascus, he said, "I also count all things loss for the excellence of the knowledge of Christ Jesus" (Philippians 3:8). The same Kingdom spirit that Paul exemplified is the spirit God desires from us. The day is late. Our world grows weary while creation waits for the manifestation of the sons of God.

How long will creation wait? Must we wait until famine has destroyed the lives of millions of people? Will we wait until a nuclear holocaust kills millions of people? Or will we say, "It is now God's hour to manifest His Kingdom"? We must say with Paul, "I count all things as loss that I might gain Christ."

Young people who "seek first the Kingdom of God" will challenge the current contention of educational institutions that the purpose of education is to make money and become economically and socially successful. Education is subtly controlled by a desire for more possessions, higher social status and more easily acquired wealth. Mammon motivates people to learn by promising them security and happiness through knowledge.

Kingdom people must expose Satan's stronghold in education by resisting the innate competitiveness which schools foster in motivating students to achieve. Competition and achievement are separate and distinct motivations. God blesses achievement, which means being fulfilled in God's calling in an individual life. Achievement is pressing toward the "goal of our high calling," or spiritually hungering and thirsting to be conformed to the image of Jesus Christ who is our ultimate role model. Competition dictates the "winners and losers" mentality that puts people in bondage to fear of failure long after their school days are past. The self-seeking attitude in competition requires comparisons between ourselves and others which causes us to judge ourselves as either inferior or superior. Neither concept enables us to live out God's purposes in our lives.

Many Kingdom churches are beginning to open schools to demonstrate prototypes of education under godly, scriptural principles. Kingdom schools help individual students meet their full potential academically, emotionally and spiritually. These schools become that witness to other educational institutions that money and competition are not the proper motivations for learning. They challenge the prevailing humanistic doctrines subtly infiltrating classrooms today which imply that man is his own god, able to decide for himself what is right and wrong, good and bad, moral and immoral. The "I'll have it my way," or "anything goes as long as you don't hurt anyone else" attitudes have done great damage to society's order and have caused confusion and frustration in young people who want guidelines and answers before they make choices for their lives. The attitude can be traced to curriculum content taught in schools across the nation.

Kingdom teachers and young people must infiltrate current educational institutions with a bold witness of scriptural motivations for learning and Kingdom life goals. They need to challenge humanistic values subtly conveyed in social sciences, literature, pure science and the arts. They need to confront the mind of reason with the Spirit of God as they become God's light and salt in secular institutions that they rightfully claim for Christ's Kingdom. The zeal and anointing of God in those He raises up as His witnesses in academic environments will set new standards of excellence in the modern world and will offer alternative choices to those who are truly seeking for answers and who claim a sincere dedication to truth.

KINGDOM OF COMMERCE AND FINANCE

Business, commerce and finance are three closely related kingdoms where Satan dwells. Few kingdoms are as closely knit together as finance and commerce. In the book of Revelation, the great city Babylon is symbolic of the commerce of the world. A Babylon spirit is prevalent in the marketplaces of the world today. One needs only to observe people to recognize that they have made commerce their god. Possessions become idols as people focus their concern on how to handle and invest their finances.

The business and financial world can do great things with money in the name of progress. Occasionally they will even contribute money to religious institutions to prove that they are "good citizens" of the community. The commercial philosophy of private enterprise emphasizes the pursuit of wealth. I prophesy that needy people who are hurting in impoverished conditions are going to rise up when they realize that they number more than those who are affluent. These conditions may result in revolution unless the Church of the living God wakes up and identifies where Satan dwells in the world's financial structure and begins to influence with Kingdom principles those who control the world's wealth.

Revolution waits for the right moment to explode. Working people fear becoming indigent, and they save their money for emergencies because they are obsessed with becoming financially secure. Understand that this is a financial kingdom that is owned and directed by Satan. God's people must recognize that commerce, business and finance, when properly understood and practiced, can represent godly stewardship.

What appears to be stewardship in Christians is sometimes greed. We approach life like the rich man who filled one barn and was not satisfied until he filled another. He planned to take his ease and rest and he felt that he would live forever. Unexpectedly, however, his life was taken from him. Satan tries to make us feel that we are immortal but our humanity is the same as the rich man's in this parable. When one is dying, earthly possessions will have no value. We must know where Satan lurks and refuse his control of our finances. Satan must not deceive us concerning our stewardship to God. Our finances go for one of two purposes. Our money goes either to the kingdoms of this world or to the Kingdom of God. We must be in control of our finances and know where our money is going.

We find a lesson concerning finances in Leviticus 27:28. "Nevertheless no devoted offering that a man may devote to the Lord of all that he has, both man and beast, or the field of his possession, shall be sold or

47

redeemed; every devoted offering is most holy to the Lord." This a matter of Old Testament law, but Paul's letter to the Hebrews tells us that the Law was given to us for an example. Leviticus 27:28 speaks about a sacrifice, but the spirit of stewardship is the same as sacrificial offerings to the Lord.

"Every devoted offering" means something that has been set apart for God. The tithe is a requirement of the law, but the New Testament goes far beyond the tithe by encouraging us to give as God has prospered us. The tithe is only the first requirement. Anything set aside, or devoted, or earmarked for God is a holy thing. One may say that this scripture is referring to sheep and goats, but God said that a man shall devote unto the Lord all that he has, both of man and beast, of the field, and all of his possessions.

A person is a part of a Kingdom Church only if that church is doing those things that God said a Kingdom Church will do. God's Church can never usher in the Kingdom of God until all the people begin to practice financially what the Word says to do. Christians must not be capricious, but should always be consistent concerning the money that belongs to God. One cannot call himself a "Kingdom person" when he pays tithe only part of the time. Satan has deceived people into thinking that tithing is their own decision. That deception keeps the Church from demonstrating God's Kingdom. The kingdoms of this world are so strong that they deceive even God's people, especially concerning money.

Someone says, "Pastor, you're under the Law." I

know that some call tithing "legalism," but Jesus said, "This ye ought to have done."

It is not easy to transfer money from the realm of Satan to the realm of God because we are dealing with Satan himself whose kingdom is darkness. When I unmask Satan by preaching in these matters, I can feel the very powers of hell, but I know that "greater is He that is in me than he that is in the world." We've been victimized long enough by the financial structure of our society. The time has come for the sons of God to stand up and say, "I want to expose what is taking place!"

Concerning a church which needs financial help, Paul wrote, "First they gave themselves to the Lord"(II Corinthians 8:5). God does not want our finances until He has us. Some people feel they please God by giving the church a small offering or tithe. That offering can even become an abomination. When we give something to God—a tithe, an offering, alms or a gift—we must be certain that we can say that we belong to God first. Take the holy part that belongs to God and freely return it to Him. Kingdom people should be willing to stretch themselves beyond expected requirements to give to God.

We must demonstrate spiritual principles that the world does not follow. Several years ago a man drove up to my house in a very expensive car. He said to me, "Preacher, I've been watching you on television. I operate a certain business in this town and I hear you preach against the things that I do and the products that I sell." I said, "That's right, you've got the right

49

man." Then he said, "I want to give you several thousand dollars for your church so that I can claim it as a tax deduction. It may sound crazy, but somehow I think I'm supposed to give this to your church and I don't know what else to do other than come tell you that."

I'm sure he thought I was going to say, "That's the devil's money and you take it and go your way with your business!" But I looked him straight in the eye and said to him, "You've come to the right man. The devil has had that money long enough. Now it belongs to God." Money itself is not evil. The danger in churches receiving money from outside sources (such as this man) rests in any controls which may be imposed on how the money is to be used.

When Israel started leaving Egypt, the Spirit of the Lord told them to do a strange thing. God said, "Go among the Egyptians and spoil." That means to go among them and steal what they have. Steal their gold and their silver, hide it in little bags and get ready to go. God said, "Spoil them." That command of God is right in our Bibles. When Israel arrived in the desert, people who had been paupers and indigents with no possessions whatsoever in the land of Goshen had enough gold and silver to build a tabernacle. They spoiled the Egyptians because God said that the gold and silver of the Egyptians belonged to Him.

The kingdoms of this world have deceived us long enough. We are not to steal our neighbor's silver and gold, but some things have indeed belonged to the devil long enough. The time has come for the Kingdom of

God to take back the things that belong to God. We can take our gold and silver and do one of two things. The children of Israel are symbolic of our choices. Gold and silver can become a god of Mammon to us, or we can do as God commanded so that He can use our offerings as sanctified money.

While Moses went to the mountain top, some of the Israelites took golden earrings and made an idol, the golden calf. Today the same spirit prevails within the Church among those who choose to use God's money for their own pleasure. They are certain to give an account to God for their actions. The financial system will eventually belong to God and not to this world. Satan's control of the world's wealth signals the time for us to understand that worldly business cannot run the Church. The Church must demonstrate God's power to the business world. The Church of the living God under the direction of the Holy Spirit will establish God's Kingdom through revelation of innovative business practices.

In the same way that God told Joseph what, when and how to prepare for a famine, He will also tell His Church to prepare for events that are going to happen. The mighty power of God knows and reveals the kingdoms of this earth. They will become the Kingdom of God when we recognize where Satan dwells, how he manipulates and controls, and what we must do to unmask him.

Jesus told us to choose whether we serve God or Mammon, which is a powerful antichrist spirit. The spirit of Mammon has tried to manipulate God's people in financial extremes or mixture with worldly financial concepts. Mammon tries to destroy our witness as the world closely watches how we spend money. Some Christians regard poverty as "holy" and have become bound to proving their righteousness by deliberately being poor. Other Christians have insisted that God's people must be wealthy and materially prosperous.

Believers must test their own spirits in regard to money. Jesus is our King and He rules our lives according to His plans and purposes. Are we really seeking the Kingdom of God and its righteousness first, trusting that all our needs will be met?

The alternative to Satan's kingdom of commerce is a mentality of wealth which meets every need of human life. God's people rejoice when Babylon falls (Revelation 18:20), while the merchants of the earth weep and mourn (Revelation 18:11). We rejoice because greed and human exploitation for financial gain have ended at last. Justice finally reigns under God's authority in finance and commerce and business.

Until that day, Kingdom people need to be open and sensitive to meeting the needs of others in the Body of Christ throughout the world. Churches which God has blessed with material resources need to move joyfully by the Spirit in providing for churches which need equipment and supplies to spread the Gospel of the Kingdom. My own ministry in Atlanta, Georgia, has at times provided television and audio equipment, medical supplies and financial support to ministries in need in places such as Nigeria, Jamaica, Honduras, Brazil and Haiti. At times of greatest financial need in my own church, we will take an offering for some other ministry because the Spirit of God will specifically tell me about an existing need in the Body of Christ. God's power is released when we meet the needs of others. That is a Kingdom principle that works repeatedly when the motive and the spirit of the giver are in obedience to God.

The world watches carefully over Kingdom finances. We must demonstrate purity and faith in spending without becoming defensive or apologetic to worldly criticism over how our money is spent. We spend as God directs us. The world under Mammon's control hates any use of its idol for any purpose that honors God, and it will always attack, distort and misrepresent the finances of the Church. Kingdom people must be wise as serpents and harmless as doves in financial decisions. Remember that people are choosing daily between God and Mammon, and we want to confront and influence their decisions for the Kingdom of God.

KINGDOM OF THE ARTS

Another kingdom of Satan exists in the arts: music, dance and drama. Among Pentecostal and holiness groups, dancing unto the Lord used to mean what we called "the holy jerks." The holy jerks is not dancing unto the Lord. I'm not saying it's not of God, but dancing unto the Lord is a response of flowing in worship and praise.

Don't be offended by dance or drama in worship. Jesus said when He dealt with some of these areas,

"Woe unto you if you're offended at Me." The arts open our spirits to God's beauty and majesty. We respond to Him in expressions of worship from our spirits. Both the soul and the body respond to intimate communion with our Maker.

The arts should express God's creation rather than interpret it. Interpretation can be a subtle challenge to God's design through man's powers of reason. Christian parents need to take a firm stand for their children's sake against the sexual perversion and distorted role models that many rock stars and movie stars project. Satan is even able to imitate worship in many rock concerts that sell out large city auditoriums and stadiums. The large crowds at these concerts make the lifestyles of the "entertainers" seem both glamorous and acceptable. These concert events unmistakably imitate the worship of God by the spiritual, emotional and physical participation of the audience. The similarities are so blatant that many Christians fear lively music and active physical participation during worship in the house of God. Can't we see how Satan is trying to rob God's people of high praise and worship of the King, Jesus Christ, by promoting his own shocking counterfeits?

Much of modern art also reflects distortion and confusion rather than the natural order and beauty of God's creation. Kingdom art captures the expression of the source of true creativity, the Creator Himself. Examine the spirit of a work of art. Does it express the Creator or interpret the creation?

God's Word contains some of the most effective

drama that has ever been written. The story of David and Goliath depicts the warfare of every believer and the victory of God's anointing on one who fights in the name of the Lord. The drama of Abraham putting Isaac on the altar to sacrifice him to the Lord is a timeless example of unquestioning obedience. Jesus spoke in parables and used symbols of seeds, coins and trees to represent reality in people's lives. He would sometimes go through a process of demonstration requiring faith to heal someone, and other times He would only speak a word to accomplish the healing.

Drama is a powerful teaching tool that Satan uses to instill his own values and paths of destruction. Children watch violent and pornographic scenes each day on television in their own homes. Imagine the impact of those scenes on tender, highly impressionable young minds! How can God's people allow the mental and emotional destruction of an entire generation with our silence and passivity? We are accountable to God for our silence! We must sound the alarm and blow the trumpet while at the same time, offer a life-giving alternative to the world.

THE KINGDOM OF SPORTS

God's Word says to "train a child in the way he should go." God's way is reverence for sacred things. The kingdoms of this world have a tremendous opportunity to influence youth. Sports, while innately beneficial to the physical man, can actually become an addiction. No church in the city of Atlanta has a better athletic program or athletes than my church, but I would prefer our athletes attend another church than to have spirits built on premises of competition that lose sight of what athletics is all about.

When any activity in one's life so consumes a person's time and energy that he can't honor the house of God or the things that belong to God, that activity has become Satan's kingdom. Satan has so subtly preoccupied people's minds with "wholesome" activities that people cannot identify a work of Satan.

Until we know where Satan is, we will never establish the Kingdom of God. Satan will not boldly introduce himself to us. He will come in subtle ways saying, "If you want to win people to the church, go with them to see the Falcons play on Sunday. Tell them, 'I'll go to the game with you this Sunday, if you'll go to church with me next Sunday.' " Such thinking is the subtle trap of Satan and his kingdom of darkness.

People begin to look to athletes for advice on personal matters from recommendations on which products they purchase to endorsements of political candidates. Suddenly a star athlete is an authority on life. Some athletes who should be examples to youth in areas of discipline and achievement display hostile, competitive attitudes and immoral lifestyles and openly admit they are playing only to make money. How subtly Satan captures those areas of our lives that could honor God! Sports enthusiasm without proper spiritual perspective can so easily become an example of false worship and idolatry.

The Bible says that our bodies are temples of the

Holy Spirit. Kingdom people are instructed to lay aside every weight (hindrance) because we are running a race each day of our lives. The Body of Christ is intended to be a shining example of teamwork—every member doing his best at the place God has called him to serve. Discipline is inherent in our call to discipleship as we present our bodies as living sacrifices to God. This is the day for Kingdom men and women who are outstanding athletes to boldly exemplify these principles to the world as they give glory to God for their abilities and talents.

KINGDOM OF FALSE RELIGIONS

Another of Satan's kingdoms is false religions. False religions are usually religions of the mind which subtly creep into the Church under the disguise of "positive thinking." Not all positive thinking is wrong, just as not all of the financial or educational kingdoms are corrupt. Any focus, however, that fails to magnify Jesus Christ or establish the Kingdom of God can become a false religion.

False religions are bound up in forms of godliness, traditions and doctrines. Entire denominations are built on nothing more than traditions and doctrines. Members of these churches often have no Biblical answers for what they believe. Some emphasize makeup and jewelry and certain types of clothing. They don't understand scriptures in proper context. They quote scriptures concerning Jezebel to prove their point about makeup. Satan deceptively emphasizes areas such as forms, traditions and doctrines which have nothing to do with establishing the Kingdom of God.

Most false religions are based on fear and they control people's behavior by manipulating and threatening them. Control of people is an essential element of false religions. These religions disregard two basic ingredients of living for Jesus Christ—free will and grace. Mental, emotional and spiritual bondage is the fruit of lives controlled by false religions. These people constantly strive to adhere to rigid, even abusive rules. They are driven as zealots instead of being motivated by the meek, yet powerful zeal of the Lord. The zeal of the Lord does not drive us; it produces joy which is our strength and empowers us to sow seeds of peace and righteousness in the Holy Spirit.

False religions foster dishonesty with others and oneself. Some religions literally whisper their doctrines and build walls around their compounds so that only those people whom they thoroughly indoctrinate can get inside. Beware of ministries that are closed off to the outside world. God's true Church is bold enough to shout His praises from the housetops. Truth always sets people free and makes them want to share the good news of Jesus Christ!

Deceived people are religious and sincere. Jesus's strongest opponents were the religious leaders of His day who despised His authority and truth. Test the spirit of "religious-sounding" words. Do they honor and lift up Jesus Christ? Do they reflect the goodness and love of God's character?

Unfortunately, the influence of religious spirits has infiltrated the Church, causing mixture, divisions and prejudices in the Body of Christ. God is shaking and purging the Church to purity today so that we can sound the clear voice of God to the world. God's chosen people are tuning their ears to hear the voice of God's anointing on His called apostles, prophets, evangelists, pastors and teachers. We can expect persecution because the world despises the purity and goodness exemplified by Jesus Christ. Deceived members of false religions will attack the true Church with the greatest persecution, but God will win!

The eyes of God look upon the the earth, searching for mature groups of people to whom He can show Himself strong, a people who are willing to be a first-fruit of His Kingdom. I am hungry to see the things of God take place and to see God's Kingdom established now. I want to be among those who answer that prayer that Jesus prayed,"Thy kingdom come, Thy will be done on earth as it is in heaven." That prayer is my meat and my purpose!

The Kingdom of God will be birthed when God finds a foretaste, a prototype, a lead domino, or a showcase who will be His witness to the world. When God can find that group of people who take seriously His original intentions when He created us, the Kingdom of God will be established.

God has given us the Holy Ghost with unlimited power. He has given us the name of Jesus Christ like a blank check which we are empowered to use for His glory. He has given us weapons for spiritual warfare.

He has given us the Body of Christ in which He has placed the five-fold ministries. He has given us the enlightenment of the written Word and the image of the living Christ. Then Jesus said, "Take these tools and subdue the world." We sit back and wait for God to do it, but God wants us to manifest Kingdom principles. His plan is for us, His people, to subdue the kingdoms of this world. God wants the world to see His children bring His glorious plan to success.

3

OVERCOMING HINDRANCES TO THE KINGDOM

Jesus Christ, God in the flesh, proclaimed, "The Kingdom of God is within you!" A Christian's comprehension of the Kingdom of God can easily be measured by whether he worships a God Who serves him, or one Whom he serves. Who is our King? Who is in control of our lives? What are our goals? What kinds of fruit do our lives produce? These questions uncover the subtle deceptions which hinder the Kingdom of God from coming on earth as it is in heaven. The "few who find the Kingdom" are those who have learned to lay aside every hindrance in a tenacious pursuit of an unseen prize which will even cost them their lives. Few people will ever applaud such a pursuit. Worldly critics of Kingdom motivation call it "madness," or "fantasy," or "a waste of great potential for success."

Complacent Christians, steeped in their traditions and doctrines, are often suspicious of those who are willing to give all to follow the Lord. Most Christians choose comfort and security. The Church shouts, "Amen!" over hearing the salvation message of eternal life. They look forward to white robes and golden crowns. They desire the day when they will walk on streets of gold and live in mansions in heaven. But why do so few Christians enter the dimension of Kingdom living in their daily decisions? Few obediently drink of His cup or willingly partake of His baptism of death (their wills) on the cross which is required to rule with Him. "It's too hard! Too complicated! Too demanding! It hurts too much," they say. "God would never ask me to sacrifice like that!"

So instead of living the Kingdom life, Christians usually settle for respectable lives, middle class (or better) standards of living, well-educated children and promises of heaven when they die. They easily separate the values of church on Sunday and work during the week. God is someone "up there"; heaven is "over there"; and Jesus is someone who is simply "there when you need Him."

Those who decide to pursue the Kingdom of God "on earth" and establish Jesus as King in every area of their lives begin to enter into Kingdom demonstration. Kingdom people follow the leading of the Holy Spirit in their daily experiences. They discover that when Jesus is the King of their lives, His "yoke is easy" and His "burden is light." Many people unintentionally complicate the definition of the Kingdom of God. Kingdom truths are simple. The simplicity of the Kingdom message is the key to its becoming a definable reality in our lives and in the world. The Kingdom of God is righteousness, peace and joy in the Holy Spirit (Romans 14:17). Jesus instructed us to reach out, grasp and implement Kingdom reality in everyday experiences. He said, "The Kingdom of God is within you! The Kingdom of God is at hand! The Kingdom of God is near!"

The Kingdom of God is basic Christianity lived out —loving one's neighbor, blessing an enemy, forgiving as God forgives, and loving God with all our hearts. Kingdom hindrances are attached to our selfish natures, appealing to our powers of reason, personal ambitions, public opinions, traditions, sensual appetites, our desire to rule others or to take an easy path which avoids self-denial. We worship other gods which serve our purposes rather than becoming the "living sacrifices" created to glorify God and enjoy His fellowship forever.

The one intent and purpose of Jesus Christ's coming to the world was to establish a new order, a new Kingdom. Some would say that Jesus came solely "to seek and save that which was lost." Why did He come for that purpose? Just to save people? To leave them saved? No, Jesus came to establish a new order. Everything that He said or did was for that purpose. Some people miss this truth and they will eventually look back and say, "I was close to it, but I never totally comprehended the meaning of the Kingdom of God."

John the Baptist came preaching that the Kingdom of God was at hand. After John the Baptist preached the Kingdom proclamation, immediately the first Kingdom Man walked on the scene. He was the first Man to represent bodily all the principles that God wanted His people to understand about the new order He would establish. Jesus Christ personally exemplified the perfect specimen of a Kingdom Man in the flesh. John said, "The Kingdom of God is at hand." Jesus Christ could have established the witness necessary to totally establish the Kingdom of God on earth. Certain hindrances were the reasons He did not and could not do it then, but feasibly, the Kingdom could have come on earth two thousand years ago.

After John preached the Kingdom of God was at hand, Jesus lived a demonstration of the principles of the Kingdom. Jesus Christ was the perfect Demonstrator. He lived out all the teachings, attitudes and purposes of God's plan that one man could possibly fulfill. Jesus said, "I cannot do it alone, and since I am the firstfruit of the Kingdom, I am going to leave the Holy Spirit for those who will come after Me. When the Spirit comes, He will enable each one of you to do what I am doing, and even greater works you shall do." Today the Church is in a holding pattern, needing to become the witness to the world which God requires. Jesus sits at the right hand of the Father waiting until His mandates are accomplished in His Church (Acts 2:34,35).

Jesus personally demonstrated all the principles of the Kingdom of God. First of all, He single-handedly confronted and conquered Satan by bringing him to a dimension of defeat. Though much must yet be lived out, Jesus reduced Satan's authority to a defeatist mentality. Satan refuses to believe that he is defeated and knowing that his time is short, he battles desperately. Since Satan is not only a deceiver but also deceived, he thinks that he will win in the end.

Jesus Christ demonstrated the power of the Kingdom. The Word says that when we "cast out devils," the Kingdom is present (Matthew 12:28). Casting out devils was visible evidence of Jesus's great power. We cannot separate power from the Kingdom or the Holy Spirit from the Kingdom. Not only did Jesus come to cast out adversaries, He personally defeated the last enemy which is death. He defeated death in principle for us, but we have not yet experienced that defeat except in the Spirit. Jesus defeated death as an individual, and in that victory He became the firstfruit of many who will follow Him. Now He says to us, "You have a job to do in relation to death." Jesus personally defeated death by coming back after His death in the resurrection. The Bible said that He was upon the earth for forty days after the resurrection (Acts 1). What did Jesus choose to do for those forty days when He returned to the earth?

"The former account I made, O Theophilus, of all that Jesus began both to do and teach, until the day in which He was taken up, after He through the Holy Spirit had given commandments to the apostles whom He had chosen, to whom He also presented Himself alive after His suffering by many infallible proofs, being seen by them during forty days and speaking of the things pertaining to

the kingdom of God." (Acts 1:1-3)

Jesus was totally committed to talking about the Gospel of the Kingdom. He talked about a coming new order, a new society lived out "in" the world but not "of" the world.

Then Jesus gave power to His disciples to complete His work. The ministry He had personally demonstrated was now corporately demonstrated by His followers. That demonstration is the key issue. Everything that Jesus Christ did, the Church must do. Everything that Jesus Christ performed, His Church must perform, including challenging and overcoming death! Paul said a time would come when the saints would not depart from this life, but they would be changed. Understand that we must do everything that Jesus Christ did. He gave us the power to complete the work that He began. Only that generation that precedes the coming of the Lord will experience this "change."

Jesus left tools for us to use to accomplish our glorious mission. First, Jesus called out leaders. The Bible says (Ephesians 4) that when He came out of hell, He gave to the Church apostles, prophets, evangelists, pastors and teachers. Someone says, "I have the Holy Ghost, therefore I can teach." Not necessarily so! "I have the Holy Ghost, I can be a prophet." Not necessarily so! One may be moved upon by the spirit of prophecy and not be a called prophet at all.

"Therefore, indeed, I send you prophets, wise men, and scribes: some of them you will kill and crucify, and some of

them you will scourge in your synagogues and persecute from city to city that on you may come all the righteous blood shed on the earth, from the blood of righteous Abel to the blood of Zechariah, son of Berechiah, whom you murdered between the temple and the altar. Assuredly, I say to you, all these things will come upon this generation." (Matthew 23:34-36)

People today do not crucify God's messengers on a cross, but they kill God's voice by character assasination, refusing to listen to them or making them commonplace through insults and disrespect. Jesus said that when the generation comes who will experience the Kingdom in that final thrust, God's leaders will consist of prophets, wise men and spiritual scribes who will be crucified, killed, ridiculed and scourged. These leaders will be persecuted from city to city, but according to Jesus, their generation will experience the revelation of the Kingdom.

Jesus sent the Holy Spirit to us. The outpouring of the Holy Spirit at Pentecost was the consummation of God's spiritual manifestations in the Old Testament. In the Old Testament, the Holy Spirit moved through individuals such as Ezekiel and Elijah, but until Pentecost the Holy Spirit had never before moved upon an entire body of people. We now live in that spiritual dispensation where we may accomplish what God has called us to accomplish by the Spirit.

Jesus said that He would send the Holy Spirit among us to teach us, guide us and give us gifts. He makes callings among us. He comforts us. God promises all of these things to His Church today. Why? Not so we can get puffed up, lift our hands and praise God, or even speak with tongues. No! Why did Jesus send the Holy Spirit? Jesus spoke to His disciples of the Holy Spirit in answer to their question, "Will You now restore the kingdom?" He said, "The Holy Spirit will help you to do it." This answer is the key to unlocking the Kingdom. We must not lose out on Jesus's meaning. The reason for the Holy Spirit's coming was to take the arms of the Church, like Aaron and Hur lifted Moses's arms, and enable the Church to perform the demonstration of a corporate move of God.

Not only did Jesus send us the Holy Spirit, He gave us the use of His name. When we walk in the will of God, whatever we ask in Jesus's name, He will perform by the Spirit. Jesus did whatever He heard His Father say. Through Him we can do all the things that Jesus did if we keep His commandments and do the things that are pleasing to Him. We usually don't receive our petitions because we ask things for our own kingdoms. One of the greatest deceptions in the Church today is the misuse of the name of Jesus. His name cannot be spoken flippantly. When we walk in the light as He is in the light, we will have fellowship with Him and have the right to ask what we will. If one has not had a personal experience with Jesus, the only prayer he can pray is for salvation. Once we are in the Kingdom and begin to follow the Father's plan, the Holy Spirit guides our lives.

Finally, Jesus left us promises, direction and further revelation. Many of the things prophets preach today have been held in mysteries for centuries. In these last days, God is beginning to open new dimensions of understanding. I am writing some things now that I have heard only by the Spirit. I have not conferred with flesh or blood. The spirit of wisdom and revelation is becoming more evident in the Church today.

The Kingdom of God was and is always "at hand." John the Baptist came proclaiming that the Kingdom of heaven was at hand meaning that the Kingdom is touchable (Matthew 3:2). The Kingdom is within our grasp (Matthew 4:17). Jesus told His disciples, "Now you go out and preach the Gospel of the Kingdom" (Matthew 10:7). Notice the sequence. John came saying, "The Kingdom is at hand." Jesus came saying, "I am the demonstration of the Kingdom." Then Jesus told His disciples, "Now go and preach the Gospel of the Kingdom."

Someone says, "I just thought we were supposed to preach 'Jesus'." Please understand that the sequence of announcing the Kingdom of God is significant. Jesus told His disciples, "Go out and perform the work of the Kingdom which you saw Me do so that we will have an adequate witness in the world."

Some people were near the Kingdom of God then, and some are near it today. A certain scribe got very close to the Kingdom.

Then one of the scribes came, and having heard them reasoning together, perceiving that He had answered them well, asked Him, "Which is the first commandment of all?" Jesus answered him, "The first of all the commandments is: 'Hear, O Israel, the Lord our God, the Lord is one. And you shall love the Lord your God with all your heart, with all your soul, with all your mind, and with all your strength.' This is the first commandment. And the second, like it, is this: 'You shall love your neighbor as yourself.' There is no other commandment greater than these." So the scribe said to Him, "Well said, Teacher. You have spoken the truth, for there is one God, and there is no other but He. And to love Him with all the heart, with all the understanding, with all the soul, and with all the strength, and to love one's neighbor as oneself, is more than all the whole burnt offerings and sacrifices." So when Jesus saw that he answered wisely, He said to him, "You are not far from the Kingdom of God." And after that no one dared question Him. (Mark 12:28-34)

Jesus said that the first commandment is "to love God," the second commandment is "to love your neighbor." The scribe added to Jesus's answer by saying that God wants love more than He wants sacrifice. The scribe had an instant revelation into the Kingdom message and stood right at the door of the Kingdom. Jesus Himself acknowledged that the scribe was close to the Kingdom. Many people have seen the Kingdom, but they are reluctant to enter because of their own individual selfishness. God is saying, "Hear the Word of the Lord, housewife." "Hear the Word of the Lord, spiritual father." "You are near to the Kingdom. Don't back away. You are too close. You will never be happy with anything less!"

Others were also close to the Kingdom, but they chose to shut the door and walk away.

Then Jesus spoke to the multitudes and to His disciples, saying: "The scribes and the Pharisees sit in Moses' seat. Therefore whatever they tell you to observe, that observe and do, but do not do according to their works; for they say, and do not do." (Matthew 23:1-3)

Jesus had numerous confrontations with the scribes and Pharisees. Don't overlook a very key point that also applies today. Pulpits today are filled with people who sit in Moses's seat, speaking the laws of God. The Church has a lot of "saying" the right things but very little "doing." Candler School of Theology at Emory University, the seminary where I graduated, has invited me to participate in a series of lectures during the spring quarter of next year. The seminary will join ranks with pastors who are involved in ministry demonstrations. Those young Methodist ministers are not just going to be looking at the lifestyles of people in Chapel Hill Harvester Church and the demonstration that God has given to this ministry; they will be specifically studying how lifestyles are affected by the baptism of the Holy Spirit. The message of the Kingdom is world-changing, and we need to understand what is happening in the Church today. Institutionalized religion is beginning to say, "There is something more. Our eyes must be open to see what God is doing on the face of the earth today." Charismatic Christians are not the only spiritually hungry people in the world today. Christians everywhere are beginning to grow hungry for the reality of what God is doing in the world.

"For they bind heavy burdens, hard to bear, and lay them on men's shoulders; but they themselves will not move them with one of their fingers. But all their works they do to be seen by men. They make their phylacteries broad and enlarge the borders of their garments." (Matthew 23:4-5)

"Woe to you scribes and Pharisees, hypocrites! For you shut up the kingdom of heaven against men; for you neither go in yourselves, nor do you allow those who are entering to go in. Woe to you, scribes and Pharisees, hypocrites! For you devour widows' houses, and for a pretense make long prayers. Therefore you will receive greater condemnation." (Matthew 23:13-14)

"Blind Pharisee, first cleanse the inside of the cup and dish, that the outside of them may be clean also. Woe to you, scribes and Pharisees, hypocrites! For you are like whitewashed tombs which indeed appear beautiful outwardly, but inside are full of dead men's bones and all uncleanness." (Matthew 23:26-27)

"But woe to you, scribes and Pharisees, hypocrites! Because you build the tombs of the prophets and adorn the monuments of the righteous, and say, 'If we had lived in the days of our fathers, we would not have been partakers with them in the blood of the prophets.' Therefore you are witnesses against yourselves that you are sons of those who murdered the prophets. Fill up, then, the measure of your fathers' guilt. Serpents, brood of vipers! How can you escape the condemnation of hell? Therefore indeed, I send you prophets, wise men, and scribes: some of them you will kill and crucify, and some of them you will scourge in your synagogues and persecute from city to city."

(Matthew 23:29-34)

Jesus admonished religious leaders for proudly quoting Isaiah and Daniel, while calling God's chosen men and women "heretics," "cultists," "blasphemers," or "extremists." They warned, "Don't listen to that, or you will get into trouble." God has not sent Isaiah to prophesy to people in the 1980's. God set forth the principles and patterns of prophecy in His Word, then Jesus said, "I shall send you prophets." The problem with the Church today is that people don't want to submit to God's ordained spiritual authority. One thing which stops people from pursuing the Kingdom and causes them to walk away is when a prophet of God tampers with individual kingdoms. People walk away saying, "I won't hear that any longer." Jesus turned and looked into the faces of those twelve disciples and asked, "Are you going to leave also?" Some of the most capable men that God ever gave to my church walked away because they could not bear to hear the truth. And yet it is the good pleasure of God to give us the Kingdom (Luke 12:32).

What has kept the Kingdom from coming? Jesus demonstrated it, empowered the Church, and spent forty days teaching and preaching the secrets of the Kingdom. So why hasn't His Kingdom come? The Spirit impressed me that there are five reasons that the Kingdom did not come in the days of Jesus.

First, the people's familiarity with Jesus's flesh caused great unbelief. This same principle hinders the Kingdom from coming today. They said, "This is

Joseph's son." Jesus could do no mighty miracles among His own people because they said, "We know His flesh."

Secondly, the dullness of the people's hearing hindered the Kingdom. When the Spirit of God descended upon Jesus at the time of His baptism, the one thing the Spirit said was, "Here ye Him." God still says today, "Hear what the Spirit is saying to the Church."

Thirdly, Jesus's followers lacked oneness. Why did Jesus pray in John 17, "Father, make them one," if they were already one? The Kingdom could not come in the days of Jesus because He could never get His disciples to come into unity. When Jesus walked among men, He could have demonstrated the Kingdom adequately to have taken total control of the earth from Satan, but there was lack of unity.

Fourthly, they were steeped in religious tradition. They followed what their fathers had said. They did not hear what Jesus was saying because they always reverted to saying, "Abraham is our father. Moses gave us the Law." They refused to hear the young prophet from Nazareth.

Fifthly, the Kingdom could not come then because of a betrayal spirit among Jesus's intimate group. Personal betrayal hindered Jesus from establishing His Kingdom.

Why then did the Kingdom not come during the Apostolic period? I prayed, "God, I must have some answers." God revealed to me that the Kingdom did not come in the Apostolic days because there was too much prejudice. Mighty Peter, who preached at Pentecost, was full of prejudice when Cornelius came to take him to the Gentiles. Religious as well as racial prejudices abounded in the Apostolic Church so that the Kingdom could not be demonstrated.

God will never demonstrate His Kingdom in a church that is not totally racially and culturally integrated. A Kingdom Church must overcome racial prejudices, religious prejudices, or any other prejudices which exist. The pastors in my church wear clerical collars and put on vestments during Communion as an outward demonstration of a lack of prejudice. We also have a woman pastor on our staff who has been divorced. The Holy Spirit is leading Chapel Hill Harvester Church to demonstrate a total confrontation and defeat of spiritual prejudices, but the Apostolic Church never moved beyond their own prejudices.

The second reason that the Apostolic Church could never experience or demonstrate the Kingdom of God was because of mutiny in the ranks. When God called spiritual leadership, certain rebels in the ranks like Ananias and Sapphira said, "We will deceive the church leadership." People like that today are deceiving no one but themselves. The Apostolic Church never experienced the ability to listen to their spiritual leaders.

The third reason the Kingdom did not come during the Apostolic era is revealed to us in I Corinthians 3:1-4. Because of carnality, the Corinthians chose their own leaders and refused to follow the leadership God established. Some people chose Paul as their leader, some chose Apollos, and some chose other leaders. Paul said, "Are you not yet carnal?" God cannot do His work when people are following men's personalities instead of following the Spirit. Many people today choose leaders who will say exactly what they want to hear. They have itching ears which cause them to run from place to place to hear what they want to hear, not necessarily what God is saying today.

The next reason that the Apostolic Church could not bring the Kingdom to pass was because they developed "another world" mentality. They underwent great persecution and instead of maintaining the Kingdom concepts, they began to say, "It will be better 'over there'." The Christian Church has been deceived into believing that something will happen "over there." "I'm going to join Grandma who's over there." God is looking for people who are excited about what is taking place under their feet. This "other world" concept continues even today. People fervently worship God because it will be wonderful "over there" even though Jesus never said that, not even once.

Though the Kingdom did not come in Jesus's day or during the era of the Apostolic Church, why couldn't it have come during the first three centuries when the message of the Church literally took over the world and even the emperor of Rome became a Christian? The first reason the Kingdom did not come was the powerless mixture that replaced the purity of the persecuted Church. The Church felt proud because the world began listening to them. Being a Christian became very popular, and that mixture produced a lifeless Church.

The next reason the Kingdom did not come in the first three centuries was because of men's greed to rule. Such misuse of government did not properly display Kingdom principles. They called themselves "Christian" emperors, but they did not live out their convictions. A notable lack of demonstration characterized the Church in the first three centuries. The true Church was being buried in the catacombs. A Church state may have existed, but it never represented the true principles of the Kingdom of God.

Why didn't the Kingdom come during the Reformation? The Reformation seemed to be an ideal time for the Kingdom of God to finally be established upon the earth. Three reasons prevented its establishment. First of all, the Reformation was man's effort to purge the Church instead of a genuine purging by the Holy Spirit. I am not suggesting that Martin Luther was not moved upon by the power of the Holy Spirit, but many changes in the Church turned out to be a reformation of efforts. Much of the purging turned out to be righteousness brought on by man's works. Protestants stopped the sale of indulgences and challenged many of the immoral practices in the Church, but many of their actions were motivated by a purging of the flesh and not of the Spirit.

The second reason the Kingdom could not happen during the Reformation was the tremendous division within the Body of Christ which has continued into this century. This schism focused on Catholics and Protestants. The time has now come for Catholics and Protestants to lay down their separate identities and be identified as one Body of the Lord Jesus Christ.

The third reason the Kingdom did not come to pass during the Reformation was a lack of the outpouring of the Holy Spirit. As we read the writings of Martin Luther, Wycliffe and other reformers, the obvious missing ingredient in their movement was the Holy Spirit's power as it was at Pentecost.

Then came the rise of Pentecostalism at the turn of this century. The Holy Spirit was poured out upon "backwoods" preachers, whom the world would later call the little "nothing" people. This little group of people in the mountains of north Georgia and North Carolina — Spurling, Tomlinson, Lee and some of the old-time Pentecostals — were the generation just before my dad who followed in their footsteps and preached in their pulpits. Why didn't the Kingdom come then? Why wasn't it demonstrated by this little group of people who were physically driven from their churches because they spoke with other tongues? They believed in the power of God, so why didn't it happen then? I prayed, "I've got to know, God," and He gave answers to me which I now give to you.

First of all, God could not establish His Kingdom at the turn of the century in the classical Pentecostal movement because of exclusivism. Rather than turning themselves to the world as a shining light, Pentecostals built up walls and said, "We have the truth." They forgot about the rest of the world and the rest of the Church.

Secondly, they developed an attitude of condescendence toward the rest of the Church. I'm not referring to something I've only heard because when I grew up, I believed that if a Baptist woman wore make-up she would go to hell. I grew up believing that if a Methodist man went to a movie, he would go to hell. I thought if a young man played football on a high school or college team, he would probably go to hell because I was taught that those activities were "of the world." Pentecostals had the truth of the message, but they did not understand how it fit into daily life in the world. They had a condescending attitude and thought if people didn't do things their way—no make-up, no jewelry, a certain kind of dress—then they were bound for hell.

I saw my first movie ever—*Ben Hur*—when I was thirty-three years old in Phoenix, Arizona. My father forbade me to play on a basketball or football team because those activities were worldly, but in college at Furman University I was allowed to run on the track team because nobody would know about it. God has such a sense of humor! I broke some school records and my picture was on the front page of the "Sports" section of the Sunday paper. God was trying to say to Pentecostals then, "Wake up and stop trying to please yourselves! Broaden your perspective and see what I want to do in the world."

Pentecostal churches could not bring about the Kingdom because of their errors in discipline. Their doctrines for the most part were accurate, but they confused doctrine and discipline. They believed they were "holy" if they looked a certain way. I used to preach at camp meetings and at the end of the sermon I would open the pulpit for questions. I remember being asked, "Brother Earl, tell me this: Will a woman who wears make-up go to heaven?" I asked, "What color make-up?" You see, their faces looked like they had just gotten out of a powder bowl, but as long as their faces were white, make-up was permitted. If a woman painted herself with red, she was going to hell for sure. Pentecostal people were trapped in confusion about discipline and God says, "Don't concentrate on these things." Paul implied that everything he said about the outward man was by permission, not by commandment.

Pentecostals preached about the length of hair and the length of the dress, but they missed the greater truths. They had the Holy Spirit and they should have changed the world, but they spent their energies on matters of discipline!

Another reason the Kingdom did not come about in the Pentecostal church was because they became mindful of "another world." They began to sing "Over There," "In the Sweet Bye and Bye" and "I'll Fly Away" and abandoned the covenant God ordained with the earth. Because of this error, God went beyond old-time Pentecostalism so that He could birth His Kingdom to touch the world. Pentecostal churches could not bring about the Kingdom of God because they lacked Kingdom vision.

Concentration on personal salvation causes many churches to forget the Kingdom message. Their sole message becomes, "Just as I am, without one plea." I admire and acknowledge the calling of men like Billy Graham and Cliff Barrow, both of whom I know personally. They are absolutely, indisputably men who were raised up by God to preach the message of salvation, but that will not bring the Kingdom of God to this earth. The message of repentance actually causes some people to become almost self-centered. "Well, I am saved," they say, while their attitude implies, "So let the rest of the world go to hell." Personal salvation alone, without the Kingdom concept, is not enough. We are saved for a purpose—to change the society in which we live.

Even the Pentecostal purpose focused on "missing hell." They had no Kingdom concept of changing the world. They were determined to stay here saved, battle through as pilgrims, and after awhile go home to be with Jesus.

The Church has come to the end of the Pentecostal reign, as far as the traditional Pentecostal Church is concerned. We are now in what is called the great Charismatic movement which introduced the baptism of the Holy Ghost beyond the traditional Pentecostal Church to many other denominations. Doctrinal fences began to fall down as Catholics, Lutherans, Methodists and others received the Holy Ghost. The traditional Pentecostal denominations still serve a vital place in the Church world today.

We must never forget to honor the perseverance of those early Pentecostals who went before the mobs, without food, enduring suffering and sacrifice. We are their seed, but we simply cannot stop with that heritage. My father used to tell me, "I didn't get to go to school, but I am going to see that you go so that you can sit with anybody, even kings or governors, and look them straight in the eyes and say, 'I went to the same schools you did, and I still believe in the baptism of the Holy Ghost.' " I honor my father for that encouragement, but to go back to the message of his day would be a grave error. God is saying, "Look at the new horizon. Now is the time to change the world around you."

Unless something happens to prevent it, I will meet soon with the outstanding black leadership of the United States and perhaps of the world. If God gives me that opportunity, my one message to them will be, "Don't get caught up in another movement. You don't need another movement. You need a move of the Holy Spirit that will make God's people one all over the earth."

I sat recently with the Christian Council of Metropolitan Atlanta as one of their newly-elected members. I was very honored by a spokesman who said, "Earl was here during the Civil Rights movement. Twenty-five years or so ago, he was one of the pastors who had the guts to put his name on a Manifesto that said, 'You can't keep our little black children from going to white schools.' " I did sign that Manifesto and I'm proud that I did because today I enjoy the fruit of taking that stand. I spoke out when racial unity wasn't popular, and when society took away pulpits and laughed at preachers who defended human dignity. I had fire bombs thrown at my house, but I spoke out because I knew we had to break down prejudices in a corrupt society. When we began to move in these areas of confrontation, people in high spiritual leadership warned me of what was going to happen to me. Many people turned and walked away from my church. Many people today are preaching unity, but now my church desires more than unity. We want to demonstrate God's Kingdom to the world.

I prayed, "God, I must know what to do. If the Kingdom has never been adequately demonstrated except in the person of Jesus, only the Holy Spirit can tell me how the Church can do it." I took my Bible and began reading some of the scriptures we usually use when we speak of the Kingdom.

I read the Beatitudes in Matthew 5 which reminded me that the Church needs all the attributes Jesus described such as mercy, purity of heart and humility. I read Matthew 25:31-46 where Jesus said, "You can't enter because you didn't feed Me when I was hungry, or clothe Me when I was naked, or visit Me when I was in prison." In other words, "You weren't there to help me when I was captured by society, or when the worldly system around me had taken everything I had." I read Luke 9:62 where Jesus said, "Having put your hand to the plow, don't turn around," and how well I know that the Church needs perseverance. We can't give up or grow weary in well-doing. I read John 3:3, where Jesus said to Nicodemus, "You must be born again. You must leave the kingdom of darkness and move into the Kingdom of light. You must be circumcised in heart." I read Acts 14:22 where endurance is clearly one of the keys to producing the Kingdom. Then I went to James

2:5, where "faith" and "love" are two of the secrets of the Kingdom.

These scriptures could have been enough insight, but I said, "God, I must have deeper understanding. These scriptures are still the milk of the Word. I must know more." The Spirit of the Lord said to me, "You have asked for understanding, so I will give it to you. The Church has never heard the message I gave two thousand years ago to the beloved Apostle John. Turn to Revelation and I will show you the message that lists the hindrances to My Kingdom coming."

Again I took my Bible and after the Spirit of the Lord led me to the second chapter of Revelation, He said, "The same Word I gave to the seven Asian churches is the message the Church has never heard. If you will fulfill the message I gave to the Church years ago, the Kingdom of God will be birthed in your generation."

I first read about the Church at Ephesus (Revelation 2:1-7). I said, "Holy Spirit, what was the message to Ephesus?" God said to me, "You have left your first love." Can we say that our love and zeal are the same today as they were when we first fell in love with Jesus? Can we say that we are still on fire for God since we drive better cars and wear better clothes than we once did? Better things are not wrong, but do we have the same zeal that we had when we were first converted? Do we still get up in the morning saying, "God, this is Your day. If it weren't for You, where would I be?" We can talk about the Lord to other men, but do our works show our love for Him before God? Do we love the man imprisoned by his circumstances? Do we clothe people who are naked? Do we feed hungry people who are members of God's Church?

The struggle is raging today because God is making His Church a witness in eternity. I prophesy that some people who neglect attending a Kingdom Church are making a choice before the throne of God. How can God prove a person without trying him? Some people complain that God speaks too harshly. If Jesus Christ were preaching today, He would look into the faces of people and ask, "Where is your first love?" Jesus said to His disciples, "Forsake everything to follow Me. Don't call yourself a disciple unless you take up a cross and follow Me." Otherwise, we are fooling ourselves and playing games.

God told the church at Smyrna, "Some say they are Jews but are not. They are of the synagogue of Satan" (Revelation 2:8-11). God said to me, "That refers to both national and spiritual Israel." Some who claim to be "the Jews" nationally are not Jews, they are merely a group or race of people. Many who call themselves "spiritual Israel" are not Jews at all because they do not understand circumcision of the heart. God is looking for a peculiar people, a priesthood, a people worthy of kingship. He said to Smyrna, "You don't understand. You claim to be something you're not. You claim to be 'sons of Abraham,' but you don't have faith." If God told us to leave everything we own, would we do it? Would we be willing to sacrifice a son like Abraham did?

To the church at Pergamos (Revelation 2:12-17), God said, "You are mixing with the world by marrying

among the Moabites." When Christians join themselves with the world in business or social activities
and become so involved that they do not have time for a
covenant community, they are in trouble. When business deals become more important than individual
relationships with God, then we don't understand
what the Spirit is saying. Mixture makes us indifferent
in our love toward God. He told the church at Pergamos, "You are teaching the doctrine of Baalam." The
study of Baalam shows that when Satan could not
defeat God's people any other way, he had them marry
foreign wives. They were in such confusion from mixing with worldly systems that they didn't know truth
from error or darkness from light.

I've heard Christians say, "I'd rather do business
with a sinner than with someone in the church." If that
is true, then something is wrong with that person's
spirit. If a Christian's character is not such that he will
pay his bills, then we should address the matter of
discipline. People need to be taught Kingdom principles.

God's charge against the church at Thyatira was
that they were teaching spiritual fornication — going
to a church for convenience instead of conviction
(Revelation 2:18-29).

People will soon have a difficult time finding a place
to sit in churches which preach Kingdom principles.
God already has hundreds of people in Kingdom
churches where Jesus is lifted up and He will add to
them other people who are hungry for the things of the
Lord. If others want to commit fornication by search-

ing for a preacher who will say what they want to hear, they can find themselves a soft pew of convenience somewhere, but they will never see the Kingdom.

Then I asked, "God, what did you say to Sardis?" (Revelation 3:1-6). Sardis had grown weary in well-doing and failed to be watchful. They did not want a watchman on the tower and they did not want to pray or have a shepherd to watch over them. They wanted their preachers to be quiet. They didn't want to hear sermons on shaking up worldly systems and thought patterns.

What has happened to the "watching spirit" parents used to have over their children? Many parents decide it's much easier to give their children $5.00 and send them to the movies than to take care of them. They find parenthood easier when they put their children in a sports car and turn them loose. Their conscience assures them that they have fulfilled their responsibility to their children. If we are not teaching our children stewardship, we are sending them straight to hell. Young men today need to learn how to work. They do not need to marry until they learn how to assume responsibility by holding down a job.

Once again I asked, "God, what did you say to the church at Philadelphia?" (Revelation 3:7-13)

Indeed I will make those of the synagogue of Satan, who say they are Jews and are not, but lie — indeed I will make them come and worship before your feet, and to know that I have loved you. (Revelation 3:9)

The Holy Spirit told me, "They say they are Jews, and my Church supports them as God's people, but they have denied the Cornerstone." The Church of Philadelphia denied that Jesus was the Christ. They called themselves spiritual Jews, even natural Jews. What did God say to them? "I will make them come and worship me." The Word declares that every knee shall bow and every tongue shall confess that Jesus Christ is Lord. Whether we are Jews, Gentiles, Samaritans or Greeks, the only way to the Kingdom of God is through Jesus Christ, the Cornerstone. I support any denomination or persuasion that proclaims that Jesus Christ is the Chief Cornerstone.

The church of Laodicea represents more people than any other church that I have covered (Revelation 3:14-22) because it describes the Church today. Jesus said, "You are lukewarm. You are not consumed with zeal." The Church was content because it felt it had everything it needed and it had become complacent. Many people stare eternity in the face, feeling satisfied that they have everything, yet failing to realize that they are not ready to move into the Kingdom of God.

The Lord gave me seven insights that summarize the churches of Asia Minor. God's message then and throughout the ages applies to us today, and this message is the only one that will bring the Kingdom of God into reality.

First of all, we are hindered by a lack of commitment. We are committed to jobs and to our own welfare, but what about our commitment to God and to His ministry?

The second hindrance is claiming righteousness because of traditions or heritage. Some people claim righteousness because they have the Holy Spirit. Many traditional Christians have joined a church, yet they have never experienced the new birth in Jesus Christ. Circumcision of heart is not properly understood. Many think that circumcision of heart is "just an outward sign of an inward grace." To bring the Kingdom to earth, we must be circumcised of heart and in covenant with God. Only then will water baptism take on its proper meaning in the Church.

The third hindrance is mixture with the world. Jesus instructed us to come out from worldly influences and be a separate people. How can we keep from being affected by worldliness? We must learn how to be "in" the world, but not "of " the world.

The fourth hindrance is having another god based on our own gratification. That god is Mammon. The Holy Spirit addressed that issue with total accuracy two thousand years ago.

The fifth hindrance is growing weary. Some have said to me, "I have worked so long on the parking lot." "I have ushered so long." "I have been in the television ministry so long." "I have counseled people so long." But God says to us, "I want a people who will not grow weary, but will get up in the morning saying, 'I belong to God today, and whatever God wants me to do, that I will do to know true joy and fulfillment.' " We become restless because we do not want to occupy the place in the Kingdom to which God has called us.

The sixth hindrance is rejection of Jesus Christ as the Chief Cornerstone.

The seventh hindrance is a lack of zeal. The performance and demonstration of the Kingdom of God will be birthed in zeal. Where is our zeal? Where is our excitement?

God showed me clearly three major principles which are necessary in seeking His Kingdom. Seeking the Kingdom of God is simple and basic. Anyone can live a Kingdom lifestyle.

The first principle in seeking first the Kingdom of God is that we will meet human needs around us. We cannot seek first God's Kingdom and not meet human needs whenever and wherever we find someone needing Jesus's touch and His love.

The second principle is that we cannot seek the Kingdom of God without establishing lasting relationships. Where are the friends we had two years ago? The closest friends who surround my life are those who have been my friends for many years. I thank God for all the new relationships I have made, but I never have had any desire to close off relationships that I've had for years. Close friendships should not be established with worldly people. We can have certain levels of friendships and even be called "a friend of sinners" as Jesus was, but we are not to fellowship with the world. Though Jesus was a friend of sinners, when He wanted to enjoy fellowship He would go to the mountains with His disciples. When He wanted true intimacy, He took Peter, James and John aside to talk with them.

The third principle in seeking first the Kingdom is that we cannot seek God's Kingdom without giving ourselves to hope and faith. Hopelessness is never the Kingdom mentality. We must always believe that God is greater. No matter how dark the day seems to be, as in Paul and Silas's situation in prison, we have hope. Tribulation is just beginning for God's Kingdom people. Wait until people begin to comprehend the difference between the message of personal salvation and the message of living by Kingdom concepts. A reaction will sound from many Christians because of this distinction, but it is still God's truth. Personal salvation is necessary to begin a "new life," but unless salvation becomes a door to daily Kingdom life, it falls far short of demonstrating and seeking first the Kingdom of God.

What then shall we do? First of all, listen to what the Spirit of God is saying today and don't be offended by God's voices in the earth. Just as Jesus said, "Do not be offended by what I am saying," I tell my congregation, "Do not be offended by what I am saying, but apply it to your personal life."

The second action we must take is to practice being overcomers; practice taking dominion. Begin with small personal things like shining shoes. Sometimes we get our heads so high in the clouds that we forget to do little basic things that make us a demonstration of the Kingdom in our lives. We need to focus on where God is addressing our personal lives, such as how we relate in our marriages, to our children and to those over us in the Lord. If we are uncomfortable with spiritual leadership, we need to admit that we have problems. When the convenient time to do something or to be somewhere coincides with the teaching or preaching in God's house, we are in trouble. Most children hide from their fathers when they are not doing what they are supposed to do.

The third action we must take is to pray for the laborers of the harvest. Jesus didn't tell us to pray for houses, jobs or cars. He told us, "Pray for laborers." If we seek first the Kingdom of God, He will take care of those other things.

We must not go to sleep waiting for the Kingdom to come. When we are asleep, we are vulnerable to things around us. A thief or robber could easily come in and steal God's promises from us. Today I find too little excitement about Jesus among His people because the devil has lulled them to sleep. The most exciting time of the whole week should be when God's people go to His house. We need to tell our physical bodies, "It is time to praise God! It is time to serve the Lord!"

The Kingdom of God is at hand! Since Jesus came into the world, it has always been at hand. But it is truer now than ever before that the Kingdom is within our grasp. It is touchable. It is attainable for this generation — for the Church and for our families. Don't miss it! Grasp the secrets of Kingdom manifestation!

Part 2

"Yet who knows whether you have come to the kingdom for such a time as this?"

Esther 4:14

4

A MORE SUBTLE HINDRANCE TO THE KINGDOM

Satan dwells in the kingdoms of this world and he prevents God's people from taking dominion over his domain through subtle hindrances that thwart, cripple and defeat believers. One of the subtle hindrances to the Kingdom of God today is the lack of spiritual comprehension. Except for Jesus Christ Himself, no one had a greater comprehension of Kingdom concepts than the Apostle Paul. In Ephesians 3, Paul dealt with the mysteries of the Kingdom that are now being revealed.

That Christ may dwell in your hearts through faith; that you, being rooted and grounded in love, may be able to comprehend with all the saints what is the width and length and depth and height . . . (Ephesians 3:17-18)

For this reason I, Paul, the prisoner of Jesus Christ for you Gentiles — if indeed you have heard of the dispensation of the grace of God which was given to me for you, how that by revelation He made known to me the mystery (as I wrote before in a few words, by which, when you read, you may understand my knowledge in the mystery of Christ), which in other ages was not made known to the sons of men, as it has now been revealed by the Spirit to His holy apostles and prophets: that the Gentiles should be fellow heirs, of the same body, and partakers of His promise in Christ through the gospel, of which I became a minister according to the gift of the grace of God given to me by the effective working of His power. (Ephesians 3:1-7)

Revelation is ongoing. The first part of the revelation, the first mystery unfolded, is that the Gentiles should be fellow-heirs of the promise. Before this revelation, the assumption held that only the Jews could have access to God and only through a family relationship could the natural sons of Abraham receive the promise.

To me, who am less than the least of all the saints, this grace was given, that I should preach among the Gentiles the unsearchable riches of Christ, and to make all people see what is the fellowship of the mystery, which from the beginning of the ages has been hidden in God who created all things through Jesus Christ; to the intent that now the manifold wisdom of God might be made known by the church to the principalities and powers in the heavenly places. (Ephesians 3:8-10)

Paul wanted people to comprehend two things: first, that the Gentiles are to be fellow-heirs, and secondly, fellowship is a spiritual family relationship. God has called us to witness or to demonstrate the Kingdom to the heavenly beings. Paul said, ". . . that now the manifold wisdom might be made known by the church to the principalities and powers in the heavenly places." Our warfare today includes the whole universe, not just the earth.

Faith in Christ's life, death and resurrection resolves the problem in the spirit, but this truth has not been lived out on earth. We are challenged to live out Christian principles through the strength that God has given us.

We can become witnesses to the world as Job, a type of the Church, became a witness to Satan. God said, "Satan, have you observed Job?" The conflict between God and Satan was lived out in Job's life. Today the Church becomes that same witness to the principalities and powers in heavenly places. The whole universe stands in awe of Kingdom believers. We are encompassed about with a great cloud of witnesses who wait to see what the Church of Jesus Christ is going to do today.

I do not believe that we comprehend the battle, nor do we comprehend where we are in the history of mankind. God's mystery has always been to have a family who are His people. Paul said in Ephesians 3:9 that one of the mysteries of God would be spiritual relationships. From the very beginning, one of God's original intentions was to share His dominion and glory with mankind. Adam and Eve were placed in the Garden primarily to fellowship with God, and God also had fellowship with heavenly beings such as Lucifer and the angels. God created man in His image so He could enjoy fellowship with him, and He gave man power to subdue and take dominion over the earth.

Until we comprehend dominion, we will never manifest an adequate witness to the principalities and powers in heavenly places. Some preach about speaking the Word with authority, but this teaching causes disillusionment after awhile because we find ourselves in the same situations. As we attempt to struggle out of the same frustrations, God must correct our concepts and give us comprehension of why and where we take dominion. Because we have not fully understood the meaning of dominion, Satan has subtly stopped the full revelation of Jesus Christ, causing the Body of Christ to be fragmented and powerless.

God wants to establish and unfold the mysteries of the Kingdom today. He wants us to internalize truth and live it out in dominion and glory so that the powers in heavenly places will recognize the authority of Jesus Christ. Man was created with the potential for God-likeness.

Adam and Eve were placed in the world as the seed and expression of God. Just as dogs have puppies and cats have kittens, so God has little gods. Seed remains true to its nature, bearing its own kind.

When God said, "Let us make man in our image," He created us as little gods, but we have trouble comprehending this truth. We see ourselves as "little people" with very little power and dominion. Until we comprehend that we are little gods and we begin to act like little gods, we cannot manifest the Kingdom of God. We can talk about the Kingdom, write about it and preach about it, but we cannot demonstrate it until we comprehend who God created us to be.

The Kingdom of God does not come in observation; it comes in demonstration. The Church talks about demonstration and we have seen some firstfruits, but we lack powerful implementation of the things that Jesus told us to do. We are new creatures in Jesus Christ when we are born again, and our spirits are made alive in God. To move from the mind of the Spirit into the soul (our emotions and intellect) is a very difficult transition. We must reach a dimension of comprehension that will enable our decision-making processes to be controlled by the Holy Spirit. (Even more difficult than truth flowing from the spirit to the soul is taking dominion over the physical body to such an extent that total physical healing becomes reality.) Until the Holy Spirit controls us, death will never be challenged. We know that Christ, the firstfruit of a generation which will be changed in a moment, overcame death. We must overcome it also. Death, the last enemy, must be conquered by the Bride of Christ. Indeed, we experience death with Christ by faith, but the generation that precedes the coming of Jesus Christ must follow the example of Enoch who was changed.

Satan subtly tries to convince us that nothing can be done to hasten the coming of the Lord. We must comprehend that Jesus Christ is a firstfruit of the life which the Church must demonstrate. Jesus went into hell and took the keys from Satan. When He came back to the earth, He said, "I have the keys to death, hell and the grave, and I give them to My Church so she too can conquer death." When we understand that we have been delegated that authority by Jesus Christ, we can then move from semantics into realities. We are still debating over words instead of moving into the reality of demonstration which is what God desires.

God's plan for man was defeated in the Garden of Eden, but a promise was made in Genesis 3:15 that a renewal of power and authority would come from the seed of a woman. The heel of the woman will bruise the head of the serpent. The entire Bible is concerned with that promise. If we take away Genesis 3:15, the promise of the seed, the Bible has no meaning. The Old Testament deals with the Seed of God that began with Abraham, a man whose faith ultimately produced Jesus Christ whom Galatians 3:16 calls the Seed of God. In his Galatian letter Paul spoke of how Israel, the natural seed, rejected the promise. Jews of natural origin must now be grafted back into God's covenant through Jesus Christ. Paul said in Romans 11 that if the Gentiles (who were not a part of the natural seed) were grafted in, how much more easily Israel could be restored. But Israel must be grafted in again (just as the Gentiles are) because salvation can come only by accepting Jesus Christ as the Chief Cornerstone. God provides no other way.

As He says also in Hosea: "I will call them My people, who

were not My people, and her beloved who was not beloved.
And it shall come to pass in the place where it was said to
them, 'You are not My people,' there they will be called
sons of the living God." Isaiah also cries out concerning
Israel: "Though the number of the children of Israel be as
the sand of the sea, the remnant will be saved. For He will
finish the work and cut it short in righteousness, because
the Lord will make a short work upon the earth." And as
Isaiah said before: "Unless the Lord of Sabaoth had left
us a seed, we would have become like Sodom, and we
would have been made like Gomorrah." (Romans 9:25-29)

The promise of God is maintained in the Seed where
God left His incorruptible power. His power has been
invested in His Church which is a spiritual, rather
than a fleshly family. It is important to comprehend
that natural family ties can imprison us if not properly
understood. Once we know that we are not bound to the
natural family, we can even be freed from inherited
infirmities. That does not mean that we forsake our
families, but we must comprehend that our responsibilities to our natural family and our spiritual family are
different. Only keen spiritual minds understand that
the spiritual family transcends the natural family.
Paul wrote concerning the Jewish people who were his
own family:

For I could wish that I myself were accursed from Christ
for my brethren, my kinsmen according to the flesh.
(Romans 9:3)

Attachments to natural families often place us in

99

bondages which must be broken as we move to the spiritual dimension to which God has called us. This comprehension can remove infirmities from the flesh and soul. Inherited illnesses like migraine headaches, or emotional traits such as uncontrollable tempers can be broken by understanding how to move from the natural family to the spiritual family. "According to the flesh" means that we have not broken the ties which bind us to the family of the flesh and we cannot manifest the incorruptible seed of Jesus Christ which dwells within us. Transcending earthly relationships does not mean that we walk away from them. It means that we understand the difference between earthly and spiritual relationships. In I Corinthians 7, Paul addressed this same issue. He said that the marriage bed is sanctified and we must be faithful to that earthly relationship, but we should not be enslaved by it. We must know who we are and not be constrained by natural ties because God's people are related by more than their natural relationships. Jesus is a prime example of the Seed in relationships.

> *Brethren, I speak in the manner of men: Though it is only a man's covenant, yet if it is confirmed, no one annuls or adds to it. Now to Abraham and his Seed were the promises made. He does not say, "And to seeds," as of many, but as of one, "And to your Seed," who is Christ. (Galatians 3:15-16)*

The fulfillment of everything that the Old Testament taught is found in Jesus Christ who became the Seed.

> *Another parable He put forth to them, saying: "The king-*

dom of heaven is like a mustard seed, which a man took and sowed in his field, which indeed is the least of all the seeds; but when it is grown it is greater than the herbs and becomes a tree, so that the birds of the air come and nest in its branches." (Matthew 13:31-32)

The fulfillment of the promise of Abraham is Jesus Christ, whose Seed came forth as a firstfruit and began to grow. As we comprehend the Kingdom of God and begin to move like the King, our firstfruit will grow and flourish until it becomes the greatest of all cherished trees. That tree began with one Seed, Jesus Christ.

Then some of the Sadducees, who deny that there is a resurrection, came to Him and asked Him, saying: "Teacher, Moses wrote to us that if a man's brother dies, having a wife, and he dies without children, his brother should take his wife and raise up offspring for his brother. Now there were seven brothers. And the first took a wife, and died without children. And the second took her as his wife and he died childless. Then the third took her, and in like manner the seven also; and they left no children, and died. Last of all the woman died also. Therefore, in the resurrection, whose wife does she become? For all seven had her as wife." And Jesus answered and said to them, "The sons of this age marry and are given in marriage. But those who are counted worthy to attain that age, and the resurrection from the dead, neither marry nor are given in marriage; nor can they die anymore, for they are equal to the angels and are sons of God, being sons of the resurrection." (Luke 20:27-36)

Jesus was talking about two totally separate concepts in His answer to the Sadducees. One had to do with earthly families which are bound by limitations because God cannot trust them. Jesus said in order for the sons of this age to become the "Sons of God" and usher in the age of the resurrection, they must enlarge their concepts. No longer will they be bound by earthly relationships, but they will enjoy relationships in a heavenly family. The sons of this age understand responsibility in natural relationships, but the sons of the Kingdom of God comprehend that relationships can mean something far greater. Indeed the earthly family has its purpose, place and plan, but the family of God exists for far greater eternal purposes.

Then His mother and brothers came to Him, and could not approach Him because of the crowd. And it was told Him by some, who said, "Your mother and Your brothers are standing outside, desiring to see You." But He answered and said to them, "My mother and My brother are these who hear the word of God and do it." (Luke 8:19-21)

The crowd so pressed around Jesus that His mother and His brothers could not get near Him. This did not lessen His sonship to Mary, nor did it mean that others were not His brothers and sisters whom He loved. Jesus's answer meant that He comprehended greater relationships. People who are possessive of husbands, wives or children will never know how to relate to others in a spiritual dimension. Until we learn to embrace spiritual relationships on a "Church family" level, the Kingdom of God cannot be established upon the earth. Failure to comprehend spiritual relationships absolutely cuts off the revelation that will eventually bring the family of heaven and earth together under God. Comprehension of spiritual relationships gives real meaning to the concept of "brothers and sisters in the Lord."

Then Peter began to say to Him, "See, we have left all and followed You." So Jesus answered and said, "Assuredly, I say to you, there is no one who has left house or brothers or sisters or father or mother or wife or children or lands, for My sake and the gospel's, who shall not receive a hundredfold now in this time — houses and brothers and sisters and mothers and children and lands, with persecutions — and in the age to come, eternal life." (Mark 10:28-30)*

In this scripture, Jesus was saying that no competition should exist between earthly relationships and the relationships that He calls us to have. If we are led by God's Spirit, we will not compromise. The major priority of our lives will be centered around the Kingdom of God. Learn the difference between natural relationships and spiritual relationships in the family of God. Many people who stand today at the door of the Kingdom cannot enter because they are bound by earthly relationships.

Although we are citizens of heaven, that citizenship does not exempt us from legal authorities upon this earth. Paul said that even the authorities upon the earth are given by God because He desires order and design. "That which belongs to Caesar, give to Caesar, and that which belongs to God, give to God." We must never allow the two governing authorities to become confused in our spirits. We must always know the difference.

Natural family ties working apart from a proper understanding of the spiritual relationship between Jesus and the Church always create conflict. Some women want to own their husbands. They tell the head of the household how much money to give to the church and what meetings they may attend. Some men make selfish demands of their wives, failing to realize that women are repulsed by such possessiveness. What most husbands do not know is that a wife may act as though she belongs to him, but she doesn't. We need to understand that possessiveness will not work in the Kingdom of God.

"He who finds his life will lose it, and he who loses his life for My sake will find it." (Matthew 10:39). The most binding spirit in God's Church is one that perpetuates our inability to know how to break free from natural ties so that we can soar in the Kingdom of God.

When we are born again, we are born of the Spirit and become citizens of a new Kingdom as we are risen in newness of life. Living out that new creation in the soul of decision and the mind of reason is very difficult and requires great maturity. Living out a walk of faith in the physical body means taking authority when the body rebels. Instead we usually say, "I have a right to get weary. I have a right to get sick. I get sick because my mama got sick and my daddy got sick and I live in a sick world." As long as that mentality dominates us, we will never challenge the devil's power on the earth.

We come to understand our new citizenship as we live it out daily. We put off the old man and put on the new man which is created after God in righteousness and true holiness. We have assumed that our Kingdom citizenship is only spiritual by faith and that we must walk through the world with sickness of the body and mind. That reasoning prevents the Kingdom of God from prevailing. We have already concluded that this is the only path we can choose. Peter writes about the precious faith and the divine power which is given to us.

By which have been given to us exceedingly great and precious promises, that through these you may be partakers of the divine nature, having escaped the corruption that is in the world through lust. (II Peter 1:4)

How much have we escaped? As long as we admit that we are under the control of these forces, we have not escaped anything. This scripture very clearly points out that we are partakers of the divine nature. The Seed has been revitalized.

The elders who are among you I exhort, I who am a fellow elder and a witness of the sufferings of Christ, and also a partaker of the glory that will be revealed. (I Peter 5:1)

Peter realized that he was already a partaker of the glory that would be revealed as he came to know the Seed principle at work within him.

Having been born again, not of corruptible seed but incorruptible, through the word of God which lives and abides forever. (I Peter 1:23)

Corruptible seeds consist of our families and natural relationships such as our parents and grandparents. Peter experienced something new working within him, not the old family lineage but the incorruptible Seed. The lack of comprehension of this principle stagnates us in moving forward in the Kingdom of God. The incorruptible Seed is available now!

Behold what manner of love the Father has bestowed on us, that we should be called children of God! Therefore the world does not know us, because it did not know Him. (I John 3:1)

People around us may know our names, but they don't know about the Kingdom within us. They don't know who we are in Christ if they know us only through social or business relationships. The world does not know us because it did not know Jesus Christ either.

Anyone who says we have already received all of God's revelation hasn't read the scriptures. Some things are yet to be understood and we do not yet comprehend that measure of stature which we shall attain. Just as Jesus was in the world, so also are we. Until we are able to implement that likeness of Jesus within ourselves, we will not be able to move in the areas of Sonship to which God has called us. God wants us to ascend to higher spiritual concepts leaning totally on the Holy Spirit. He said, "My sons will be led by the Spirit." We must not be led by genealogies or inherited infirmities. We are led by the Spirit through whom fleshly infirmities can be overcome. We have the incorruptible Seed within us which we acknowledge and pursue. Through life in Jesus Christ, we can move from situations of the flesh to life in the Spirit.

There is therefore now no condemnation to those who are in Christ Jesus, who do not walk according to the flesh [the genealogies, the old line, the old family ties], but according to the Spirit. For the law of the Spirit of life in Christ Jesus has made me free from the law of sin and death. (Romans 8:1-2)

But you are not in the flesh but in the Spirit, if indeed the Spirit of God dwells in you. Now if anyone does not have the Spirit of Christ, he is not His . . . He will give life to your mortal bodies through his Spirit who dwells in you. (Romans 8:9-11)

The Apostle Paul said that a generation would be born that would not die but would instead be changed in a moment, in the twinkling of an eye (I Corinthians 15:52). That generation will face the devil and say, "You have no control over me because I am the incorruptible Seed of God." The Church must move as a corporate Body as Jesus did as an individual. Our failure to move in unity hinders the Kingdom.

I beseech you therefore, brethren, by the mercies of God, that you present your bodies a living sacrifice, holy, acceptable to God, which is your reasonable service. And do not be conformed to this world, but be transformed by the renewing of your mind, that you may prove what is that good and acceptable and perfect will of God. (Romans 12:1-2)

107

A transformed mind is possible. Paul and Silas's minds were so transformed that even when they were physically confined in prison stocks at midnight, in their minds they were free. In the midst of enslavement Paul and Silas could sing, "Thank God, I'm free at last."

Their natural minds knew that they were still in prison, but their minds were so spiritually transformed that God released them from prison. The transformed mind activates miracles on the earth. The transformed mind follows the Spirit with positive power and demonstration in a negative world. Today God is looking for people whose minds can be released in Kingdom power. Our inheritance has been made clear to us now not only in this world but in the future Kingdom as well.

For this reason we also, since the day we heard it, do not cease to pray for you and to ask that you may be filled with the knowledge of His will in all wisdom and spiritual understanding; that you may have a walk worthy of the Lord, fully pleasing Him, being fruitful in every good work and increasing in the knowledge of God, strengthened with all might, according to His glorious power, for all patience and longsuffering with joy; giving thanks to the Father who has qualified us to be partakers of the inheritance of the saints in the light. (Colossians 1:9-12)

We are becoming qualified to be partakers with the saints of our inheritance. We must begin to live as the mature Body of Christ because that identification enables us to receive our inheritance. As we begin to live that life, our spirits must be quickened by the power and the anointing of God because until we are quickened to these truths by the power of God, we will not be able to move to the next dimension. The quickening within the Body of Christ helps us to understand our potential and to comprehend what we can do for God. We are that Seed, incorruptible through Jesus Christ, with the authority and power of God at work within us.

The Bible says that when Mary became pregnant with Jesus, the incorruptible Seed of Abraham, she went to see her cousin, Elizabeth, who was pregnant with John the Baptist. When Mary entered the house, Elizabeth's baby leaped within her womb. The presence of the incorruptible Seed quickened the life in the womb of Elizabeth.

When we understand that the incorruptible Seed dwells within the dedicated believer, we will experience an internal quickening from God. We will recognize that we have been bound to the flesh and bound by things that harass our minds and bodies. We will know that Jesus Christ is the incorruptible Seed and that we can become everything He is (I John 3:2).

The difference between an earthly relationship that is active and working properly and one that is dead is that a good relationship causes a physical quickening within the body. When David was old, a young woman was taken to him to see if she would bring him life. When her beauty did not draw a response from David, they knew that David was dying. Lift that physical concept to the spiritual realm. When we comprehend the person of Jesus Christ and the power of God and the anointing of the Holy Ghost, our spirits are quickened. We know that with Jesus Christ, we can do anything. That quickening brings life. I suggest four areas where we can begin to live out and comprehend Christ's power. After we comprehend it, we can begin to live it out.

The quickening of the Spirit first begins with Philippians 4 which refers to our thought patterns. Paul declares, "Think on things that are of a good report." A transformed mind does not dwell on contemplating people who have wronged us. Instead we spend time meditating on the blessings the Lord has given us, such as our church or our relationship with God. A transformed mind transcends the flesh. Until our thoughts are controlled by the Holy Spirit, the Kingdom can never become a reality in our lives. Trust, not suspicion, characterizes a pure mind. Husbands and wives must believe the best about each other. Relationships must be built in trust. God will give us spiritual relationships if we will walk in the Spirit.

If our attachments focus on earthly things and we are not committed to a heavenly vision, we lose that which is incorruptible by putting earthly relationships above those in the Body of Christ. When we recognize our heavenly family and know who we are in Jesus Christ, God will give us the relationships that we need.

Brethren, my heart's desire and prayer to God for Israel is that they may be saved. For I bear them witness that they have a zeal for God, but not according to knowledge. For they being ignorant of God's righteousness, and seeking to establish their own righteousness, have not submitted to the righteousness of God. For Christ is the end of the law for righteousness to everyone who believes. For Moses writes about the righteousness which is of the law. "The man who does those things shall live by them." But the the righteousness of faith speaks in this way, "Do not say in your heart, 'Who will ascend into heaven?'" (that is to bring Christ down from above). (Romans 10:1-6)

Christ will not come until the meek move with maturity to inherit the earth and we perform what God has called us to do. Then He will come and receive His Bride.

"The Word of God is near you even in your mouth and in your heart, that is the word of faith which we preach." We have a responsibility to speak by the Spirit. The word of God is in our mouths. If a wife says, "My husband is a crook," the chances are that he will be. Instead she should say, "My husband has the potential to be a man of God, and I'm going to stand by him until I see that potential manifested in him." The Kingdom of God will not come to pass until we let God use us to perform his work.

Jesus bore the cross for us, and even though we talk about carrying the cross ourselves, we want to choose which cross. Jesus said that unless we forgive others, He cannot forgive us. Once we learn to deal with our thought patterns and our conversations, we can begin to live in proper relationships.

Can we honestly say, "I have no relationship on earth that I need to correct?" Do we play games with our relationships? Until we allow our relationships to be controlled by the Holy Spirit, we can never know the full possibility of the Kingdom. While Jesus was on the cross, He was saying, "Father, forgive these people, they don't know what they are doing." Jesus's prayer didn't necessarily change those people standing near Him, but He was right in His relationships. He didn't curse them or ask God to destroy them. Instead He said, "Father, forgive them," because He wanted to be right in His relationships regardless of the response of the people.

If we try to get in God's way in the Kingdom walk, He will quietly move us to the side. We need to consider our relationships. Are they ordained of God? What about relationships with our children or with those over us in the Lord? We don't choose who God uses to deal with us. Those dealings are God's business.

Learn to build a spiritual history instead of a medical history. When one enters the hospital, the first question the medical personnel ask is, "What diseases did your parents and grandparents have?" We become so frightened by these questions that we can actually become ill with the same diseases. We must meditate upon the miracles that God has performed because He is abundantly able to break every inherited trait of the old man. We need to prepare our spirits for a glorified body that will overcome the power of death.

"And do not think to say to yourselves, 'We have Abraham as our father.' For I say to you that God is able to raise up children to Abraham from these stones." (Matthew 3:9)

We must say, "The incorruptible Seed, Jesus Christ, dwells within me and if the Spirit of Him that raised up Christ from the dead dwells in me, He shall quicken my mortal body." We must fill our minds and spirits with that concept.

Another parable He put forth to them, saying: "The kingdom of heaven is like a mustard seed, which a man took and sowed in his field, which indeed is the least of all the seeds; but when it is grown it is greater than the herbs and becomes a tree, so that the birds of the air come and nest in its branches." Another parable He spoke to them: "The kingdom of heaven is like leaven, which a woman took and hid in three measures of meal till it was all leavened." All these things Jesus spoke to the multitude in parables; and without a parable He did not speak to them, that it might be fulfilled which was spoken by the prophet, saying: "I will open My mouth in parables; I will utter things which have been kept secret from the foundation of the world." Then Jesus sent the multitude away and went into the house. And His disciples came to Him, saying, "Explain to us the parable of the tares of the field." He answered and said to them: "He who sows the good seed is the Son of Man. The field is the world, the good seeds are the sons of the kingdom, but the tares are the sons of the wicked one." (Matthew 13:31-38)

No wonder Paul said that the whole world groans and waits for the manifestation of seeds (sons of the Kingdom) who can live according to Christian principles and can walk, live and breathe in faith. All of creation waits to see if the seed of this generation will grow and bear fruit. Another scripture speaks of the Word being the seed and the two are inseparable because the Word waters the seed. The seed is alive today and we are that seed.

The seed principle will be demonstrated around the world to this generation by young people who now sit under Kingdom ministries, if they do not forget what God is saying. We are beginning to see great moves of God here and in foreign countries which will bear much fruit for the Kingdom as God speaks to His people by His Spirit.

The devil has attacked the message of the Kingdom by creating his own imitations. God gave us a round rainbow as a sign of the covenant, and the devil has also used a rainbow to identify his "New Age Movement." The devil is no fool; he is very subtle. He was smart enough to say to Eve, "Eve, don't you know that when you eat of this tree, you are going to fulfill the plan of God? God wants you to be a little god." Even though deceptive groups such as "The Sons of God" or "The Children of God" emerge, don't doubt for a moment that the sons of the Kingdom are about to be manifested in the world! God is waiting for that manifestation to take place so that Christ can come again. The people of God must learn to walk in natural relationships while maintaining their walk in the Spirit. Because these realms of life are contrary to one another, the Spirit relationship may sometimes require us to do one thing while the flesh relationship requires us to do something else.

We must learn how to play to two different audiences,

as it were. When Peter was imprisoned, the audience to whom he played in the natural man were those who saw his plight and infirmity. He did not deny that he was in stocks nor did he deny his infirmities. He played to a natural audience, but he also played to another audience as he transcended his present circumstances by recognizing the Spirit of God within him. By playing to the audience of authority and power, Peter became a witness to the principalities and powers of the air. God said, "I am going to honor his faith," and the principalities and powers of the air stood back helplessly as an angel of the Lord broke the chains and set Peter free. When Peter realized he was free, he went to the house of Mary, the mother of John, where many Christians had gathered to pray. When they heard Peter's voice, they said, "It must be Peter's angel," because they knew he was bound in chains. The natural man may have doubt when a situation seems impossible, but that shouldn't keep us from playing to the spiritual audience. God has said, "If you will believe (have faith), I will open the windows of heaven and pour out a blessing you can't even contain."

Paul refers to playing to two audiences in Romans 14. Paul said before the Judge of eternity, "I am a free man. I can do anything." Paul had to be speaking of things of the flesh because the context of this passage concerns the subject of eating meats offered to idols. Paul said that all things were lawful for him, and when he played to the heavenly audience he danced in the sunlight of total freedom in the Spirit. He realized, however, that in the natural realm some people would be offended by his freedom.

Jesus also played to two different audiences. When Jesus received word that Lazarus was sick, He knew that His friend was going to die. Because He was an expression of the Father, He knew exactly what was going to happen. As a matter of fact, His actions were totally deliberate so that Lazarus's resurrection could take place.

To the natural audience, Jesus came so slowly that Mary and Martha were upset with Him because He didn't get there in time to save Lazarus. Martha said, "Lord, if You had been here, my brother would not have died." Jesus, who was walking in the Spirit, didn't apologize. God gives us that kind of grace. Jesus knew Who He was, where He was going and with Whom He was communicating. Because He knew the source of His Spirit, Jesus walked in total peace and patience. He knew that victory was already won, but He started playing to another audience and He wept.

The picture of Jesus's weeping is not where this story ends. Jesus lifted his voice and said, "Father, I want to say something to You, not because You need to hear it, but so that these people I'm playing to will hear it." Learn the difference between audiences. Don't cast pearls before swine! Learn how to walk in the Spirit and not to fall prey to the encumbrances of the flesh. Learn proper conduct. As Kingdom people, our lives become a beautiful balance relying on the Church, spiritual headship and counsellors as the covering who protect us from the enemy.

A major hindrance to the Kingdom of God is a lack of understanding of who we are in Christ. We must understand the difference between the incorruptible Seed and the genealogy of the flesh. We must learn how to walk by faith so that we can implement and demonstrate the power of the Kingdom of God to eternal beings, principalities and powers. We must first see the Kingdom of God and then enter into it. With force and violence, we must become witnesses to the principalities and powers of the air so that God can say, "Look at My Church! She is grown now and she is worthy of the Bridegroom."

5

BE SURE YOU HEAR THE RIGHT VOICE

Because God's voice to man is through His Word lived out in His people, local churches are the focus of Satan's strongest strategies of deception. I have already said that deceived people are religious and sincere. Proclaiming the Gospel of the Kingdom sets the Church in order so that God's voice becomes a powerful, certain sound to the world. Deception leaves the Church in weak and powerless factions. Satan creates uncertainty, disunity and confusion in the Church to delay (and he hopes to prevent) the coming of the Lord.

The local church must take on a new look in the day in which we live. The local church has often been undermined and even abused by what has been loosely called "trans-local ministries" or certain national radio or television ministries. Yet, the local pastor is the angel of the church and the one to whom God addresses messages to His people. The local pastor is the authority in that local church. He is charged under God to stand guard over the sheep that God has given to him. Because of that local pastor's grave responsibilities, we need to re-evaluate and even gain new appreciation for the work and ministry of the local church.

Apostolic ministries which go out from a church to establish new churches in various locations are indeed part of God's plan. However, in the days in which we live, large, strong, local churches will be able to minister to small congregations. The anointed five-fold ministries listed in Ephesians 4 are greatly needed for the Body of Christ to communicate and demonstrate the Gospel of the Kingdom as a witness to the world. world.

And He Himself gave some to be apostles, some prophets, some evangelists, and some pastors and teachers, for the equipping of the saints for the work of the ministry, for the edifying of the body of Christ, till we all come to the unity of the faith and the knowledge of the Son of God, to a perfect man, to the measure of the stature of the fullness of Christ; that we should no longer be children, tossed to and fro and carried about with every wind of doctrine, by the trickery of men, in the cunning craftiness by which they lie in wait to deceive, but, speaking the truth in love, may grow up in all things into Him who is the head—Christ— from whom the whole body, joined and knit together by

what every joint supplies, according to the effective work-
ing by which every part does its share, causes growth of
the body unto the edifying of itself in love. (Ephesians
4:11-16)

This passage proves the connection between the five-
fold ministry and the local church for the edification or
equipping of the Body of Christ through these
ministries.

I believe that in the past we have regarded apostles
as being either disciples who surrounded Jesus, or perhaps some unique ministers whom God ordained
across the years for some special purposes of Church
expansion. Some churches have regarded the prophet
as being an impossible ministry for our day. Clearly,
the prophetic writings of the Bible indicate that the
apostle and the prophet, along with the evangelist,
pastor and teacher, must be restored and functioning
within the local church for spiritual maturity to occur.
The Body of Christ today needs some forerunner
churches which show how these five-fold ministries
operate from the local perspective.

All of these ministries or callings may operate within
one individual to some degree, but that does not disregard the fact that just as there are identifiable pastors,
evangelists and teachers, we should also be able to
recognize identifiable prophets and apostles.

The plurality of ministries in the local church is an
area which is innovative, yet very necessary in these
last days. The old idea that every young preacher must

pay his dues by first becoming an evangelist, or beginning a new local church, is not the innovative way that God is leading us today. God's innovative method in our day is for a minister called by God to find a local church in which there is a plurality of ministries, identifiable callings and a spirit of working together in unity. I believe that a network of these large local churches where all of these ministries function will become the new force that God will use as His witness in the world today. In fact these churches will be major embassies of God's message. These embassies will demonstrate strong ministries in preaching the message of the Kingdom. They will become influential in high places throughout the earth.

It is not original with me, but I surely agree with the concept of using the hand to demonstrate the five-fold ministries. When examining the way that the hand functions, the thumb has access to all the fingers. I believe that the thumb represents the apostle. The index finger is the pointing finger. This finger represents the prophet because it points or gives direction. The middle finger is the long finger which represents the evangelist. The evangelist reaches out beyond the local church with the Gospel of Jesus Christ. The ring finger is the finger of love, which expresses the heart. This finger represents the pastor. The fifth finger is the finger which represents the teacher. When hitting a table, this is the one that is the first to feel the impact, and so the teacher implements the Gospel in the most direct way by breaking down God's revelation for comprehension on every level of understanding.

I am convinced that all of these ministries, or call-ings should be evidenced in major local churches around the world. Each one of these five-fold ministries relates to an effective ministry in the local church.

THE APOSTLE IN THE LOCAL CHURCH

The apostle is the person who is sent on a special mission. He is like an early advocate or ambassador. Great apostles in the past, even since Biblical times, might have been apostles of love, or apostles who had a particular cause they fostered. The apostle is the one who has the ability to build, and many times, a local church is built out of the vision of the apostle who becomes the father of that work. The way the thumb reaches all of the other fingers demonstrates that the apostolic ministry must be in touch with, and in some respects, responsible for the other ministries.

The apostle is the key builder in the local church since he sees that church in its broader relationship with the Church universal. The calling of the apostle is to establish order in the Church. The Apostle Paul often said that he would shortly come to a church so that he could set the church in order. The apostle is called to the joyful task of ordaining ministers. He is the one who must finally give the approval that one is ready to be set forth, or ordained, to the ministry after having proper spiritual counsel and inspection.

Also, the apostle is the one who maintains the home base. He is responsible for the other ministries and he is the one to whom the others submit in times of differences or difficulties. The apostle must become responsible for maintaining the strength of that home base, yet be released to minister in a broader perspective to the Church universal. He must also touch every other ministry in that church, whether it be prophet, evangelist, pastor or teacher with a sense of responsibility for that ministry.

In addition to the twelve men chosen by Jesus to assist Him in His ministry, we also have Paul who was referred to as an apostle (I Corinthians 15:8-11). Barnabas also was an apostle (Acts 14:4,14). We must realize that in Ephesians 4 when, "He gave some apostles," the original apostles had already been set forth.

THE PROPHET IN THE LOCAL CHURCH

The next called-out ministry in the local church is the prophet. The prophet is the person who speaks for God. Functioning like a rudder of a ship, he is the tongue who gives direction. Because he is the one to whom God speaks in relation to giving direction, often the prophet will work closely with the apostle. The prophet interacts with other prophetic ministries, not necessarily in his particular church. In other words, the prophet from a local church would be likely to preach at other churches where prophetic utterances are consistently given. I believe the prophet in the local church would aid in ministerial seminars, particularly related to the transcending apostolic ministries of that local church. The prophet establishes certain principles from the Word of God by which the Church operates.

May I also point out a difference between being a prophet and having the ability to give prophetic utterances. A prophet is not to be judged. However, the New Testament teaches that when the Holy Spirit fell upon all the people, prophetic utterances were judged by the elders. So while prophetic utterances may come from the congregation, those words must be judged. Every congregation needs the prophet, but many times that role may be served by the apostle who has the prophetic utterance. Of course, the apostle is responsible for any prophetic utterance because he is the father of the work and the one most responsible for all areas of ministry.

Paul made it clear that all may prophesy (I Corinthians 14:31), but that all are not prophets (I Corinthians 12:29). In the New Testament, Agabus was called a prophet (Acts 11:28; Acts 21:10). Prophets were called by God in both the Old Testament and the New Testament, just as prophets are called in the Church today.

THE EVANGELIST IN THE LOCAL CHURCH

The next of the called ministries is the evangelist. An important point to recognize is that the calling of an evangelist is between that of the prophet and the pastor. The evangelist is represented by the longest finger which extends to the world. The evangelist is an extension of the prophetic ministry. The evangelist may move not only as an individual, but also within group activities out of the local church where the evangelist's message touches the world. He may organize people to minister in street ministries or prison ministries. The evangelist may travel under the direction of a local assembly. The chief evangelist in a ministry should be the one who organizes other evangelists to go out from the local church. He will be the one who would be involved in training programs such as the Timothy program, a program which trains young evangelists or evangelistic groups to go out and touch people's lives.

Among those listed as being evangelists in the Early Church is Philip (Acts 21:8). He was one who proclaimed Jesus Christ and preached the Good News of the Kingdom (Acts 8:5,12).

THE PASTOR IN THE LOCAL CHURCH

The ministry represented by the finger that wears the love ring, the heart of a local church, is that of the pastor. Notice that the pastor is between the evangelist and the teacher. He or she not only feels the need to go beyond the local church, but also the need to implement the teaching of the Word of God by association with teachers whom he/she will oversee. Pastors and teachers are directly associated and interact with each other in ministry.

The pastor feeds and tends the sheep. The pastor knows how to lead people into worship. He knows best how to make them respond in praise to God because he is the one who is most sensitive to the people. He both hears and embellishes the prophetic words that are spoken. Though he will hear prophetic words, his primary calling is that of a pastor and his message is usually directed to the sheep. He is the one who stands at the door to protect the sheep against the wolves who may come among them. His job is to see that the people of the local church are equipped because he himself is an equipper of the saints. He gives direction to the deacon ministry and becomes the one who teaches the deacons how to minister to the sheep. The pastor is the one who directs covenant fellowship groups because of his pastoral sensitivity to the people. He may have several covenant groups, or he may have someone under him in charge of covenant communities.

THE TEACHER IN THE LOCAL CHURCH

The final ministry in the five-fold calling is that of a teacher. He or she is also closely associated with the pastor and the work of the pastor in equipping the local people by teaching them Kingdom principles. The teacher breaks down the message of the prophet. The teacher is the one who is able to cause the message to be understandable on the various levels at which people can comprehend God's Word. He/she breaks the message down for all age groups because he is the one who concentrates on providing food for all the sheep. In the hand illustration, this finger is the first finger which hits the table. The "rubber hits the road" in the teaching ministry because it is the one most involved with directing the minds of the people. Therefore, the teaching office must become inseparable from that of a pastor. Usually one person heads this ministry and under that person, God provides many other capable teachers.

When Jesus started to feed the multitudes, He broke five loaves of bread. I believe that these parts represent the ministries that will touch sheep or the masses of people. Christ is the bread, and we see Him broken to feed the people in five parts. I believe the five parts into which Christ is broken in ministry are these that we have addressed: the Apostle, Prophet, Evangelist, Pastor and Teacher. In order for us to have the complete ministry of Jesus Christ in the local church, we must have all five of these ministries represented. The small local churches that may not be able to have all of these ministries can draw greatly from strong local churches such as Evangel Temple, Washington, D.C.; Chapel Hill Harvester Church, Atlanta, Georgia; Rock Church, Virginia Beach, Virginia, or many other churches that God is raising up to provide the five-fold ministry to smaller churches under their auspices.

May I also point out that any man called of God into the ministry may at any given time have apostolic abilities within him. He may also have prophetic capabilities. He certainly will have pastoral and counseling abilities. He should have the ability to be an evangelist who speaks out the Word of God and brings converts to Jesus Christ. He will also have the ability to teach the Word of God. All of these qualities rest within a minister and the Holy Spirit that is within us divides as He wills, not only the gifts, but also the callings. But we have come to a time when the local church must be able to demonstrate on a local level what we have only until recently seen on an international level in the Body of Christ.

We have known some great apostles, prophets, pastors, evangelists and teachers who are recognized from the impact of their national or international ministries. The time has now come when the most innovative ministry will occur in local churches where all of these callings are represented.

The apostolic ministry of the local church should raise up new churches, and from those large local churches, pastors are assigned to smaller churches that are inseparable from the mother church.

It is my judgment that a prophet should not be the one who begins a local church. The prophet should be under the direction of the apostle who will send out an evangelist to make contact with new communities to begin these works. The office of the bishop administratively cares for other local churches that have been raised up out of his particular local setting.

Once ministries are identifiable and understood, competition is eliminated. Within one's calling is interaction and even crossing over into the ministries of others when necessary without abusing the flow of the Holy Spirit. But in these situations, the apostle becomes a very important discerner of God's direction because he knows how to regulate and relate ministries properly to one another.

STRUCTURE OF THE LOCAL CHURCH

The structure of the Church is yet another matter. First of all, the office of the deacon is clearly defined as one called to serve people who are in need. Certain men waited on tables in order to free the apostles for the work of the ministry and the study of God's Word. A higher office of authority in the spiritual and administrative structure is the elder, or presbyter. Many times, the presbyter may function also as a pastor. An interesting observation to note is that in the New Testament, each local church had several pastors. When ministries function together as a decision-making body, they are called the presbytery.

The bishop has the responsibility of overseeing both ministers and local churches. Many times the bishop may also function as a pastor. These three church offices — deacon, presbyter and bishop — are vital in the administration of the Church. I believe that if the staff of a church properly know their callings as administrators and implementors, they may also serve as deacons, elders, or even pastors. And of course, the bishop is a vital part of the local presbytery as its head.

An old method of church expansion is for a man to go to a new community and begin a church by taking a few members from an old mother church. A much more exciting and innovative method of far-reaching ministry is a strong Kingdom Church which exemplifies the five-fold ministry to demonstrate how ministries can work together in these last days. Through this demonstration of the five-fold ministry functioning in unity and power, the Church universal can be greatly blessed.

With so much misunderstanding and even criticism directed toward the "Kingdom message," I want to clarify even further the description and the character of Kingdom churches. Satan tries to defeat truth through distortions and semantics. God's people must not be intimidated by spirits which attack present day revelation (fresh insights into God's Word) that God is giving to His Church as His plan unfolds to this generation. Satan will always attack a prophetic voice because truth sets people free.

God reveals Himself by His Spirit to prophets who give God's direction to this generation of believers. Each of us knows his own desires and feelings. Another person could never truly know us inside except through spiritual discernment. Only the Spirit of God can give revelation to us. Finite man, through his mind of reason, can never fully understand and know the deep things of God. Only believers with spiritual hearts and ears can understand spiritual truth. The things of God are foolishness to the world because only God can see the the ultimate culmination of events. Since man's mind is finite, we can only see pieces of a historical puzzle. Man cannot comprehend Biblical history from the beginning to the end of the age.

We can only know the voice of God through our spirits. If we strive to hear from God with our natural perceptions, we can easily be deceived. We must listen intently to the Holy Spirit who prepares our hearts for new concepts and thoughts above our natural thinking.

For "Who has known the mind of the Lord that he may instruct Him?" But we have the mind of Christ. (I Corinthians 2:16)

Are we presumptuous when we say that we have the

mind of Christ? Of course not! The mind of Christ is promised to us in the Word of the Lord. Neither our eyes nor our ears are dependable. When we try to perceive the things of God through natural reasoning, we make mistakes. God speaks to our spirits with an assurance that transcends natural reasoning. God's ways are a certainty upon which we can stake our lives.

Revelation must come by the Spirit. The Bible says that holy men of old were moved upon by the Spirit and they wrote the things God spoke to them. The compilation of these writings are what we know as "the Bible." Why can't holy men in our day get this same inspiration from God? Is what we say any less important than God's Word spoken by holy men of old? If the Holy Spirit leads us to unchanging truth, His message today should be totally consistent with that spoken in past ages. The truth of God is not changed just because we as earthen vessels make mistakes in our flesh. Many people in Judea never received what Jesus said to them because they saw Him only as a carpenter's son. When God sends a prophet among people, they sometimes never hear the message of God because they are too preoccupied with looking at human weaknesses, (the earthen vessel).

The Bible says the last days will be characterized by many prophets and teachers. The Church must have wisdom and discernment to know who is speaking with the voice of God.

And the Word of the Lord came to me, saying, "Son of man, prophesy against the shepherds of Israel, prophesy and say to them, 'Thus says the Lord God to the shep-

herds: Woe to the shepherds of Israel who feed themselves!
Should not the shepherds feed the flocks?' " (Ezekiel
34:1,2)

The Word of the Lord says that shepherds who fleece
the flock instead of feeding them are cursed. The
Church Body has been wounded because certain leaders have taken selfish advantage of their people.

Thus says the Lord God: "Woe to the foolish prophets, who
follow their own spirit and have seen nothing!" (Ezekiel
13:3)

Who are those prophets against whom God directs
His spokemen to prophesy? They are prophets who
prophesy out of their own hearts and have no genuine
direction from God. God resists men who prophesy and
have heard nothing. God must be tired of people saying, "Abortion is evil," yet offering no alternatives.
Who doesn't know the evils of society? Anyone can
preach about those things. God is grieved because of
preachers who make big promises, yet do nothing
because they have seen and heard nothing. These
preachers are in the ministry for their own personal
gain.

God instructed His Church to prophesy against the
shepherds, not the sheep. The sheep are scattered and
God has compassion for them. God wants His prophets
to prophesy against leaders who are misleading people
and confusing them.

"An astonishing and horrible thing has been committed

in the land: The prophets prophesy falsely, and the priests
rule by their own power; and My people love to have it so.
But what will you do in the end?" (Jeremiah 5:30-31)

In those days the priests were ruling for their own gain, and people were deceived. Unfortunately, the people were content with that arrangement. Some people love to hear what they want to hear even if they know they are being led astray.

"However when He, the Spirit of truth, is come, He will guide you into all truth" (John 16:12). God left a five-fold ministry to impart His revelation to His Church Body. These ministries are the only means by which God imparts His revelation to us. When Jesus spoke of prophets, He was not speaking of Old Testament prophets. He was speaking of the prophets He would raise up by His Spirit. These prophets, He said, would disclose things to come to God's people. If God were not going to raise up new prophets, He would simply have told us to read the scripture for revelation. Modern apostles and prophets must be raised up if the Church is to fully equip the saints for the work of service.

How can we truly know which voice is the voice of God? The true prophetic voice of God was put into the world for one primary reason—to find God's people. The true prophetic voice was not put in the world only to prophesy against governments and kingdoms. Prophets are raised up primarily by God so the sheep can receive direction. Jesus said, "My sheep will know My voice." When we realize this, listening to the Spirit becomes mandatory for maturity.

A true prophetic voice will always be synonymous with the character of God. If a person claims to be a prophet, yet he separates people by racial overtones, love of money, or anything else that violates the character of God, that preacher is not a prophetic voice. God's Word is always consistent with His character.

A true prophetic voice will always share the message of the Kingdom of God: righteousness, peace, and joy. A prophet will never be influenced by the congregation, a board of directors, or a committee. A genuine prophetic voice will never be influenced by his spouse, children, or other family members. God's true prophet has the mind of Christ and the sure Word of the Lord that overrides any influences that come from his natural reason or relationships.

God puts pastors among people to comfort and to lead them. He uses His prophetic voice to correct, direct and point the way to fulfill His purposes. The prophet says, "Here is what God is saying about the future." Until we learn the difference between a pastor and a prophet, we can never understand the five-fold ministry.

Prophets and prophetic voices do not always come from expected places. John the Baptist preached, prophesied, and stood as a man of God, yet people questioned his lifestyle and message. He dressed strangely, lived in the desert, and ate unusual foods. Regardless of these things, Jesus said of John, "He is the one who recognizes God in the world." John's spirit recognized that Jesus was the Messiah.

God waited patiently while John grew up. Patiently, He waited for Jesus to assume His ministry, and now He is waiting for His Church to mature. Most people are comfortable with the Church as long as it remains only a "City of Refuge" that feeds the poor and clothes the naked of the world. People love the church that relieves them of that burden. The Church is loved when it preaches messages aimed at "unity of faith." Yet, when the Church tells people that they are in error because their congregations are not racially integrated, suddenly the message of the Church becomes very unpopular.

Opposition begins whenever the Church begins to teach and preach spiritual authority. The first true spiritual battles begin in churches when Christians enter into an understanding of spiritual authority. Satan knows that his end will come when believers understand that Jesus Christ is the King of kings with all authority in heaven and in earth and that the Church is God's authority in this world. Understanding spiritual authority makes Satan angry and he attacks God's people. Many people scatter when attacks come. God is searching for people who will hear His voice and communicate and demonstrate His Word as a witness to the world. When God finds these people, the world will be changed.

The Kingdom Church that teaches the message of maturity rather than waiting to be caught up into the clouds with Jesus will receive the most aggressive opposition. Few people like change, but growing up means change. It is comforting to an infant to drink its mother's milk. A baby never has to fight obstacles or battle opposition. With an infantile lifestyle, the Church could spend this generation waiting on Jesus to return instead of growing up and receiving Him back as His mature Bride. Until the Church reaches maturity, Jesus Christ cannot return.

Other messages taught in a mature church will meet with much opposition. For example, some believers will protest the teaching about the timeclock of God being spiritual Israel rather than natural Israel. Modern national Israel has become a sacred idol that God never intended it to be. God is concerned with people who are following His voice today whether they are in Mexico, America or Africa. Christian believers are spiritual Israel.

In the light of opposition, what if our critics are right? As God said to Jacob, "Come now and prove your cause." Let us say that our critics are right about spiritual authority. Everyone could do his "own thing," be his own authority and submit to no one. Let us assume our critics are correct and the Church should have no right to say anything about relationships or tithing. If everyone is right in his own decisions, and our critics are right, that issue is not going to keep us out of heaven. The fact that we obeyed those over us in the Lord is not going to change eternity for us. BUT, if the message of spiritual authority IS right, and God intends for people to be submitted to those who are over them in the Lord, some people are in danger of hell because they will not listen. Think of all the Christians who are living their own lives apart from what God desires to speak to them. They believe they are right because their church and their pastors are not teaching them any differently. They are hearing no clear voice from God, and they are following their own subjective opinions.

The belief concerning the "rapture," in which any moment we could all be caught up and taken away to a place where we will have no more problems, will not save a person. Salvation comes only by believing in Jesus Christ. If the Church must mature and learn how to rule and reign with Christ; if the Church must make this world Christ's footstool, then theories opposing these truths will lead people to destruction.

Before the late 1800's, the rapture theory did not even exist. The rapture is a modern-day heresy. Many of us were raised during a time when the rapture was taught by spiritual authority in our churches, so we immediately accepted it as truth. Satan has put this modern-day heresy in the minds of people to rock them to sleep. Christians sing about heaven and wait until they are called out of the world instead of understanding the prayer of Jesus. He prayed, "I do not pray that You should take them out of the world, but that You should keep them from the evil one" (John 17:15).

If the rapture theory is right, we don't have a problem. But if it is wrong, it doesn't matter how much about Jesus those believing in the rapture preach, they still are keeping a milk bottle in the mouth of the Church. The Church remains in its infancy instead of growing up. Maturation teaches us how to get along with neighbors of different races. We learn how to move into a realm in which our faith is not attached to materialism. If we are right, think of the people who are deceived and will never grow up to face the important issues of demonstrating their faith.

Satan has deceived many preachers and religious leaders of our day. Ministers repeatedly cry out against drugs and the evils of abortion when these are not the real problems at all. These issues are only symptoms of the real problems. Preachers blame the wrong people when they admonish a girl for her pregnancy or a boy for his drug abuse. Pregnancy and drug abuse are merely symptomatic of a much greater problem that began when parents failed to assume their God-given responsibilities of caring properly for the children they brought into the world.

Possibly that little pregnant girl did not have parents who cared for her. Perhaps her parents did not set an example of proper authority and respect. The boy who smokes marijuana could have had parents who told him to stay away from drugs, yet kept their refrigerators full of alcoholic beverages. The major moral problem is lack of credibility and parental inconsistency which tells the child, "Do as I say, not as I do." Parents are responsible for setting an example of godly virtues that a child can see lived out before him every day of his life. How can the blame be placed upon a child who was simply doing what he had seen his parents do? How can we expect wholesome, righteous behavior from children unless we teach it to them by example?

Preachers cry out against high divorce rates without realizing that they may be contributing to the problem. Many pastors grant permission for young couples to marry because these couples are convinced that they will be in love eternally. Pastors should say, "I cannot give you my approval to get married until you have been counselled together concerning the tremendous responsibilities that come with marriage." Couples need to know one another before they decide to spend the rest of their lives together. Their spirits must be in unity. Pastors must help the couple to determine in their spirits that God is joining a man and woman together. If more pastors required thorough pre-marital counselling of couples asking for the Church's approval for their marriages, divorce rates would decrease dramatically.

Until the Church wakes up, diligently seeks the root causes of these problems, and addresses the real evils of our society, God can never trust us as being anything other than an immature Church. Unless we correct the source of our problems, those problems will perpetually exist.

If we saw a child who was hit by a car, lying in the street, bloody and broken, we would not rush over to him and say accusingly, "My, what a mess you are! What were you doing out in the street in the first place?" We would act quickly to call an ambulance. We would get him to a hospital where doctors could attend to his medical needs.

In the same manner, the Church of the living God should never sit in judgment of those who have been injured on life's highways by divorce, abortion or chemical addiction. We do not need to tell people that their lives are in a mess. They already know that they need help because of their low opinions of themselves. The Church should be God's "emergency room" to deal with human casualties by ministering God's healing love to injured or hurt people.

For the most part, people are victims of their circumstances. Daily problems are usually only symptoms of much more serious situations. The Church must get to root causes of people's problems before we will ever see true healing of these situations. What are some of these root causes?

I began to seek God's direction and revelation to understand root hindrances in His people, and He showed me a mystery. God told me that a man could judge his relationship with the Church by judging his relationship with his wife. A woman can judge her relationship with the Church by judging her relationship with her husband. A man will treat the Church the way he treats his wife. If he is selfish with his wife, he will generally be selfish with the Church. A man who is overbearing or domineering in the marital relationship will also try to dominate decisions regarding the Church. If a man is confused about his relationship with his wife and is emotionally unstable in his love for her, he will act the same way toward the Church.

A woman views the Church as she views her husband. If her husband is a spiritual man, committed to God, under submission to the Church, and she sees him as a godly man whose judgment she trusts, she will also trust the Church. If a wife does not listen to her husband, she probably will not listen to the voice of God through the Church either.

Prejudice is another root problem. We will never know oneness in Christ with brothers and sisters in the Kingdom if we have prejudices. The Kingdom of God does not distinguish between male or female, Jew or Gentile, black or white, bond or free. We are all one in Christ. People are comfortable with the idea of Kingdom unity until it begins to affect them personally.

The third root problem is pride. God has stripped some people of material possessions and comforts because He is searching for people who will hear His voice. God touches our lives in sensitive areas until we allow Him to make us into what He wants us to be. Then we can stand up for Jesus Christ in the midst of persecution and say, "Let the world laugh. We know who we are and who has called us."

Prophets of God have always been peculiar, and prophetic churches are also different. They seem strange to the eyes of the world. Four characteristics make prophetic churches unusual. They are peculiar when they decide to mature in Jesus Christ instead of escaping from their trials. They realize that trials only bring maturity and growth as they attain the likeness of Jesus Christ.

Maturity also comes by hearing and submitting to God's voice. Maturity is manifested in an attitude that refuses to settle for less than one's full potential in Jesus Christ. As we mature, we understand that our righteousness is not ours, but His righteousness. He took our sins on the cross so that we could take on His righteousness in our lives. Jesus did not commit sins; He took them on Himself. We are not righteous because of anything we do. We take on His righteousness as we grow and mature in His likeness. This understanding leads us to true holiness.

The second characteristic that makes prophetic churches peculiar is that they are demonstrators of God's Word, not merely observers. For instance, they do not just preach about the evils that surround abortion; they offer an alternative. They do not just say that homosexuality is a lifestyle that ends in devastation; they offer an alternative. They offer alternatives to old lifestyles and patterns. Even if someone falls back into old ways, the mature Church will love and pray for that person so that he can learn that Jesus Christ and the power of God in him is stronger than sin.

The third quality that makes the prophetic churches different is that they are not spectators; they are participators in worship. People who come to church expecting to see a show have an improper motive. They could better be entertained at home. People who are aware that those who lead worship are totally given to the Spirit of God and His Kingdom can enter into that same Spirit of worship and say, "God, here I am. Use me to make a difference in Your house." The little Israelite maiden was the smallest voice in the house of the great Syrian captain Naaman, but God spoke through her because her spirit was open and receptive. She said, "I'm the one. Talk to me, God."

Fourthly, prophetic churches address all believers regardless of race, culture, traditions or denominations. God will not talk to us if we are proud, prejudiced, or closed off from hearing His voice. He will speak to us when we stand up and say, "God, I'm the one. Talk to me! Tell me how to operate my business. Tell me how to handle my relationships. Tell me how to live my life." When God finds that kind of open willingness in us, He will speak clearly to our minds and spirits, saying, "Here is what I want you to hear."

We hear many voices, but the most important thing to know is when and where we hear God's voice. We hear God's voice when we think of the welfare of others before our own comforts. We hear the voice of God when we know how to go the second and third mile in relationships. Our spirits must say, "God, whatever it takes, I'm listening."

God speaks to spiritual ears that will hear His voice. The most important questions that we must ask ourselves are, "Will I listen to the voice of God? Am I really hearing His voice? What is God saying today?" We must decide whether we are honestly questioning ourselves or if we are simply listening to someone who is preaching what we want to hear.

Jesus told His disciples, "In order to make a difference in the world, I must go to the cross. When I do, My death will fulfill God's requirements for the earth and will bring man to a place of reconciliation with My Father." Because they did not fully understand, the disciples said, "No, Lord, You can't do that." Peter probably thought, "Jesus, You must be a false prophet because nothing has ever been accomplished by some-body dying on a cross." Jesus replied to the voice speaking through Peter, "Satan, get behind me."

Only spiritual ears will understand by the Spirit of God that the Church must go to the cross before it becomes the prophetic voice that will shake the foun-dations of the earth. Out of the mature Church will sound a voice that will bring such sure and true words of God that even the elements of the earth will obey. Out of the mature Church will come the mighty, mirac-ulous power of God that will overcome the deceptive spirits that confuse the world and prevent the return of our King, Jesus Christ.

6

THEY CHOSE OTHER GODS

On a trip to Jamaica in 1983 I shared a bedroom with Bishop Harry Mushegan. Brother Mushegan was quite ill the first night we were there. In the course of the night, the Lord awakened me and I began praying for Brother Mushegan, although he was not aware of my prayers. The windows were open in the little villa where we stayed. The house was small and a breeze blew through the window. I thought that the air might be too much on Brother Mushegan, and I got up to close the window. As I did so, the Spirit of the Lord stopped me and said again, "Pray for Brother Mushegan."

I knelt at Brother Mushegan's feet to pray for him while he slept. As I began to pray, the Spirit of the Lord came upon me. I began to have a revelation in relationship to the god of this world. The god of Mammon was a message I had preached many times with some understanding, but I had never comprehended its depth until then.

The Spirit of the Lord said, "The god of this world is Mammon. The god of this world must be uncovered and he must be judged." Jesus said, "When the Holy Ghost is come, He will judge." God's judgment of worldly kingdoms will be the beginning of the fall of Mammon and Mammon's kingdom, Babylon or commerce.

I did not completely understand this revelation in my spirit, but the following morning I told the Bishops who were gathered that I would like to talk about a matter having to do with finances in the Church. For an hour or so, we shared together from the Word of the Lord concerning the god, Mammon. Mammon is a god and a spirit. Money is a spirit. When I came home I referred to this subject rather briefly in a message to my congregation. I knew, however, that God had more to speak on Mammon than I had preached. God gave me much confirmation and additional insight concerning the god of Mammon. Were I to follow my flesh, I would not address this subject. I share this revelation because God said it is a vital message to the Church.

This revelation is not of earthly origin. It comes from the royal, divine throne of God. Judges 5:8 is a verse of scripture that the Lord brought to me early one morning when I was seeking Him on this subject. I had never really noticed this passage before. I use this scripture as a background to present truth. I pray to the God of Heaven that especially people who are in business will receive the truth I write. "They chose new gods; then there was war in the gates." New gods caused war over authority, dominion and power. Jesus said, "I will build my Church and the gates of hell shall not prevail against it." War began when new gods were chosen. War began over dominion.

A person, place or thing can become a god only if we give it the place of a god in our thoughts, our actions, or our commitments.

The Lord God planted a garden eastward in Eden, and there He put the man whom He had formed. And out of the ground the Lord God made every tree grow that is pleasant to the sight and good for food. The tree of life was also in the midst of the garden, and the tree of the knowledge of good and evil. (Genesis 2:8-9)

We start in the beginning in order to get the intentions and the mind of God. "Pleasant to the sight and good for food." That was not Satan's plan, it was God's plan. God's plan was good for sight, to refresh the body and provide good food. "Life" and "Spirit" are used synonymously. Spirit was placed in the Garden and then as an afterthought, Spirit was used to bring knowledge. The tree of reasoning or the power of our own mind was also placed in the Garden.

In the Garden was that which satisfied the body, was pleasant to the sight and satisfied the appetites. The body was a recipient of the blessings of God and God's blessings were lived out in the body. He placed the tree of life, the Spirit, in the Garden. The tree of life was unquestionably the presence of God. As a result of the tree of life in the Garden, man's life reflected joy and goodness.

The battle between good and evil was possible because of the soulish area of man. The soul of man (his wisdom, reason, and decision-making process) was called the tree of knowledge of good and evil. This is the area in man where Satan still has his greatest victories. This area is the tree of understanding, the tree of knowledge, the tree where our minds become gods and we are controlled by what we think is right and wrong. People become gods unto themselves.

"And the Lord God commanded the man, saying, 'Of every tree of the garden you may freely eat; but of the tree of the knowledge of good and evil you shall not eat, for in the day that you eat of it you shall surely die.' " (Genesis 2:16-17)

Notice the following term, for it will occur again and again: "You may freely eat except for one." God wants us to give our wills, knowledge, and total obedience to Him. We must not allow ourselves to control certain areas of our lives. But of other areas, God said, "Eat of it freely. Everything you want is yours." An abundance was given to man. When we are in right relationship with God, He gives wealth and abundance. This is God's original plan and intention.

And the Lord God said, "It is not good that man should be alone; I will make him a helper comparable to him." (Genesis 2:18)

God said that He would give man unlimited joy and fulfillment in human relationships. Their "nakedness without being ashamed" (verse 25) symbolized that there was nothing that they could not enjoy. Man was totally free in the Garden. God gave them abundance, wealth and total liberty in relationships. Freedom in the Spirit is only for the spiritually mature. God gave an unlimited fulfillment in relationships and He said, "My plan is for abundance and fulfillment." After sin was committed, abundance was distorted. Shame was part of the curse. Apparently God blessed man with wealth and happiness. God said, "Be fruitful" (Genesis 1:28); be successful in everything that you do; multiply and fill the earth; subdue the earth which means, "Learn its secrets." As our creator, God gave man the ability to learn His secrets. God will give us revelation or the secret things that belong to Him. He said in Genesis 1:28, "Take dominion." At that moment in the history of mankind, however, man chose another allegiance. He chose to make himself his own god by seeking his own knowledge of good and evil.

Man's mind of reason, his accomplishments and his own fulfillment became another allegiance. Because of disobedience, productivity and prosperity must be accomplished by the sweat of the brow and by the work of man's hands. Insight from God's Word on work ethics has been a missing key. Prosperity and productivity became a curse. Possessions must be acquired by the work of man's hands. Limitations were placed on relationships and God closed off the ability for mankind to be open to all that surrounded them.

Man devised his own way to be successful and prosperous. God was no longer man's source. The culmination of the decision that man had already made in the Garden was again lived out at Mount Sinai. Moses was a man to whom God could speak as few who have ever lived upon the earth. The people were complaining and disobedient. They wanted to stone Moses, their leader. They tested Moses's credibility. When they did, God said, "It is time for My people to hear from Me, Moses. Go to the mountain top and I will give you revelation." God said to Aaron, the brother of Moses, "Stay with the people and wait in the valley."

While Moses was seeking God's revelation, which is the source of all true wealth, Aaron listened to the people. Aaron wanted to please people and have his own following. The people said, "We want a god that we can see," so Aaron made them a god. A golden calf was constructed and the Bible said that they received the golden calf saying, "Let this god go before us." They chose another god.

A large percentage of the Church today is still in the clutches of that god. For that reason, the Kingdom of God waits. Overcoming the god of Mammon is a final key to establishing God's Kingdom upon this earth. The people said, "We will choose another god."

The issue before God's people today is: Who is our God? Mammon is represented by gold and silver and the pursuit of wealth. Commerce represents our allegiance to wealth. In II Corinthians 4:4, Mammon is called "the god of this age." Who has blinded people to such a degree that they do not know the difference between man-made prosperity and God-given wealth? Heads of every Christian household must address the priorities of that family in relation to the influence of Mammon. The god of this age, Mammon, has become an alternative to every aspect of life including God Himself. Jesus said simply, "You cannot serve God and Mammon." Our service is not a matter of degree or dimension. Jesus made a straightforward pronouncement. Many will say, "But Lord, Lord, we prophesied in Your name and in Your name we went to church and did great things." And God will say, "But I never really became your god. Your god was Mammon."

A god can become the search for gold and silver, instead of the One who supplies our needs. The imaginations of some people were released to such a degree that Babel brought the confusion of languages because Mammon controlled the people. "We will make for ourselves a name. We will have a kingdom unto ourselves. People will say, 'Look what they have accomplished'." The tower of Babel was living evidence that Mammon was god. Imaginations were released. Today imaginations are released in the business community where Mammon rules as god. Mammon is being preached by the Church under the guise of "success orientation," but the message is too often directly from the god of Mammon. This area of misunderstanding causes deception greater than we have ever known before in the Church. In the house of God, people are saying, "My God is Jehovah," but they bow to Mammon every day of their lives.

Mammon is pursued by the work of our own hands. Our source of strength becomes our own ability to achieve. With the ability to have dominion in business, others become our servants so that we can lend them money on which they will owe us interest. We can give them alms and they are indebted to us. People become classified as "those who have" and "those who have not" because Mammon is god. Some say that forms of government cause economic discrimination, but forms of government have nothing to do with this situation. Whether an economy is lived out in socialism or capitalism, finances of both serve the god of Mammon. One government says that man is free, while another says that society is free to make a choice. Both, however, serve the god of Mammon. No government on the earth today is serving God, not even one. Every government on the earth is serving Mammon. I know that is a bold statement, but I will not back away from it.

In the midst of this situation, however, God shows his desire to bless people under certain conditions. Understand that God will always preserve His seed. God will never leave Himself without a witness in the earth—never! Some will say, "What about Abraham? What about Job? What about Solomon?" They were seeds of the Kingdom. They were visible evidences of what God wanted to do from the very beginning which was to give abundance to man.

The condition under which Abraham could be declared a man of wealth was that God put Himself between a man and his possessions, even with the sacrifice of a son. Never was anything allowed to come between this man and God's revelation to him. Abraham was made wealthy under the condition that he would not allow possessions of any kind to come between him and his revelation of God. Abraham was detached from his wealth. Although Abraham deserved it by the flesh, Abraham said to his nephew, "Lot, you choose the way you want to go. Whatever is left over, I will take because God is my Source."

In Genesis 13:15, Abraham received a promise, not only of wealth, but a promise of everything. God said to Abraham, "All the land is going to be yours because you gave up your first choice. You had a right to it, but you denied yourself that right. Because you rejected your right, your wealth is now in the promise." No true wealth exists apart from God's promises.

In Genesis 14, when wealth was offered to Abraham from a king, he refused those riches because he would not obligate God to them. The Church must learn that it cannot receive money from the world. The Church cannot receive money from millionaires who do not comprehend the purposes of the Church and insist on controlling how their money is used. The Church makes itself a servant by receiving income with restrictions attached to its use. Abraham knew that to receive wealth from another source would give that source power over him. When we make ourselves subservient to Mammon or our own success, we give that source power over us. Mammon begins to control our total lives. Mammon affects the perception of everything we see. We begin to perceive solutions from wrong sources and judge circumstances through misplaced power.

The issue facing Job was whether the disappearance of his wealth would affect his service to God. The whole issue with Job was that God allowed everything to be taken away from him, including his relationships. Yet through it all, the Bible said that Job did not lose his integrity. Job did not abandon his righteousness when his wealth disappeared. How many curse God when there are dark days in their lives and sickness comes? How many curse God when material things disappear? We are on the faith bandwagon as long as we "name it and claim it." Everything is fine and everyone is serving us. But what happens when everything is gone? The test for Job was that God wanted evidence of his love.

Even before God gave Solomon wealth, He tested Solomon's requests. What are we praying for? James put it simply. "You ask amiss because you want it for yourself." God told Solomon, "Ask what you will and I will give it to you." Solomon asked for understanding as to how he could help people. Solomon needed understanding to govern God's people, to show God's way, to speak God's Word. God said to him, "Because you did not ask for yourself, I will give you the blessings of wealth."

Jesus put it even more simply. "Seek ye first the Kingdom of God and His righteousness, and I will add these blessings to you." Solomon's wealth was prophetic in that it pointed to the Kingdom of God. Solomon's reign is in some ways a prototype of the Kingdom of God. Earthly wealth is a foretaste of real jewels and wealth represented in the New Jerusalem. Even the foundations of the Holy City are filled with the true wealth of God. Money is not true wealth. Money is only a system of exchange.

The Old Testament gives insights to wealth that will stand the test of time. First, wealth is a sign of God's blessings. When God is recognized as the source and man lives in total obedience to Him, man prospers. Proverbs 10:22 establishes the fact that wealth was a blessing of God. In Old Testament times, wealth was not justified because of gain through the world systems or because of improper stewardship. Wealth was given because one's relationship was right with God. Any other wealth was gained improperly. The Word of the Lord states that those who gain wealth by any other means—fraudulent actions, oppressing widows, or taking advantage of people with interest charges— were cut off.

Wealth was not justified simply because someone felt that he "earned it." God blesses us because our relationships are under spiritual authority and directly in accord with God's will. The Old Testament principle was that God is Lord and His ownership must be recognized as people become stewards of the things of God. Financial confidence must be in the source and not in the wealth. One must keep his confidence in God, the Provider, and not in the provision. We must worship the One who gives freely to us rather than that which is freely given.

Righteousness is total dependence upon God's action and not on the works of our own hands. Sin, on the

other hand, is the defiance of God's Lordship and inter-
ference in purposes that belong to God alone.

One who builds his life around material possessions
will never be satisfied. Ecclesiastes 5:10 says that he
who loves money will never be satisfied with money.
Man must have a revelation from God so that he can
judge his own spirit. Hosea 2:8-9 clearly states that
wealth is taken away because of man's disobedience.
Wealth will not last if it is not from God and acquired
with total obedience to spiritual authority. Joel 2:24-27
says that wealth comes and goes because of our knowledge of God.

"The threshing floors shall be full of wheat, and the vats
shall overflow with new wine and oil. So I will restore to
you the years that the swarming locust has eaten, the
crawling locust, the consuming locust, and the chewing
locust, my great army which I sent among you. You shall
eat in plenty and be satisfied, and praise the name of the
Lord your God, who has dealt wondrously with you; and
My people shall never be put to shame. Then you shall
know that I am in the midst of Israel, and that I am the
Lord your God and there is no other. (Joel 2:24-27)

The Apostle quoted Joel in Acts 2, saying, "In the
last days I will pour out 'wealth' from heaven," or spirit
or revelation of the Kingdom. Wealth gained through
oppression or slavery is scandalous. In Psalms 73, the
Psalmist summarizes the Old Testament concept of
wealth.

Behold, these are the ungodly, who are always at ease;

*they increase in riches. Surely I have cleansed my heart in
vain and washed my hands in innocence. For all day long
I have been plagued and chastened every morning. If I
had said, "I will speak thus," behold, I would have been
untrue to the generation of your children. When I thought
on how to understand this, it was too painful for me until I
went into the sanctuary of God; then I understood their
end." (Psalm 73:12-17)*

This scripture speaks of those who seek wealth by
wrong means. Usury, or taking advantage of the less
fortunate people as a means of making money, is bla-
tantly wrong. Wealth gained through the oppression of
God's people, in business or otherwise, is scandalous.
The riches gained by those who practice such methods
will disappear. The conclusion of the Old Testament
concept is that as long as wealth remains a sign of the
glory of God, it is regarded as being sacramental.
Wealth is, in fact, evidence of the New Jerusalem. But
when wealth is reduced to money-making, it loses its
spiritual significance as a sign of God's covenant with
man upon the earth. Mammon, or money, is the power
of exchange and comparison. Money can separate families. Wealth, however, is abundance which acknowledges that the source is God.

Our tithe belongs to God, but Jesus said, "Woe unto
you; you bring your tithes and you don't give Me your
heart." This statement moves us to the New Testament
concept. Jesus never once applauded a rich man. As a
matter of fact, He said, "Don't seek riches." He said if
we seek wealth, we won't find the Kingdom. Jesus is

the substitute for the Old Testament principle that measured blessings from God by wealth. Jesus became poor, brought His Gospel to the poor, and claimed the poor as His people.

Jesus became the Seed of the Kingdom. Abraham's seed, which is abundance from faith, is produced only in Jesus Christ. We must turn our eyes away from Old Testament principles of wealth and success and instead we must look to Jesus who is the incorruptible Seed. In fact, Jesus is the antithesis of the Old Testament concept of wealth.

Money is a god. Money takes on a personality. We make gods for ourselves when we turn away from Jesus. Mammon has become a god to the world even above Yahweh, Jehovah God. Mammon has become the incarnation of Satan. Satan's incarnation was Mammon just as Jesus was the incarnation of God. When Babylon collapses in the book of Revelation, heaven rejoices because the incarnation of Satan has fallen.

Many who call themselves Christians have never learned the difference in God, Jehovah, and the god, Mammon. They spiritualize money because it is a god. With the mind of reason, these Christians decide how to make it and use it. They justify themselves and let the world around them suffer.

We claim to be God's chosen because we tithe and feel that God is obligated to bless us. Wrong! Jesus said, "You cannot serve God and mammon" (Matthew 6:24). Serve is the key word. What do we seek most? We must not serve occupations, wealth and riches. They have power, but they must serve us rather than our being subservient to them.

The original story in Genesis included God's blessings through relationships. Today Satan aborts and prostitutes God's plan and creates, through Mammon, new kinds of relationships between the seller and the buyer.

Do not love the world or the things in the world. If anyone loves the world, the love of the Father is not in him. For all that is in the world—the lust of the flesh, the lust of the eyes, and the pride of life—is not of the Father but is of the world." (I John 2:15-16)

We are often embarrassed if our material possessions are less than our desires. People measure success by the kinds of clothes we wear, the quality of our houses, and the kinds of cars we drive. We call it "respectability," but God calls it pride. I Timothy 6:10 makes it very clear that the root of all evil is Mammon. Mammon is the antithesis of God. Previously we have thought sin was manifest only in things like adultery or stealing, and that is what the devil wants us to think. Those actions are sins which were dealt with at Calvary, but God says the love of money is the root, or the initial cause, of all evil. I have spent many years looking at that verse and saying, "God, please give me understanding of it. Let me know what You are saying. Did you mean to say it that way?" I say to God's Church by the Holy Spirit, "The love of money, Mammon, is the root of all evil!" Mammon forces us to have a totally different perspective concerning life.

Money means ownership. Jesus took a coin and said, "Who's face is on this?" and they said, "Caesar's." If we must live in worldly systems, remember that we are dealing in Caesar's market. That which belongs to Caesar is Caesar's and that which belongs to God is God's. We must separate the two. Christians are totally without hope of accomplishing God's purposes unless we address the truth of Mammon's influence as a spiritual issue and seek deliverance. There is absolutely no other way to be victorious.

Mammon is a spirit which dominates personality and societies' values are governed by it. Societies which are poor, such as those in India or Central America, are dominated by the lack of it. Concern over either having money or not having money dominates the world. Mammon is the god. Mammon decides success, power and all worldly decisions. People choose their gods, and Mammon battles to win our love. How much do we love what we wear, what we drive, or where we live? These things are necessary possessions, but Mammon is trying to win our love.

Mammon is a spirit and has power to possess and control someone. It will make people leave a community where their children are happy in search of more money. Beautiful relationships are sacrificed for jobs in distant cities because of Mammon. Most people save money to educate their children so that those children can follow the god, Mammon. With God's help and grace, the Church can offer alternatives to change the values of society. Jesus put it succinctly when He said,

(Matthew 6:21), "Where your treasure is, [your activity, your emphasis and your focus], that's where your love is." Earthly possessions are passing away. Lay up treasures in heavenly places. Set affections on things above. If we are totally in love with things above, we will not become entangled with earthly pursuits.

The problem is that most Christians have not given their affections to things above. Mammon and things consume the efforts of Christians. We follow what we love. We can follow what we love so intensely upon the earth that we will follow it into eternity, into death, and even into hell. In hell the rich man lifted up his eyes. God placed a witness at his door who asked for his help everyday. The rich man did not heed the opportunity that God placed before him. Are we understanding this story? Whatever church ministry or call for service God offers us, we must give an account to Him for our response.

The rich man prospered every day. He rode in his chariots, but at his gate lay the poor man, Lazarus. They both died. The rich man lifted up his eyes in hell while the angels came to the poor man. What does that do to our success theology? The angels took the poor man away because he had been a witness of God.

The rich farmer will say, "I worked hard while my neighbors were following the shade around the house. I have a right to be rich. Let the widow over there whose husband has left her, let the orphan who has no father take care of themselves. I'm too busy. I'm going to build a bigger barn." And God said, "You fool, tonight your soul is required of you." Jesus said that it is difficult for a rich man to enter the Kingdom of God, but all things are possible with Him.

A rich young ruler came to Jesus one day and said, "I have kept all the laws. I tithed to the letter. I have a right to my prosperity. I have a right to be rich because I've kept all the moral code." Jesus said to him, "Go and sell it and give everything you have to the poor." The Bible clearly defines the poor as those who hunger and thirst after righteousness. Jesus's condemnation was not against the possessions of the rich ruler, but against that which enslaved him. He was a slave to the god of Mammon, and the Bible said he turned and walked away sorrowfully.

Only a miracle of revelation can cause a rich man to see the Kingdom of God. The poor are the people in the Church who most often give sacrificially.

We often rationalize selfishness with the idea that we worked hard and used our abilities productively. That thinking makes us feel that we have a right to our possessions. I knew that I must have revelation, an understanding by the Spirit, to speak to the church concerning stewardship.

And He also said to His disciples: "There was a certain rich man who had a steward, and an accusation was brought to him that this man was wasting his goods. So he called him and said to him, 'What is this I hear about you? Give an account of your stewardship, for you can no longer be steward.' Then the steward said within himself, 'What shall I do? For my master is taking the stewardship away from me. I cannot dig; I am ashamed to beg. I have

*resolved what to do, that when I am put out of steward-
ship, they may receive me into their houses.' So he called
every one of his master's debtors to him, and said to the
first, 'How much do you owe my master?' And he said, 'A
hundred measures of oil.' So he said to him, 'Take your bill,
and sit down quickly and write fifty'. Then he said to
another, 'And how much do you owe?' So he said to him, 'A
hundred measures of wheat.' And he said to him, 'Take
your bill, and write eighty.' So the master commended the
unjust steward because he had dealt shrewdly. For the
sons of this world are more shrewd in their generation
than the sons of light. And I say to you, make friends for
yourselves by unrighteous mammon, that when you fail,
they may receive you into everlasting habitations. He
who is faithful in what is least is faithful also in much;
and he who is unjust also in what is least is unjust also in
much." (Luke 16:1-10)*

The man's mind of reason said to him, "Why, I was
just taking care of the man's business. How will God
trust me with spiritual wealth if he can't trust me with
Mammon?" And what was Jesus's answer?

*"Therefore if you have not been faithful in the righte-
ous mammon, who will commit to your trust the true
riches? And if you have not been faithful in what is
another man's, who will give you what is your own? No
servant can serve two masters; for either he will hate the
one and love the other, or else he will be loyal to the one
and despise the other. You cannot serve God and mammon." (Luke 16:11-13).*

The mind of reason says, "God wants me to be faith-

ful in Mammon so that He can trust me with riches."
But Jesus says, "You cannot serve both."

> *Now the Pharisees, who were lovers of money, also heard*
> *all these things, and they derided Him. And He said to*
> *them, "You are those who justify yourselves before men,*
> *but God knows your hearts. For what is highly esteemed*
> *among men is an abomination in the sight of God." (Luke*
> *16:14-15)*

The steward, with his own ingenuity in business
matters, made himself a fortune. God informed that
steward that when he had needs, his only source of help
would be himself. One can count on God when in trouble only according to the way his lifestyle has been
prioritized. When trouble comes, one will have the
same help he has previously depended upon. The man
who trusts God has an alternative source of strength
from worldly security.

People can be deceived or they can accept the revelation of God. Mammon is iniquity. Jesus came to reveal
the concept of Mammon versus true wealth. Jesus said
the Kingdom of God is not in what we can acquire. He
said the Kingdom of God is righteousness (total
dependence upon God's action), peace (the right relationship with our neighbors) and joy in the Holy Ghost
because we are serving Jehovah God and not Mammon. That defines the Kingdom.

Money passed under the scrutiny of Jesus. He said to
His disciples, "I must teach you a lesson before I leave
you." He took them to the treasury, and as He sat there,

He watched people bring their offerings. Jesus said to His disciples, "See that wealthy man? He has treasures of all kinds that he has brought, but at home he has many more treasures. He has a savings account which someone else would kill him to have. He has expensive things that his children will fight with one another to inherit. People applaud him because of his giving."

The same spirit of Jesus Christ is here today and says, "Watch them now. That nobleman left more wealth at home than he brought. In his deception he is saying, 'I've met my obligation.'" Jesus said, "Look at the little woman coming in the door. Let's see what she does. Maybe she will say, 'Somebody help me.' No, perhaps she knows who her Source is." The little woman walked timidly to the treasury. She had no money at home. She had nothing of any earthly good, only some coins that would keep her alive for a few days. She gave everything she had brought to the treasury and said, "Thank you, God. I'm glad to give this to You." She turned and walked away. And Jesus said, "She gave more than all the rest put together."

The key to finding our treasure is how much we keep back for ourselves. That principle equalizes the giving in God's Church. The abundance of one believer ought to be adequate for the supply of another. Those who have prospered should share the burden of those who lack provisions for basic needs. Jesus Christ condemned laying up treasures for ourselves. Most people feel that a good steward should have a savings account. A proper cash flow is not laying up treasures. Savings is not a New Testament principle.

The master had three servants. He gave one servant ten talents, one five, and the other servant, one talent. Most people believe that the one who made money on his talent was great. They interpret this scripture to say that making money pleases God. Oh no, that idea misses the point. The one with five talents is regarded as great because he made money. That interpretation misses the point. Jesus said the one who saved it, the one who made his talent his treasure, is an unfaithful steward. "Take away what he has and give it to him who has ten talents" (Matthew 25:15-28)

To understand what Jesus taught about money, one must always, always, side with humanity against accumulated wealth. Jesus said those who are naked represent Him. Those who are in prison represent Him. Prison doesn't mean only a penitentiary. People can be imprisoned by the circumstances of their lives. The Bible says that pure and undefiled religion is taking care of widows and orphans, those trapped by society; those trapped in racial difficulties; those trapped by the political philosophies of the nations of the earth. When God's Kingdom reigns, earth will have no poor nations.

Jesus made it very clear that our only true source is God. He emphasized this truth by saying, "Look at the lilies of the field. They don't toil or work; they are dependent upon God." Work is only the means by which God brings us resources so that we can invest them in the Kingdom of God. We have no other reason for God to be our source of prosperity unless we put our resources into God's Kingdom. God gives talent for no other reason than to use it for the Kingdom of God.

God said in the Garden of Eden, "Eat freely." Does that sound familiar? Jesus said, "I want to teach those who receive from Me how to give freely." The giving of God's grace is a continuous evidence of God's Kingdom in the world. Love and trust are not the evidence of the Kingdom. Kingdom evidence is giving, which is a constant evidence of God's grace. God so loved the world that He gave.

Grace takes the power away from Mammon because grace teaches us how to give, recognizing God as the source. The tithe should be an evidence of God's Kingdom in our lives. Offerings should be an even greater evidence of God's grace. One's spiritual concept should be, "Freely I have received, and now freely I give." We should give according to the proportion of God's grace that He has given to us.

Almsgiving perverts the truth of God's plan for giving because it creates a relationship based on money instead of love. By giving alms to a poor soul who sits by the wayside, we make him subservient to our gifts. That is the reason Jesus said, "Give unto Me." As we give to the Church, the Church is responsible to care for the poor and the needy. Individuals should not get the credit for provisions to the poor. Let the elders and God's people be the ones to care for them. When we follow this concept, one will never have a wrong source of "giver" and "debtor." Those with spiritual understanding know the difference.

Giving to God should be an act of faith to take away the power of money over our lives. Giving should be a declaration, "In God I trust and not in Mammon." It should be a declaration before Mammon, "I will not serve you. I bring prosperity to God's will. I bring it to the ministry of the Kingdom."

Some churches are filled with bankers and affluent people who want to make spiritual decisions because they feel they have paid for the privilege. Bankers would resent a pastor demanding to make their business decisions for them, but money will try to run God's Church. Men who are called of God must be allowed to be prophets of God to this generation.

I don't believe that a pastor should be regulated on a salary because it makes him subservient to his people. The Levites never owned anything but they received the tithe from all the people. If Christians don't trust prophets and pastors, they are never going to enter the Kingdom of God. John Gimenez, pastor of Rock Church, was challenged about the amount of money he was making. He told his challengers to read what the Bible says the tithe is intended to do. They studied for two weeks on the subject, and they came back to John Gimenez saying, "Pastor, the tithe belongs to you and the ministers of this church. Offerings should take care of everything else." John looked at me with tears in his eyes and said, "Earl, that was going to be over a million dollars a year. I refused to take the tithe of the church, but they insisted. Finally I agreed to allowing them to set up a ministerial account for one tenth of the tithe of the church from which pastoral salaries would come. The rest of the money in this special account is used for the work of the ministry."

People don't trust the pastor until the elders trust

him. Some churches that were once stalemated have no indebtedness today. Having hundreds of thousands of dollars in a church budget is the difference in depending on Mammon and in trusting in God.

The tithe and offering is a sign of the coming Kingdom. Christian giving is a testimony of grace to this generation. It is a challenge to Mammon. Jesus likened the Kingdom of God to a man who found a treasure in a field and sold everything in order to buy that field. Put investments in what God is doing in His Church. If God prospers us and He is our source, everything we make above necessities should be given to God's Kingdom.

Understanding of Old Testament teaching and what Jesus accomplished when He challenged Mammon is not understood in the Church. Jesus Christ will come back to this earth when He has a people who know the difference in Mammon and Who the Lord of Israel really is.

The sobering conclusion is that many are helpless and do not know what to do. Christians must be delivered from any spirit controlling their lives. If we open our wills, God will deliver us.

Children are possessed by their parents' attitudes toward wealth. Adults make their children become schemers. Parents reproduce their philosophies of success in their children. Parental values influence the choice of schools, the kinds of cars children will buy, and the importance of stylish clothing. "How will I look in society? What are people going to think about me?" Jesus said, "If you're ashamed of Me in this world, I will be ashamed of you before the Father."

Declare the source of treasure and the source of love. Security is found either in Jesus and God's Word, or in the ability to make money. Abundance, wealth for God's children, comes through God's promises. This whole world can fall apart with a holocaust, but world catastrophe will not affect those who are spiritually wealthy. Our source and abundance is in the revelation God has given to us. We must choose the God of revelation, which Moses represents. The alternative is choosing the golden calf, the god of Mammon, represented by Aaron.

In Revelation the cry was, "Babylon is falling! Babylon is falling!" Man's ability to make money is gone. Commerce is destroyed. Jesus Christ will come again only when Mammon is judged. Six-six-six on the forehead of man represents his humanistic intelligence. God's Word says, "That's the antichrist." The antichrist will not come out of the Mediterranean. He already reigns in the minds of men. The humanistic god of this world is the antichrist. The antichrist spirit is the one who says, "I don't need God. The tree of knowledge is my God." God's Word says that a day will come when only those who are subservient to humanism will be able to exchange in the world's markets.

"Babylon is falling!" is the cry. Commerce is falling and our only source is God who puts us in the garden and provides all things. God teaches us how to take dominion and how to subdue. He gives us intellect through His wisdom to rule and to reign properly. Rulership will not come because of competition in the markets, but because of compassion in our hearts.

How do we overcome Mammon? First, we must give and expect nothing in return. That's grace. Grace is the unmerited favor of God. We give without expecting to control. We overcome Mammon by giving without any reservations. Secondly, we overcome Mammon and the gods of this world when we can pray in the Spirit and not depend upon intellect or reason. The baptism of the Holy Spirit is necessary to the understanding of spiritual things. One can receive the Holy Spirit when his own pride is defeated and he begins to speak in a language he does not know. Be willing to be a fool for Christ's sake. Speak in a unlearned language to the glory of God. God hears our prayers in powerful, spiritual petitions.

The Kingdom of God is understanding that the answers we seek in the Spirit are more important than those things we ask in the flesh. That is Kingdom understanding.

Thirdly, we overcome Mammon when we learn how to fast and deny our fleshly appetites. When appetites are out of control, our bodies reflect that we have never learned the difference in the god of Mammon and the God, Jehovah. If we learn these principles, the only reason to exercise is just to firm up our muscles. The Kingdom comes in Christian fasting. We must know how to look at ourselves and say, "Sure, I can do it." Paul says, "I have the right to do anything I want to do because of revelations, but I don't do certain things because I want to bring the Kingdom to pass."

The Kingdom begins when we get out of the center of our worlds and we begin to live for others. That's the Kingdom. We overcome Mammon when we sing songs that do not satisfy the flesh, but bring glory to God. Songs of the flesh are making millions of dollars today because they sympathize with the flesh. Songs of the Kingdom are about to revolutionize worship in churches.

Kingdom music prepares us to refuse intimidation by Satan. We're no longer ashamed to do things in the name of God. If God says jump, clap our hands, or look foolish to the world, we're no longer controlled by the condemnation and judgment of the world. God's Word says, "Praise with a loud voice and with the dance." The world won't like it. Singing praise to the Lord means His Kingdom is coming. The purpose of our praise intimidates Mammon and worldly success. It intimidates social snobbery. Praise proclaims that Christ is Lord.

The cross is self-denial. God stripped the prophet Jeremiah naked. David danced before the Lord until his clothes fell off, but he just kept on dancing before the Lord.

This is the day of God's Kingdom coming to earth, and we are about to see an outpouring of the Spirit. The Holy Ghost fires are going to burn. We can be a part of the move of God, or we can hide the precious treasure of revelation that God has given to us. We must declare by proclamation and demonstration, "God is God! His grace is in the world and I will show it by my giving."

7

THEY PUT A REED IN HIS RIGHT HAND

The authority of Jesus Christ in us is our only hope of unmasking Satan. Yielding to the victorious Christ in us assures our victory in Kingdom against kingdom warfare. We battle the same areas that Jesus did. We uncover the same deception and confront the same accusations and lies that were hurled at Jesus. The mature Church must undergo and overcome victoriously every attempt of Satan to destroy the witness of Christ's Kingdom living in us. We need to thoroughly examine Satan's strategies against Jesus's authority to understand fully the direction in which we will move toward victory.

Then the soldiers of the governor took Jesus into the

Praetorium and gathered the whole garrison around Him. And they stripped Him and put a scarlet robe on Him. When they had twisted a crown of thorns, they put it on His head, and a reed in His right hand. And they bowed the knee before Him and mocked Him, saying, "Hail, King of the Jews!" Then they spat on Him, and took the reed and struck Him on the head. Then when they had mocked Him, they took the robe off Him, put His own clothes on Him, and led Him away to be crucified. Now as they came out, they found a man of Cyrene, Simon by name. Him they compelled to bear His cross. And when they had come to a place called Golgotha, that is to say, Place of a Skull, they gave Him sour wine mingled with gall to drink. But when He had tasted it, He would not drink. Then they crucified Him, and divided His garments, casting lots, that it might be fulfilled which was spoken by the prophet: "They divided My garments among them, and for My clothing they cast lots." Sitting down, they kept watch over Him there. And they put up over His head the accusation written against Him: THIS IS JESUS, THE KING OF THE JEWS. (Matthew 27:27-37)

They did not call Jesus "Savior of Mankind." They called Him "The King of the Jews." No one condemned Jesus as long as He was regarded as merely a "savior" or a "religious man." As long as Jesus stays in the place that people assign to Him or the role that people appoint Him to assume, they can say that He is a "Savior of Mankind," and they can spiritualize away any warfare over Jesus's identity. Nobody fought Jesus as a savior. That was not the primary focus of the battle between Jesus and Satan.

The battle raged when people no longer called Jesus a "priest," but began instead to call Him "a king." Then something happened! Kingship and authority are also the issue in God's Church today.

This is a message which causes some divisions of spirit, but will also bring greater unity of spirit. This message is directed toward those who have been unsure about their relationship with God, their relationship with the Church, or their identity in the world. Understanding will come if we comprehend by the Spirit.

The accusations hurled at Jesus concerned His Kingship. When He began taking dominion, He encountered warfare. No warfare threatens the lives of those who talk about Jesus being the Savior. Whenever someone talks about Jesus Christ the King, warfare threatens his life. The Kingdom of God is built in spiritual authority and the proper understanding of it. People did not mock Jesus as a savior, but they mocked His kingship. Notice, THEY gave Him the reed. Notice, THEY put the robe upon Him. Therefore, they maintained the right to take the reed away from Him and strip the robe from Him.

As long as they gave Him the reed, they could take it away from Him. When congregations can vote preachers into their pulpits, they can vote them out. If people can select their spiritual leadership, they always have the right to reject that leadership. The Church faces warfare today because spiritual headship is opposed by people within the Church who are never willing to submit themselves to God-called leadership.

Saying, "We will give you the reed as long as we can control the reed" is mockery. We don't have the right to put the reed in someone's hand or the robe on someone's back. Conflict results because these actions signify authority. The comment at the cross was, "If He is the King of Israel, let Him come down" (Matthew 27:42). No one commented about Him as a Savior. Jesus hung upon the cross, and the question was, "If He is the King . . ." Jesus as the Savior has never been a threat nor is it the concern of this generation. The question even today is, "If He is the King . . ." We try to press Jesus the same way that Judas did. Judas said, "Jesus is the King. Because He is the King, I will press His kingship into worldly politics." On the cross, the accusation was not, "Jesus is the Savior of Mankind." The accusation was, "Jesus claims to be the King of the Jews."

The battle rages over whether Jesus is the King. Is Jesus the King of our finances? Is He the King of our relationships? We do not encounter warfare as long as we simply make Him our Savior. We battle daily when He says, "I am the King of your relationships. I am the King of your life. I am the King of your occupation."

Herod sought to kill the little baby Jesus, not because He was the Savior, but because Herod knew within his spirit that a King had been born. Herod reacted to the Kingship of Jesus, not to His priesthood.

When Jesus was brought before Pilate, the Roman official asked Him one question (Matthew 27:11). He did not ask Jesus if He were a savior or a priest. Pilate asked Jesus, "Are you the King of the Jews?" The church which teaches that Jesus is Savior and Priest will be left alone as long as it talks only of His missions of redemption and intercession. That message is no threat to the world's systems. But the very moment that Pilate asked, "Are you a King?" Jesus answered, "You have said I am a King and so I am." Kingship led Jesus to the cross.

Christ's Kingship is no less controversial today. As long as the Church keeps its message of salvation purely spiritual, without demonstration, the message does not threaten people within the Church or within worldly systems. As long as the Church today fails to mature beyond the levels of salvation and priesthood that will snatch people from hell, the Church does not encounter great warfare from within or without. When we proclaim the Lordship of Jesus Christ over human existence, we confront a totally different warfare.

The Church has no conflict as long as our major purpose is to provide a breadline to feed the poor. Not only is the Church not threatened as long as we just feed poor people, the government will help us to do it. They will give us commodities such as cheese. We are no threat to social order. Reporters will even write complimentary articles in the newspaper about our bread-lines. They will tell the whole community by radio and television, "Get some canned goods together. The Church is going to feed the poor." Authorities in the world will say, "That's good, feed the poor, but be sure you keep them poor."

The Church is no threat to society as long as they build hospitals for sick people. As a matter of fact, the government will even give us subsidies to help us build those hospitals. I am not opposed to churches building hospitals or feeding hungry people. But we must understand the reasons no one opposes us as long as those things are all the Church does.

The Church will not threaten society by building orphanages and homes for the aged. The government will help us. They say, "Oh, that's wonderful! You're building places for the aged and for children who have no parents. That's a beautiful work of God."

Having day-care centers for children will not put the Church in warfare. As a matter of fact, the government will help us have day-care centers for children so mothers can go to work.

Songs about going home to be with Jesus will become best-sellers. Especially if they sing, "I've got a little grandmother leaning over the fence of heaven, bidding me to come home." Or some sing, "The table was spread in that beautiful place, and there's one vacant place at the table. The evening sun is sinking. All you children come to the table." People cry over these words.

People say, "Look what a beautiful funeral." A funeral becomes a beautiful celebration when a soul has arrived in God's eternal Kingdom, but just to put somebody in the ground is not beautiful. The Bible says that death is an enemy to be conquered! As long as we send flowers, play soft music and walk around on tiptoe, death is not going to be conquered.

The world says, "Isn't that church building beautiful? Look at their stained glass windows. They have a pipe organ that will blow your mind. Look at those beautiful soft seats. Look at the esthetics!" These comments mean that the Church is not challenging anybody. The government will even help us do our projects. The world places the reed in our hands and says, "There now, you be a beautiful little church in your community but be sure you keep your place." I prophesied years ago that we would have a congregation about half and half racially balanced. I can say this with authority. Many people weren't afraid of black people twenty-five years ago as long as they "stayed in their place," but society wanted to define that "place."

Likewise, the Church is no threat to the world as long as we "stay in our place." The world tells the Church what and where its place is. Let the Church challenge the social order of our day, or oppose corrupt practices that are perpetrated by the government, or support a civil rights movement and I assure you that we will enter into conflict.

We never had any problems in this ministry as long as we simply fed the poor. But one day my brother, Pastor Don Paulk, and I joined ranks with Martin Luther King, Sr. and stated, "We will go to jail with you if it is necessary. We will oppose markets that are making some people rich while they take advantage of others who are poor." The next week, we got a subpoena informing us that we had been sued for one million dollars. Why? Because we touched the gods of this world by refusing to allow poor, innocent people to be abused any longer. We became a threat to the god of Mammon.

If the Church does only those things that the world wants us to do, we seldom threaten anyone. But if we condemn the laws that abuse the rights of women or children, we are suddenly attacked by the media. Even so-called religious groups will condemn a protest concerning military bases or the nuclear arms race. If Christians express opinions against those things, conflict erupts. If the Church condemns government practices concerning drug and alcohol traffic in our nation, we become a threat. If our government were less corrupt, it could close down or at least reduce the drug and alcohol traffic in our nation. In Georgia alone, the majority of drug busts involve governmental officials on the local level. I contend, under the anointing of Almighty God, that the time has come for the Church to stand up and say to governmental officials, "We are not going to elect you until we find out your interest in us and our children. We want laws that will end abusive practices in our nation."

The Church's lack of influence is shown in our attitude toward those who are in the ministry. Some of the most stringent educational requirements today are placed upon ministers, yet pastors rank at the very bottom of the professional pay scale. Those facts reflect the world's attitude toward the ministry. As long as the Church keeps pastors humble with holes in their shoes and poorly dressed, the world will say, "My, how humble he is!" If that pastor is God's servant — a prophet, a priest, or a man or woman of God — we should reverence him as God's representative upon the earth. I write this as a Bishop who oversees many churches: Shame on churches that muzzle the ox, which the Bible says treads out the grain! Shame on you!

People cannot put the reed of God into the hand of a man called by God, nor can they take the reed out of his hand. When people begin tampering with God's anointed servants, the road they travel is like the one that Judas traveled. One day they will wake up and say, "My God, where did I go wrong?"

A pastor can be a "gopher." A "gopher" is a man they tell to "go for this" and "go for that." A preacher can be a gopher and everyone says, "Isn't he beautiful? He is the most beautiful gopher I have ever seen." Or the pastor can be a taxi cab driver and just drive people all over the city. People will say, "He is the best pastor in the world. He is the best cab driver I ever hired."

When I was the pastor of a church in this city several years ago, I had been there about two weeks when a lady called me on the telephone. She said that she was at the supermarket, and asked me to come to get her and her groceries to take them home. I said, "Uh, uh, uh, who are you?" She said, "Well, my husband is so and so." I was only 25 years old and I thought, "Well, this will be good submission." I got into my car, went to get her, and took the lady and her groceries to her big beautiful house. The next week the same thing happened. When the same thing happened the third week, God said to me, "Are you a cab driver?" When she called me the next week, I said to her, "Please call a taxi. I am not a cab driver." I didn't become the most popular preacher to that family, but I was no longer a cab driver. If a person has a need, any compassionate pastor will crawl to his people to help them. But as long as people have a mentality that a pastor is a cab driver, they don't understand the ministry of God.

A pastor can be a nursemaid. He can sit and hold someone's hand through an operation. The pastor is loved as long as he will do that, but let him look into someone's eyes and say, "I have noticed from your attendance record that you don't come to Wednesday night services. You are never at church on Sunday night, and the Bible says, 'Forsake not the assembling of yourselves together.' I have also noticed that you do not tithe." All of a sudden, that pastor becomes a threat because he takes on kingship.

The world cannot tolerate kingship. A pastor can be an athletic director with the finest softball team and people will say, "Oh, isn't that a great pastor!" He can be a missionary to Africa, and people will say, "Great, look what he is doing." But let that pastor speak as a prophet or let him speak with authority, and many people will reject him.

People said of Jesus, "He doesn't talk like anyone else. He is a man who speaks with authority." At the end of the road a cross was waiting for Him. A cross! Let a preacher challenge spiritual principalities and powers, and all of a sudden people reject his message. When a preacher tells a king, a governor, a president, a senator, or a local representative that he is immoral and he should resign his office in government, that preacher will endure a cross. John the Baptist said, "King Herod, you know you are living like the devil wants you to live." John preached by the Jordan River. He didn't even have a pulpit, but he preached truth. He was imprisoned and murdered, and his head was brought to Herod on a charger.

When the Church speaks to issues that affect the economy, it will become an enemy. Elijah said, "It is not going to rain, King, until you get straightened out." The king only cared about one thing: no rain, no crops; no crops, no money. The king was only concerned about how the prophet touched his economy. As long as the Church doesn't touch society's money, we are great! We are wonderful little taxi drivers; we are wonderful little healers laying our hands on the sick. God's ministers need to aggressively say, "Get your house in order!" "Become the spiritual head of that family!" "Become the mother you should be!" "Get your act together for God!" But those exhortations will cause grumblings. When the Church questions the easy way of life, or challenges people in the marketplaces, we must say to them, "Is Jesus Christ your Lord or not?"

As long as Jesus healed the sick and did good things for people, He had no opposition. But when Jesus began to cast out devils, He moved toward the cross. He went to the temple and said to the merchants, "This is God's house of prayer. You have made it into a den of thieves!" I see Jesus as a young, strong, thirty-three year old man. His strength showed in His muscular shoulders as He lashed the whip saying, "You get out of

God's house!"

Jesus's action against the money changers was as much God's will as feeding the poor or holding a little baby to bless it. Jesus said, "God's house has been made a house of thievery. You have stolen from God and from widows and orphans. I will no longer tolerate such activity. God's house of prayer will remain the house of prayer." Jesus's stand accelerated His journey to the cross because He became a threat to the world systems.

What makes a Kingdom Church different from any other church? Please understand that the Body of Christ is one. Those who name the name of Jesus Christ are brothers and sisters. God's Word, however, always addresses local congregations. For example, Jesus had words for Thyatira that were not the same as the words that He had for Philadelphia. Words God gave to Sardis were not the same as He had for Laodicea. Every church, though members of one Body, are members individually. Each church has an individual expression.

Unfortunately, much of the Church has lost its identity. Many churches have lost their unique purpose. Churches have become slaves because they have allowed the world to put the reed in their hands. As long as a church determines a pastor's salary, it can set his level of service. That church can place requirements on the preacher that limit him as the pastor, the preacher, or the prophet of that church. A church like that can always take the reed out of that preacher's hands. But God is doing something new in the church world today. Kingdom churches are surfacing because men of God are beginning to wake up. They will not be shackled by traditions any longer. In some of the largest churches across this country, pastors have said to me, "Earl, I can no longer sign the pledge of that denomination because it breaks my authority with God." If an organization puts the reed in someone's hand, they can take the reed out of that person's hand.

For our purposes, I am going to make a distinction between a Salvation Church and a Kingdom Church. Some prefer a Salvation Church. A person always has that option, but with that choice comes a warning from God. This message can make a difference in our eternal understanding of God and our responsiveness to Him.

What is the difference between a Salvation Church and a Kingdom Church? Some Christians are called to occupy, and some are are called to attack. I have never hidden the fact that my church is an "attack" church. A Salvation Church is content to snatch souls from hell. Their favorite songs are ones like "Just As I Am." Sometimes that song takes on more meaning than we realize because many Christians stay "just as they are" for the rest of their lives. They walk down the aisle to an altar and repeat after a preacher, "I believe that Jesus is the Christ." Forty years later, that prayer is all they have ever prayed. The message of salvation characterizes a Salvation Church, and that message is important to the world.

The Kingdom Church not only snatches people from hell, but disciples Christians to subdue the world around them. Kingdom concepts demand discipleship.

187

People are receptive to preaching which teaches them to say, "I give my life to Jesus. I want Him to save me from hell." But when Christians are told to attend a new members class or a discipling group to learn about the Kingdom of God, only a small percentage of those people attend.

The second difference between the Kingdom Church and the Salvation Church is that the Salvation Church waits for deliverance from this world and their present circumstances. Most of their singing is about how God is going to deliver them from this world. A Salvation ministry brings the message of deliverance from this world and creates a mentality of waiting for deliverance. The Kingdom Church seeks to change circumstances in the world to become co-laborers with Christ. The Salvation Church says, "Wait for deliverance, and the Deliverer will come!" The Kingdom concept is that we have the power to change the circumstances where we live. We can take dominion over our circumstances through Jesus Christ. We can begin to claim who we are in this world and take authority over our lifestyles.

The third difference between the two kinds of churches is that the Salvation Church is very eager to offer us the comforts of retirement. The mentality within the Church is to make it until the time of retirement and then become inactive. One of the greatest evils in America is compulsory retirement. There is a lack of understanding of how detrimental retirement can be. A person should be honored at the end of his chosen profession, but he should continue to be productive in another dimension of work. Don't tell anyone that he is no longer needed. Our present concept of retirement should be abolished.

The Kingdom Church says, "When we leave the land of Egypt, don't leave my bones there! Take my bones to the Promised Land. Though my body has gone back to the dust, I want my bones where the promise is." That is Kingdom mentality. The Apostle Paul said, "I have fought a good fight. I have run a good race. I'm going to finish my course." Regardless of what the government says about retirement, the Kingdom Church finishes the course that God ordained.

Another difference between the two churches is that a Salvation Church has evangelism as its main thrust. I thank God for that message. The salvation message is beautiful and great and we must send out that message. We must tell people that Jesus loves them and will save them. The thrust of a Kingdom ministry, however, is to become a witness by addressing people's lifestyles. We can go to other countries and preach that Jesus Christ will save people from hell, but until we demonstrate power and authority in Jesus Christ, we will never change wicked governments. Kingdom people actively attempt to change adverse circumstances.

Kingdom churches are not popular, but people love Salvation churches. People love churches who put Band-Aids on their hurts without pressing them for a cure. People hate a church that questions lifestyles and says, "If you don't straighten out your life, you are going to lose your self-worth, your family and your job."

The Kingdom of God will never be established by Salvation churches. They have a beautiful place in God's plan. Salvation is the first step toward God. The Kingdom will come, however, when people are challenged in their lifestyles, when they acknowledge spiritual authority, and become obedient to their callings. The greatest hindrance to the establishment of the Kingdom is our lack of submission. These concepts have nothing to do with salvation. Jesus told His disciples to tarry in Jerusalem until they were endued with power! Power for what? In the first chapter of Acts, Jesus said He would send them power to restore the Kingdom. Only the power of the Holy Ghost will restore God's Kingdom. The Kingdom of God is righteousness, peace and joy in the Holy Ghost. The Holy Ghost is essential to entering the Kingdom of God.

A Salvation Church will not preach and teach the baptism of the Holy Ghost. If a Spirit-filled Christian goes to a Salvation Church, that church will give him a Sunday School class or make him a deacon, but they won't let him teach and preach the baptism of the Holy Ghost. The Holy Spirit brings the Kingdom of God to the world. Jesus said to His disciples' salvation minds, "Stay in Jerusalem until you get authority." The difference between those who "talk" about Jesus and those who "act" like Jesus is the baptism of the Holy Ghost.

Jesus said, "The Kingdom is near when we cast out devils." What does casting out devils have to do with salvation? Jesus was referring to Kingdom authority. Go to a Salvation Church that does not believe in the baptism of the Holy Ghost with the evidence of speaking with other tongues, and ask them, "Can you cast out a devil? I have someone who is possessed that I want to bring to you." I promise that they will say, "No." Pastors have had their secretaries call me and say, "Pastor Paulk, we have a mentally deranged person we would like for you to minister to." Do you know why? Most churches don't have the authority and the power of the Holy Ghost to cast out devils. People walk among us who say, "Oh, what's the difference? There is nothing special about Kingdom churches." We don't claim to be "special." We just claim to have a special God who grants us the anointing and power of the Holy Ghost so we that can do great things in the name of the Lord.

Jesus said in Luke 10:19, "Behold, I give you the authority to trample on serpents and scorpions . . ." I thank God for everyone who preaches Jesus, but Jesus said to those who walk in Kingdom authority, "I am going to give you power to walk on serpents. If you drink any deadly thing, it will not harm you. God's purposes will be fulfilled. Many will make disparaging remarks, but God will give you authority."

"Obey those who rule over you, and be submissive . . ." (Hebrews 13:17). This verse has nothing to do with salvation but has everything to do with bringing the Kingdom of God into reality. When we cannot love people whom we see, how can we love God whom we have not seen? When we cannot trust those whom we see that are our spiritual leaders, how can we trust God whom we have not seen? If we cannot submit to those whom the Lord puts over us, how can we submit to an eternal God? Those principles have nothing to do with basic salvation, but they are necessary for the manifestation of the Kingdom of God. We are God's prototype to the world and should obey those who are over us in the Lord. What does the scripture, "The Kingdom of God is like unto a mustard seed," have to do with salvation? What does the scripture, "Find the pearl of great price and buy the field" have to do with salvation? These scriptures have everything to do with the Kingdom of God.

The Holy Spirit and I came to some conclusions about Salvation churches and Kingdom churches. If the Spirit and the Bride say, "Come," then the Holy Spirit and I have a right to confer. First, if the world (or any flesh power) places the reed of authority in our hands, they can control our authority and take it away. If they tell us what to preach and how to minister, they can take authority away from us. Secondly, Jesus gave the scepter to the Church when He said, "I went to hell and back, and I have brought the keys of death, hell and the grave with me. Whatever you loose on earth, I will loose in heaven, and whatever you bind on earth, I will bind in heaven."

When we have the divine call of Jesus Christ upon our lives and we receive the scepter from the hands of Jesus Christ, the world cannot take that authority away from us. When the scepter comes from Jesus's hands, we don't have to worry that someone will take that scepter away from us. We are God's people. Anywhere God grants an opportunity, we will preach the

Kingdom of God, and salvation will come.

God's people were having a great revival, and God said to Philip, "Get out from among this Alpha group and go to a desert place." God could have been speaking to Chapel Hill or any other Kingdom Church. God's command to Philip was to go to the desert. Why would God send a Spirit-filled man to a desert? Because Philip had the scepter of Jesus in his hand! A chariot came riding by, and the Holy Spirit said, "You're my man! Join that eunuch, and see what he is doing." When Philip got closer, he saw that the man was reading the scriptures. Philip used the scepter of authority that God had given him to open the spirit of the eunuch. He began to teach the Gospel, and the eunuch's life was changed. He was a man of high authority in the government. We should not be afraid to take God's message to those in high authority.

There should be no fear of sharing with legislators, mayors or other influential people. Take the **Ultimate Kingdom** or another good book, walk into an influential place and say to a legislator, a mayor, or the head of the highway department, "Sir, I would like to give you a gift. Would you take time to read this book?" Some people will throw us out. Jesus said not to fret about how people react to our message. When we make the witness that God would have us to proclaim, then their reaction is God's business.

The Kingdom Church is God's Garden in the world. When God put Adam and Eve in the Garden, He said to them, "Subdue the world." The Kingdom ministry is God's Garden that reveals to the world how God operates. That is the reason for such internal warfare. The devil can never defeat us from outside the Garden. Inside the Garden the serpent lifts his head, just as when Judas began to question the authority of Jesus.

The Church is a Garden prototype for the world. Jesus said, "Love, so the world may know" (John 17). One may go from a Salvation Church emphasis to a Kingdom Church emphasis, but one cannot retreat from the Gospel of the Kingdom and its authority to a Salvation Church without running into conflict.

Therefore, leaving the discussion of the elementary principles of Christ, let us go on to perfection, not laying again the foundation of repentance from dead works and of faith toward God, of the doctrine of baptisms, of laying on of hands, of resurrection of the dead, and of eternal judgment. And this we will do if God permits. For it is impossible for those who were once enlightened, and have tasted the heavenly gift, and have become partakers of the Holy Spirit, and have tasted the good word of God and the powers of the age to come, if they fall away, to renew them again to repentance, since they crucify again for themselves the Son of God, and put Him to an open shame (Hebrews 6:1-6).

Some will leave a Spirit-filled church and return to churches that will make them like kings. These circumstances may make it appear that "Kingdom" teaching is wrong. But God says, "You put Me to open shame and have taken My sacred things and returned them to a level that is foundational rather than progressing in Kingdom truths."

194

Jesus said that those who were once enlightened by the Holy Spirit and the power of God, but then go back to the level of repentance will begin to bear thorns. They will bring persecution and agony to God's people because they reject God's complete truth. Hebrews 6:8 states, "But if it bears thorns and briars, it is rejected and near to being cursed, whose end is to be burned." I didn't say that. God said it.

But, beloved, we are confident of better things concerning you, yes, things that accompany salvation, though we speak in this manner. For God is not unjust to forget your work and your labor of love which you have shown toward His name in that you have ministered to the saints, and do minister. And we desire that each one of you show the same diligence to the full assurance of hope until the end and that you do not become sluggish, but imitate those who through faith and patience inherit the promises. (Hebrews 6:9-12)

What things accompany salvation? They include casting out devils, Kingdom preaching and taking authority. Paul says in this scripture that God's pleasure is to give the promise to His children. What is the promise to God's people who were in Egypt? What is the Promised Land of spiritual Israel? The promise is the Kingdom of God when Jesus Christ has come again. God said that when we have tasted of the heavenly manna, we have tasted of the age to come. God instructs us to pursue the promise. That promise of things to come is not the same as salvation in Jesus Christ.

195

No one fears a church if it has no authority. When Jesus spoke as One who had authority, people became afraid of Him. Some pastors console people in their immaturity and thereby stagnate their growth. Because leadership is afraid to speak to the spiritual needs of the people, they remain on the same level of immaturity. When the authority of apostles and prophets is not acknowledged, perfection of the saints is impossible. One should seek for a place of worship where the Word of God is quick and powerful and sharper than a two-edged sword and where carnality is confronted. The god of Mammon must be chiseled away from the lives of God's people if the Kingdom of God is to be established within us.

The Bible says that the soldiers crowned Jesus with a crown of thorns and put a reed in His hand. But Chapter 19 of Revelation gives the end of the story. The eternal revelation is that no longer is a crown of thorns placed upon the head of Jesus.

Then I saw heaven opened and behold, a white horse. And He who sat on him was called Faithful and True, and in righteousness He judges and makes war. His eyes were like a flame of fire, and on His head were many crowns. He had a name written that no one knew except Himself. He was clothed with a robe dipped in blood, and His name is called The Word of God. And the armies in heaven, clothed in fine linen, white and clean, followed Him on white horses. Now out of His mouth goes a sharp sword, that with it He should strike the nations. And He Himself will rule them with a rod of iron. He Himself treads the winepress of the fierceness and wrath of Almighty God.

And He has on His robe and on His thigh a Name written: KING OF KINGS AND LORD OF LORDS. (Revelation 19:11-16)

Jesus wears crowns that no man put on His head and no man can remove because God Himself placed them there. No longer does He bear the accusation, "King of the Jews." God's immaculate pen has written on His thigh,"He is King of kings and Lord of lords." No man can take His authority away from Him.

The hands bearing the reed of man's authority were to be nailed to a tree. His head, filled with the knowledge of God, was crowned with thorns. He was stripped of His clothing and indecently displayed before the world. They pulled off His garments and left him nude. They clothed Him with a scarlet robe. How prophetic! A scarlet robe clothed Him and a reed was placed in His hand.

The reed of authority they handed to Jesus was not His authority. But Jesus, knowing who He was, continued to take the abuse of the world. Woe to the hands that mistreated Him! He sat with the reed in His hand. They bowed before Him, sarcastically saying, "Oh, King Jesus! Prophesy about me. Show me all of Your great power." Jesus made no reply because He knew who He was. He knew He was a King. They took the reed out of His hand and began hitting Him over the head. The crown of thorns buried deep in His brow. They took the reed of their authority from Him and beat Him with it. When God's people give their authority to anyone else, it will be used against them. When

197

one compromises his convictions, he will be defeated because he has forfeited his reed of authority from God.

God says, "I'm going to speak to this earth so that my people will know who they are. They are either rebellious or submissive." God will never establish anyone as an authority until that leader learns how to submit.

"Judah, you are he whom your brothers shall praise; your hand shall be on the neck of your enemies; your father's children shall bow down before you. Judah is a lion's whelp; from the prey, my son, you have gone up. He bows down, he lies down as a lion; and as a lion, who shall rouse him? The scepter shall not depart from Judah, nor a lawgiver from between his feet, until Shiloh comes; and to Him shall be the obedience of the people." (Genesis 49:8-10)

God said that He was going to place a scepter in the hands of Judah, who is Jesus Christ. No one can take it away from Him until Shiloh, the Kingdom of God, comes.

The reed placed in Jesus's hand was later used to beat Him, but God said that the Lion of Judah will prevail.

And I saw in the right hand of Him who sat on the throne a scroll written inside and on the back, sealed with seven seals. Then I saw a strong angel proclaiming with a loud voice, "Who is worthy to open the scroll and to loose its seals?" And no one in heaven or on the earth or under the earth was able to open the scroll, or to look at it. So I wept much, because no one was found worthy to open and read the scroll, or to look at it. But one of the elders said to me, "Do not weep. Behold, the Lion of the tribe of Judah, the Root of David, has prevailed to open the scroll and to loose its seven seals. (Revelation 5:1-5).

A Lamb, who was worthy, came forth and received the scepter from God who then placed the Book in His hand. The Book is the revelation that God gives to us. It is the revelation of Jesus Christ to mankind.

No more reeds will be placed in the hands of the true Church, the family of God. God wants to give the Church His scepter of authority, place His royal crown on their heads, and clothe them with His royal robe of righteousness. As God clothes His Spirit-filled Church, we will begin to see a new dimension of ministry. Chosen men and women of God around the earth are becoming prophets of God. We are that generation which was prophesied. The Kingdom of God is much nearer than we believe. The generation now lives who, if they remain faithful, will see the demonstration of God's Kingdom.

Two thousand years ago, Jesus said, "It is time for Me to act like a king." Jesus could have gotten a chariot with horses from governmental officials, but they would have been the chariots and horses of the world. Jesus would have been under governmental authority. Jesus said to His disciples, "Go find Me a colt on which no man ever sat. I'm going to show the people God's authority." Anyone can ride in man's chariot. Jesus showed mankind where God's authority rides. He rode upon an unbroken colt while the people waved palm branches.

Horse trainers say that if palms were waved in the face of an unbroken colt, he would go wild. As Jesus sat upon the colt, some people expected it to start bucking. But when Jesus sat down, the colt recognized Him as the King of kings and the Lord of lords.

Some people have been so overexposed to the Gospel of the Kingdom that they have been blinded to who the King is. Instead they continue to serve Mammon. They bow to the opinions of others. They are influenced by wrong relationships. The time has come to bring the royal robe and scepter to the King. The time has come to crown Jesus King of kings and Lord of lords.

The Church is complete wherever it is. Two or three who are gathered in the name of Jesus Christ constitute a complete church. But the Kingdom of God is incomplete. Because the Kingdom awaits, God must raise up John the Baptist ministries, firstfruits of Kingdom people, as a witness to the world. As Kingdom people, we must move on to the task before us with an awareness of our mission and a willingness to be open to the leading of the Spirit of God.

8

BEWITCHED

The word "bewitch," according to **Webster's Dictionary,** has two meanings. The first one is "to use witchcraft, magic, or to cast a spell." Paul did not use the word in that context in his Galatian letter. The second definition is the definition that Paul referred to: "to attract and delight irresistibly, to fascinate, to charm." The Galatians had received the Spirit of God, but they reverted to the bondages of the law. Paul asked them, "Who has bewitched you that you should not obey the truth? Who has charmed you or fascinated you so that you would leave the Spirit walk and go back into the walk of the flesh?"

Oh, foolish Galatians! Who has bewitched you that you should not obey the truth, before whose eyes Jesus Christ

*was clearly portrayed among you as crucified? This only I
want to learn from you: Did you receive the Spirit by the
works of the law, or by the hearing of faith? Are you so
foolish? Having begun in the Spirit, are you now being
made perfect by the flesh? Have you suffered so many
things in vain — if indeed it was in vain? Therefore He
who supplies the Spirit to you and works miracles among
you, does He do it by the works of the law, or by the
hearing of faith? — just as Abraham "believed God, and it
was accounted to him for righteousness." Therefore know
that only those who are of faith are sons of Abraham.
(Galatians 3:1-7)*

Satan is always trying to accomplish his mission
which is to steal, kill and destroy (John 10:10). That
may be over-simplifying warfare, but the intention of
Satan is to prostitute God's plan on planet earth in any
way possible. Satan uses many methods and devices.
II Corinthians 11:22 records some of the methods he
used to try to defeat Paul.

*Are they Hebrews? So am I. Are they Israelites? So am I.
Are they the seed of Abraham? So am I. Are they ministers of Christ? I speak as a fool — I am more: in labors
more abundant, in stripes above measure, in prisons more
frequently, in deaths often. From the Jews five times I
received forty stripes minus one. Three times I was beaten
with rods; once I was stoned; three times I was ship-
wrecked; a night and a day I have been in the deep; in
journeys often, in perils of waters, in perils of robbers, in
perils of my own countrymen, in perils of the Gentiles, in
perils of the city, in perils in the wilderness, in perils in the*

sea, in perils among false brethren; in weariness and toil, in sleeplessness often, in hunger and thirst, in fastings often, in cold and nakedness — besides the other things, what comes upon me daily: my deep concern for all the churches. (II Corinthians 11:22-28)

Satan came in sickness and in all kinds of attacks against Paul's ministry, but Paul was a man who understood the mission that God had called him to fulfill. Satan still comes to war against the Kingdom of God with sickness and rebellion. He entices people to make golden calves or pursue idolatry. Satan now manifests himself in many religious circles. He has charmed and bewitched people with religious activity.

The Church has experienced tremendous growth in spiritual discernment through the power of the Holy Spirit in the last twenty-five years. This move of God in spiritual things has been associated with the term "charismatic." Discerning of spirits is a gift-oriented ministry. A mighty move of God's Spirit today in all denominations of the Church has caused Satan to move forward also with greater force. He has become more subtle and more deceptive in his strategy. One of Satan's strategies is to charm or to cause the flesh to be responsive.

Satan is charming people today with what we might call "good things." First of all, he is charming God's people by allowing them to wear his clothes. I am not opposed to current fashions per se, although I do believe that Satan is in charge of worldly markets. Satan is basically in charge of "fashion parades."

Don't be deceived by the world. Clothing itself illus-
trates the point I am making by demonstrating a truth
that also applies in the spiritual realm.

Remember the story of David. After hearing the cry
of Goliath, he said, "I will go and fight" (I Samuel
17:32). He went to the household of King Saul who tried
to charm him. Saul said, "David, you're a charming
fellow. You're fresh from the pasture land with a fresh
anointing, and you're great and mighty. I believe
you've heard from God. Wear my clothing into battle."
Saul wanted to put his clothes on David so that he
would receive credit for winning the battle.

Saul was a coward. He had already lost out with God
and with the leadership of Israel, but he wanted his
clothing to be credited with the victory. Satan wants to
impose these same methods and deceptions on God's
people. Satan wants us to be clothed in his armor.
David finally had courage enough to stand up to King
Saul and tell him that he wasn't going to wear his
clothing. David decided to go in his own armor. David
knew that he had to go in the name of his God and the
clothing God had given to him.

God does not want His Church to compete with the
world — in dress, fashion, or even methods. He desires
a people who are clothed in the holiness and righteousness of Almighty God. God is looking for a people who
know how to be clothed in prayer and sanctification.
Without holiness, no man shall see God. Until we stand
in the blazing holiness of Almighty God and purge
Satan's influence in our flesh, we will never walk in the
armor of God or fight in the name of the Lord Jesus

Christ. Satan comes to us saying, "Clothe yourselves with the standards of the world. Clothe yourself with the fashions of the world. Do things the way the world does." The spirit within me says, "Love not traditions or the systems of the world, but walk in true humililty before Me."

Satan's first attack is to put us in his clothing so God will not receive the glory. If David had gone in the clothes of Saul, Saul's clothing would have gotten the credit for victory. After David had slain the giant, no one could say, "Look what Saul's armor did." Everyone knew that God had accomplished this feat through a little shepherd boy. We must learn how to be clothed in Christ's righteousness and holiness. If we walk in the clothing of worldly systems, the world will get glory and not God.

The second way that Satan charms us is seating us at tables of honor. I never go to Washington without getting calls from Congressmen or Senators who say, "Come and sit with us." I usually go. I thank the Lord for that privilege and opportunity. But I warn the Church that we cannot be charmed by sitting at tables of honor which may lead us into spiritual deception. We cannot be charmed by sitting at tables of honor and forgetting who has really honored us. We are not honored because someone places us at an honored table. We are honored because God Almighty has lifted us out of a pit and put us upon a solid rock, Jesus Christ.

When Daniel, Shadrach, Meshach and Abednego were taken to the table of the King (Daniel 1:8), Daniel purposed in his heart that he would not defile himself with the king's delicacies. Daniel knew that lavish living was not a proper lifestyle for them. He said, "Give us vegetables to eat and water to drink, then let our countenances be examined." God forbid that His Church should start eating from the tables of the world! Let us remember that our table is the table of the Lord. If we cease eating at the Lord's table, our countenances will not shine, and no one will want to follow the example of God's people.

Jesus walked simply among people. He dressed simply and His closest friends were simple fishermen. A very simple man, yet His life was to change the destiny of planet earth. The Church today must return to its simplicity. We must return to a table of unity. The charms of the world take us from the table of the Lord to the tables of the world.

The third charm of Satan is the attraction of exotic relationships based on fleshly desires, even among Christians. A million miles separate a fleshly relationship from a spirit relationship. If any woman had lain at the feet of Boaz other than Ruth, the circumstances would have implied a fleshly relationship. They look a lot alike, but Ruth was under the anointing and direction of God when she slipped under the covers and lay at the feet of Boaz. Her action was honored of God. Some walk among the family of God who attract people by the flesh. God is not pleased. We must learn the difference between a spiritual attraction and a fleshly attraction.

Samson was a showpiece of God. The enemy searched for ways to cause this "showpiece" to compromise. Demons had their conclave and decided the best way to trap Samson was to try to discover his secret of strength. They knew he had a secret with God, and they had to find out his source of power. They decided to attract him by a beautiful young woman. It might surprise some to know that it was not an illicit sex act that trapped Samson. He had just left the house of harlots, but he could prophesy and he still had power with God. But when someone tried to find out about his physical strength and his secret before God, all of heaven began to take notice.

Where was Samson trapped? On the lap of a harlot —not a sexual harlot— a religous harlot. With his head on her lap, she asked him in whispering tones, "Why are you so strong?" Then came the moments of jesting. Sometimes moments of jesting lead to Kingdom destruction. Moments of jesting in the wrong places can lead to hell on earth in God's Church. After those jestings, he was weakened in his spiritual fiber and forgot who he was. She leaned close to his ears, touched him slighty on his hair and said to him, "What is your secret?" We hear him as he says, "A razor has never cut my hair." More importantly, Samson revealed his covenant with God. At that very moment he was estranged from God.

Then came the cry, "The Philistines are upon you, Samson!" He stood up and shook himself as he had done in prior times, but nothing happened. He did not know at that time that the Lord had departed from him. The Church today is shaking herself, but nothing is happening. The Church has been at the table of the world too long. We have lived with the traditions of men and have been involved in exotic relationships far too long. God is saying, "Will you be a people who will be called by My name? Will you give a pure Gospel to the world and walk humbly before the Me?" Samson's eyes were put out, and he became a grinder in the prison because of a wrong relationship.

Solomon, the great wise man of the Bible, married strange wives. In his closing days, Solomon's wives offered strange sacrifices. Idolatry tarnished what could have been God's glory. What a horrible way to end in life!

We need to have keen discernment so that we will not enter relationships that are not of God. We need to ask, "God, is this relationship of You?" We need discernment, not just in marriage relationships, but also in the alignment of ministries. We need to know whether something is a move of the Holy Spirit or a move of the flesh.

The fourth charm of Satan is glamorizing warfare. Glamorized ministries send out their front troops to the mission field. They go in, hold one little baby in their arms, and then appeal to millions of people to give millions of dollars to help them. Have they changed any lives? Lifestyles usually have not been challenged. When we send teams to other churches or to other countries, I instruct them to start drama teams and discipling programs. I desire that they share everything possible to bless the work of God in that place. Years from now, I want people to look back and say, "I remember when Chapel Hill Harvester Church sent a ministry team here. They made a difference in our church. We're different because they taught us how to minister in the name of the Lord."

We hear so much about world evangelism, but we need to hear something about changing lifestyles. We need to give people hope in their governments by telling them that they can do something to change things. We must teach people how to change ungodly circumstances. Instead of arming countries with more missiles and guns, we need to arm them with the Gospel of Peace and the Gospel of Love. The power of the Gospel will change the society in which people live.

Gideon called for men to go out against the enemy. I can see his young men kissing their sweethearts goodbye, standing with their chests out, saying, "We're going to war. We're going to go out and make it safe for you women." Thank God for men like Gideon. I can see Gideon walking around, looking into their eyes. "What are you glamorized soldiers doing out here with me?" They probably responded, "Well, you said you wanted an army." More than likely, Gideon asked them, "Are you ready to give your lives for this cause? Are you willing to die if necessary?" I can hear them saying, "Well, we didn't think about that part of it. If that is what you want, you probably don't want us. We want to see what is going on, but we don't actually want to be in the battle."

Through methods of elimination that God instructed Gideon to use, he ended up with an army of three hundred. God is looking for a core of people who understand the difference between real warfare and glamorized warfare. God is looking for some people who can intercede and supplicate before God so that the heavens will be shaken. The ballot boxes are not in charge of elections. God is in charge of politics if His people, who know how to call upon Him, will humble themselves and pray. God can move by miracles to make governments go the way that He wants them to go. If that is not true, the Bible is a lie. God's Word says, "He will exalt whom He will exalt." What God needs is three hundred warriors who will get on their faces before Him and say, "We beseech You, Father. Night and day we are before You that we may have Your blessings among all the nations of the world." No, it's not glamorized warfare we need. We need real warriors!

Finally, Satan has charmed many people by making them become prosperous in a strange land. Satan has charmed the Church in such subtle ways. Satan has placed people in worldly places and caused them to become prosperous, so prosperous that they don't want to honor the simple things of God. While in Babylonian captivity, Israel became very prosperous. They became rich with fine houses, chariots, horses, gold and silver.

God said to Nehemiah and Ezra, "I want you to go back to Jerusalem and build the walls and re-establish the temple. I want you to go back to a place of worship." The prophets of God began walking among those in captivity and saying to them, "Let's go back and rebuild the walls of our homeland." The Bible said that Israel was so prosperous that the people didn't want to go back to Jerusalem to do what God called them to do. After awhile, they found a few people to go with Nehe-

210

miah and Ezra to rebuild the walls of Jerusalem.

The wicked prosper and forget God. People in God's house even prosper when their motives are wrong. When people do not use money according to Kingdom principles, the devil lets them prosper in a strange land. The writer in Psalms said that in a moment wealthy people are cut off and cast into hell, but not so with the man who dwells by the rivers of life. His roots go deep into the Word of God. His roots go deep into sacrifices for God's Church.

God is looking for a people who understand what it means to walk in truth and sacrifice before God. Man has a tendency to forget God in times of prosperity. If the Lord prospers a Christian, that prosperity is for the sake of the Kingdom of God. Kingdom prosperity helps the helpless and supports the causes that God has on earth. On the authority of God's Word I say that possessions will rise up as a witness against us if we forget God because of riches. What about the wealth of wicked people? They are not under God's covering or covenant as God's people are. Satan will make us prosper in a strange land. That's one of the charms Satan uses. Meanwhile, God is saying, "Don't be deceived. I'm looking for My Bride."

The charmer's strategy is to find, appeal to and expose a person's weaknesses. Godly men and women cover the weaknesses of their brothers and sisters. Christians being charmed in the flesh will live to see the day when they will say, "My God, I've exposed my weakness to the world!" When Samson exposed his weakness to Delilah, that's all Satan needed. Had he

confided to a godly woman who understood the problem, she would have bowed her head in solitude and
prayer before God and said, "By God's help, I'll put you
back on the right path." People need to quickly learn
the difference. Charmers who know nothing about the
spiritual things of God walk among the family of God.
We all have weaknesses, yet in those weaknesses we
can be made strong if we submit to spiritual leadership,
humble ourselves and ask God for spiritual covering.
But if we walk around arrogantly saying, "I don't need
God's covering," the day will come when we will be
exposed. These people will say, "My God, where did I
miss your direction?"

Secondly, Satan's strategy is to appeal to the flesh
instead of to the Spirit. There is a vast difference
between a dance company who dances in a spirit of
worship, and one who dances to whet the appetites of
the flesh. There is a great contrast between an orches-
tra or a choir who submits to God with talents dedicated to Him, and one which blazes its own personal
glory and achievements across the stages of churches.
We must know the difference. Appealing to the flesh
brings heartache, sorrow and devastation.

While God is working out His plan and building
character in us, Satan will charm us with an "easy
way." No short cuts exist in experiences with God.
Quick and easy solutions will in no way develop character. God builds people. We cannot be charmed. We
must learn to say, "God, is this the way that You want
us to go? Is this the solution You offer to us? Is this Your
plan, God?"

I sat with some people recently and heard a grandmother say, "We made such a queen out of our girl. We would move her from one room to another to watch television. Now she does not know how to make a bed, wash dishes or cook a meal because we have made her irresponsible." Our government has spoiled us by saying, "Here is a quick and simple solution." Easy solutions appeal to the flesh. The hour has come for responsible citizenship and responsible people. The hour has come for responsible Christianity. Kingdom theology means responsible Christianity.

Imagine what it would be like if every church in a city took care of its own people. By common concern the early Church took care of its own. Responsible Christianity would ease the pressures of our national budget. Do you realize how much it would ease our national budget if God's people prayed with such confidence that we would not be afraid to cut back on military defense expenditures? We hear, "Don't you know about those godless Communists? They are going to destroy us." What about God? He stands in heavenly places with all power. The problem with the world today is not the world — it is the Church. "If My people, who are called by My Name, will humble themselves, and pray, I will hear from heaven, and will forgive their sins, and I will heal their land" (II Chronicles 7:14). Ecologists cry out against the misuse of the planet when God's people should be the ones cleaning up the streams and the air.

America lagged behind spiritually at the turn of the century, at the beginning of the Industrial Revolution.

However, something was happening in little churches in the mountains of North Carolina, Tennessee, and north Georgia, and on Azuza Street on the west coast. God released a mighty move of His Holy Spirit. Early Pentecostals were laughed at and scorned. My dad, now an eighty-year-old preacher, was in the second generation of those preachers who preached the mighty outpouring of the Holy Spirit. Some of us who came after that generation went to colleges and seminaries. Schools refined us bit, but we preached with the same power. " 'By my Spirit,' says the Lord " (Zechariah 4:6). God's anointing does not come by the mind of reason or by the abilities of the flesh.

Then God began to move in what we called the great Pentecostal explosion. Out of that movement came some great denominations which I honor. Mighty churches preached messages about the outpouring of the Holy Spirit in the latter days.

In the fifties we began to see something new take place. No longer were only the little churches on the back streets receiving the Spirit of God. Suddenly, the Holy Spirit began to move in Rome as Catholic Christians began to receive the baptism of the Holy Spirit. In one meeting at Notre Dame, eighty thousand people gathered in a public place testifying that they had received the baptism of the Holy Spirit. Great universities such as Steubenville were established out of that movement. Almost everyone on that Catholic university campus has the baptism of the Holy Spirit with the evidence of speaking in new tongues.

The Holy Spirit was received by people in great

churches such as the Episcopal Church. God raised up men like James Robison, a Baptist preacher, to cry out against the evils that are taking place in the world. In the Methodist Church in one gathering four or five years ago, one hundred Methodists preachers received the baptism of the Holy Spirit. That event was reported on the front page of newspapers in Atlanta. Great and mighty things took place.

The Spirit of God began to disregard denominational lines and divisions. God began to move in a mighty way. The result of the move of the Holy Spirit began a world evangelism explosion. Preachers like T.L. Osborn and many others said, "Let's take the Gospel to the nations of the earth. Let's preach Jesus." And they did.

Then came great missionaries from every denomination. I thank God for everything that they accomplished. People's lives were changed. Millions of people came to know Jesus Christ, but too often their lifestyles were not changed. They knew the grace of God, but they did not know the power of God to change the way they lived. They were so deluded by diversionary tactics that they regarded the state as one area of concern and religion as another. They did not realize that the same men who sat in church pews on Sunday sat in places of influence on Monday. Satan created a dualistic attitude, and too many of God's people backed off and said, "Well, that's them, and this is us."

God was longing for a witness on planet earth. God always works by the witness principle. Both Deuteronomy 19:15 and Matthew 18:16 say, "By the mouth of

215

two or three witnesses, every word may be established." The book of Revelation represents the final picture of the Church as the two witnesses. The Church is God's final witness to the earth. When Jesus sent out the seventy, He sent them out two by two as a witness. God is saying, "The time has come that the Gospel of the Kingdom must become a witness so that the Holy Spirit can judge the world of sin." Today God is uncovering His Word with a tremendous understanding that until now has been held in mystery. God is raising up His Church as a witness.

God has raised up at least one local church as a conscience to Atlanta. I came to the South DeKalb area several years ago. We had originally begun a church in the Inman Park section of downtown Atlanta to minister to people in the inner city who were a part of a subculture. When we came to South DeKalb, the racial balance was changing swiftly from a white community to a black community. God said to me in my spirit, "That's where I want a witness. I want my witness to spread from Atlanta to the world." In a place where people were saying, "It's another changing society," God, through His Church, challenged everything that was taking place. God raised up a church that has challenged everything some people were saying could not be changed or dealt with successfully. We turned around the trends of society in South DeKalb. We also demonstrated that blacks and whites could not only live together but worship together as well. I prophesy that undeveloped land in South DeKalb will someday be a showpiece to people around the world as witness of what Christian people can do.

We are still small in the witness God has called us to be. That is the reason the attack is great. To be that witness, the Kingdom of God must come in individual lives. God desires a witness who shows the world that they love the unlovable. They take care of widows and orphans. They care for those who cannot care for themselves. Paul said in Romans 12:1, "I beseech you therefore, brethren, by the mercies of God, that you present your bodies as a living sacrifice, holy, acceptable to God, which is your reasonable service." Paul was not talking about salvation. Once we have been born again of the Spirit of God, we need to say, "God, I present my body to you as a living sacrifice."

The time has come for responsible Christianity. God is saying, "I want a demonstration." No government can give the demonstration that I am talking about. God's people must become a demonstration of His love. Governments will change because our legislators will be people from our churches. God is looking for a people that He can trust, a people who will not allow themselves to be bewitched or charmed.

Part 3

"But when the fullness of time was come, God sent forth His Son, made of a woman, made under the law, to redeem them that were under the law, that we might receive the adoption of sons."

Galatians 4:4-5

Part 2

9

THE SEED OF GOD

Today we stand on the frontier of some of the greatest occurrences mankind will ever know. Our generation can possibly activate Kingdom faith principles to the point that Christ can come again. We stand ready, without intimidation, to cooperate with God and to open ourselves to His spiritual revelation. We boldly proclaim that God's truth will make a difference. Going beyond understanding, we may be both givers and receivers of the Word of Life. God is in great need of intimacy with His People. From the hour when he chose the tree of the knowledge of good and evil, man has had a tendency to lean upon his own knowledge and to rule as a self-centered god.

But these are written that you may believe that Jesus is the Christ, the Son of God, and that believing you may have life in His name. (John 20:31)

Christians enter the Kingdom of God at all levels of understanding. In churches everywhere unbelievers sit among believers, while other Christians believe only to certain levels. All Christians experience salvation in order to have eternal life. Not all Christians, however, are willing to participate in bringing the witness of the Gospel of the Kingdom to pass.

Jesus said, "I am the way," but He never said that our understanding should end with salvation. He is "the way" toward revelation which will come through Him. Many Christians incorrectly believe everything God would have us know has already been written. The book of John says that many things are yet to be spoken that are not written in the Bible. Spirit-led insight is necessary to understand God's intentions.

A seed provides preservation of its kind. Farmers store seeds in the fall in order to preserve life. In the spring when seeds are planted, the life within them produces a product true to their genetic nature. Corn seeds produce corn, bean seeds produce beans. Life is captured and stored in the seed.

Two forms of seed are planted in the world today: The seed of God and the seed of Satan. God said, "And I will put enmity between you and the woman, and between your seed and her Seed; He shall bruise your head, and you shall bruise his heels" (John 3:15). Out of God's

Seed comes ultimate victory. Satan, with his limited authority, causes problems in many areas of our lives, but in the seed of the woman rests the authority to deal Satan the death blow.

Satan began the warfare against mankind immediately. When Adam and Eve, the seed of God, were attacked by Satan, the woman was deceived and the man sinned. Today God requires a constant union of men and women in the household of faith. Without this balance, the enemy will bring deception in some areas and sin in others. Only through the combined spiritual unity of both men and women will God's desires be accomplished. When God spoke of warfare between "your seed and her Seed," he was talking to the devil. "He [the seed of woman] shall bruise your head, and you shall bruise His heel." Satan has bruised our heels today. God is saying that from human seed He will have victory and Satan will be crushed.

The first battle was between Cain and Abel. Sibling rivalry has not ended to this day because Satan wants to destroy the seed. Battles of envy and strife often exist between blood children concerning identity and inheritances. Cain and Abel fought over recognition. Cain was jealous of Abel's sacrifice to God. Jealous rage caused him to kill Abel, but the underlying force was Satan trying to kill the seed. After Cain killed Abel, God held the seed in abeyance until Abraham came.

God had to wait until the right time to identify the seed. God probably called others also, but Abraham obeyed and became the seed of faith because he returned his seed to God. The Bible proclaimed that through Isaac all the earth would be blessed. Covenant with God was preserved in Abraham's obedience as he placed Isaac on the altar of sacrifice. Only dedication like Abraham's will establish a household of faith who understand the Kingdom of God.

> *And the Lord said to Abram, after Lot had separated from him: "Lift your eyes now and look from the place where you are — northward, southward, eastward, and westward; for all the land which you see I give to you and your descendants forever." (Genesis 13:14-15)*

To understand Abraham's seed is to know to whom the world belongs. God was not referring to a narrow strip of land by the Mediterranean. God told Abraham, "Look to the north, south, east and west. I will give all of this land to your seed." God promised the entire earth to His people.

> *Let the heaven and earth praise Him, the seas, and everything that moves in them. For God will save Zion, and build the cities of Judah, that they may dwell there and possess it. Also, the descendants of His servants shall inherit it, and those who love His name shall dwell in it. (Psalm 69:34-36)*

> *Christ has redeemed us from the curse of the law, having become a curse for us (for it is written, "Cursed is everyone who hangs on a tree"), that the blessing of Abraham might come upon the Gentiles in Christ Jesus, that we might receive the promise of the Spirit through faith. Brethren, I speak in the manner of men: Though it is only*

222

a man's covenant, yet if it is confirmed, no one annuls or adds to it. Now to Abraham and his Seed were the promises made. He does not say, "And to seeds," as of many, but as of one, "And to your Seed," who is Christ. (Galatians 3:13-16)

There is neither Jew nor Greek, there is neither slave nor free, there is neither male nor female; for you are all one in Christ Jesus. And if you are Christ's, then you are Abraham's seed, and heirs according to the promise. (Galatians 3:28-29)

For this Hagar is Mount Sinai in Arabia, and corresponds to Jerusalem which now is, and is in bondage with her children — but the Jerusalem above is free, [which represents the spirit of freedom] *which is the mother of us all. For it is written: "Rejoice, O barren, you who do not bear! Break forth and shout, you who do not travail! For the desolate has many more children than she who has a husband." (Galatians 4:25-27)*

No woman in bondage is beautiful to behold. The freewoman is beautiful. Only the mature understand that. Men who insist on possessing women lose them. Possessiveness is an attitude of the flesh and God made us free.

This scripture in Galatians is an allegory. Hagar produced bondage. The freewoman, Sarah, produced the promise. The two women represent two covenants. Hagar was from Mount Sinai, which represents bondage. Many people stay in bondage even to the Word of God. They are not freed by the Word because they go back to old patterns, traditions and laws.

We, like Isaac, are the children of promise. Those born of a fleshly relationship persecute those born of the Spirit. Scripture states that people who are in bondage and who do not understand the spirit of freedom continue to persecute those who learn the truth of freedom.

> *Nevertheless what does the Scripture say? "Cast out the bondwoman and her son, for the son of the bondwoman shall not be heir with the son of the freewoman." So then, brethren, we are not children of the bondwoman, but of the free. (Galatians 4:30-31)*

Abraham accepted God's promise. As he became old it seemed to him that faith was not going to produce the seed. A prophetic lesson exists in what God did through Abraham. Sometimes we become anxious and afraid that faith will not produce the seed, and we try to help God. There is great danger to God's Church today in trying to help God instead of obeying Him. There is a vast difference between "helping" and "obeying."

God finally said to Abraham, "I do not see faith in the birth of Ishmael." But Abraham said, "God, I am an old man now." God replied, "I have to wait until your ability to have children is gone." God cannot work in human possibility. He can only work in human impossiblity. This truth applies to all areas of our lives. When Abraham finally realized his human impossibility, he accepted God's promise to bear a seed child with his wife, Sarah.

Satan's plan was to allow Ishmael to be the child of

promise instead of Isaac. After Isaac was born, God insisted that Hagar leave Abraham's household. That seems like a hard decision to us, but God will not tolerate mixture. God's Church must avoid mixture. Although Hagar and Ishmael were separated from the true seed, notice that God still cared for them.

Another example of God's plan and mercy was the promise He made to Joseph in Egypt. Joseph continued to care for his brothers although they hated him. The brothers also reaped some of Joseph's inheritance. Every believer will not go along with God's plan, but a Joseph ministry, a Sarah ministry, or an Abraham ministry will produce the royal seed of God and the pure spiritual race God desires. In the Old Testament, God warned Israel about marrying foreign women. God was trying to have a pure Jewish race and forbade marriage to foreign women because they worshiped pagan gods. If they accepted God Jehovah, they became Jews. Ruth was a Moabite who believed in God. Through her lineage came the royal seed, Jesus. Ruth entered into covenant with God and became a Jew through this covenant. Men who joined the worship of Yahweh God had to be circumcised in order to enter into covenant with Him.

Because Solomon's wives and concubines were involved in idolatry, they stole his heart. The difference between David and Solomon was that David's heart remained true to Jehovah God. He never embraced idolatry. Solomon accepted the idol gods of his women and God turned away from him.

For Solomon went after Ashtoreth the goddess of the Sid-

225

onians, and after Milcom the abomination of the Ammo-
nites. Solomon did evil in the sight of the Lord, and did not
fully follow the Lord, as did his father David. Then
Solomon built a high place for Chemosh the abomination
of Moab, on the hill that is east of Jerusalem, and for
Molech the abomination of the people of Ammon. And he
did likewise for all his foreign wives, who burned incense
and sacrificed to their gods. (I Kings 11:5-8)

God spoke through the prophet Hosea:

"Ephraim has mixed himself among the peoples; Eph-
raim is a cake unturned. Aliens have devoured his
strength, but he does not know it; yes, gray hairs are here
and there on him, yet he does not know it. And the pride of
Israel testifies to his face, but they do not return to the
Lord their God, nor seek Him for all this." (Hosea 7:8-10)

The Church is weakened today because of mixture
with those who do not understand the difference
between faith and the mind of reason. Ephraim turned
away from God and became a stranger to the Lord
because his faith was diluted and mixed with pagan
worship.

An enlightened household of faith must pull the
mask off Satan and reveal where mixture exists before
the Kingdom of God can be established. Rather than
making the following scripture a letter of the law with
dates, places and people, we must see the spirit of what
God has said.

Now, brethren, concerning the coming of our Lord Jesus

*Christ and our gathering together to Him, we ask you, not
to be soon shaken in mind or troubled, either by spirit or
by word or by letter, as if from us, as though the day of
Christ had come. (II Thessalonians 2:1-2)*

People continue to say that Jesus is going to return to
earth at any moment. Jesus said that we should not be
upset by people who do not understand the Word of
God. Most people preach the letter of the law and say,
"Look up, for your redemption draweth nigh." Jesus
did not say that redemption was to be the final indica-
tion of His coming. Deception will be the last sign
before the Kingdom comes. Jesus said that the Gospel
of the Kingdom will be witnessed before the nations of
the earth, and then the end will come. He also said not
to be upset about earthquakes, famines and pestilence
because these catastrophes must first occur.

*Let no one deceive you by any means; for that Day will not
come unless the falling away comes first, and the man of
sin is revealed, the son of perdition. (II Thessalonians 2:3)*

The antichrist will not appear with 666 on his forehead because he would be much too obvious. Satan will
be unmasked and exposed by the Spirit of God. As the
seed of Abraham, God's Church must recognize and
reveal the spirit of the antichrist. Scripture states that
first a falling away will occur and then the man of sin,
the son of perdition who opposes and exalts himself
above all that is called God, will be revealed.

*For the mystery of lawlessness is already at work; only He
who now restrains will do so until He is taken out of the*

way. (II Thessalonians 2:7)

Deception hinders the revealing of Satan. Only by the Spirit can we understand who he is. Satan will continue to hinder God's plan until he is taken out of the way. The wicked one will be revealed and destroyed by the prophetic voice and God's power and authority at work in His mature Church.

God withdraws from people who refuse to listen to revelation and truth. Judgment comes to those who take pleasure in unrighteousness and do not believe in the truth. Lacking the desire for a right relationship with God and the brethren is unrighteousness.

Joseph was the most hated among the sons of Jacob because he was a dreamer who had a vision of restored Kingdom authority. Likewise, visionaries will be hated in the last days. As in the story of Joseph and his brothers, strong delusions and great hatred will prevail because of wrong relationships. Satan must be unmasked and deception put aside.

Satan sits in his temples of humanism, religion, education and industry while deception prevents his full exposure. Because spiritual discernment is the mark of a mature Church, a discerning Church recognizes what is or is not of God. They are obedient to walk in God's truth, line upon line and precept upon precept. When the Lord speaks, the discerning Church listens and accepts what He says. Spiritually mature Christians who understand this concept will experience a release to a victorious life. Recognition of who they are in the Lord will move them into a new spiritual dimension. When the Lord gives instructions, His true followers obey.

Victorious Christian living begins through praise, good stewardship with money and allowing the Holy Spirit to direct all areas of our lives. We must not permit the Seed of God, the household of faith, to become contaminated by doubters who won't listen to God and are disobedient to His plan. Such actions prevent the freedom of the spirit of faith among God's people. Faith is not strength without crutches. Faith is the ability to walk before God when we need crutches. Faith is an awareness of who we are in the household of God, even in our infirmities. Faith lifts us to a place of authority in the Kingdom. We know that we are of the household of faith by the way we perceive our circumstances. Circumstances in the Kingdom of God are interpreted within the framework of faith.

God wants a pure race that is free from idolatry. God kept a pure seed to produce the remnant which brought forth the Seed, Jesus Christ. Paul wrote,

"O Corinthians! We have spoken openly to you, our heart is wide open. You are not restricted by us, but you are restricted by your own affections. Now in return for the same (I speak as to children), you also be open. Do not be unequally yoked together with unbelievers. For what fellowship has righteousness with lawlessness? And what communion has light with darkness? And what accord has Christ with Belial? Or what part has a believer with an unbeliever? (II Corinthians 6:11-15)

Relationships should be carefully made. God wants us to be people of faith. The scripture does not speak about mixed marriages or social problems, but the scripture is very clear concerning His seed not being unequally yoked with unbelievers. God wants a household of faith, people who know how to walk in faith, and to be a family of praise. The question that should be asked of those who contemplate marriage is, "Are you both believers?"

Homes with spiritual leadership are secure. Romans 8:19 states that the whole world waits for the manifestation of the sons of God. Satan attempts to corrupt faith and godliness in the Church with an institution of philosophy. God wants a seed of faith that fully trusts in Jesus Christ because He is the Cornerstone.

Belief that Jesus is the Christ determines whether we are in covenant with God. Through Jesus, we become sons of Abraham, covenant people who want to do the works of Abraham. Jewish custom requires circumcision. Baptism, a spiritual circumcision of the heart, fulfills the covenant in the household of faith. Desire to follow God's instructions should consume the child of God.

How do we know that we are the seed of Abraham?

First, we know because we are in Jesus Christ. Galatians 3:29 says that if we are Christ's, we are Abraham's seed.

Secondly, we must be in covenant with God. Our covenant is reflected in our lifestyles. Salvation and water baptism are the initial covenant, but we must account to God with our entire lives. Seeking first the Kingdom of God with our minds, souls, and energy is covenant.

Thirdly, the sons of God are led by the Spirit of God. (Romans 8:14). The Spirit of God is the only standard of spiritual measurement. The Holy Spirit allows us to understand revelation. People accept Christ by faith, but Kingdom revelation comes only by seeking the mind of the the Holy Spirit. When Jesus was asked when He would restore His Kingdom (Acts 1:6-8), He said, ". . .You shall receive power when the Holy Spirit has come upon you." The Kingdom of God resides in the Holy Ghost.

For the kingdom of God is not food and drink, but right-eousness and peace and joy in the Holy Spirit. (Romans 14:17)

Fourthly, our covenant relationship with God requires us to be peacemakers. Scripture says that Jesus Christ came to bring a sword (Matthew 10:34). God's Word, which is quick and powerful and sharper than a two-edged sword, makes the division. We become peacemakers in the household of faith even though we will be persecuted by the children of the flesh. We must be willing to suffer to be in covenant, but if we suffer with Christ, we will reign with Him (Romans 8:17).

Fifthly, we must continue to mature as the Bride of Christ. The Bride of Christ must have an awareness that spiritual maturity is selfless, not selfish. Circumstances must not control our faithfulness. Self-control of emotions should be constantly maturing us to the measure of Christ. We must ask ourselves whether we are still on the same spiritual level that we were fifteen years ago, last year or even last week. The maturing Bride looks in her spiritual mirror often, questioning her appearance because she must portray Christ's nature. Maturity is spiritual stability and knowing who we are in Christ. Our faith must be anchored in the person of Jesus Christ and the Word of God.

Finally, I Peter 1:23 tells us that we are born of an incorruptible seed. Mixture cannot corrupt the lives of covenant people. Because God's incorruptible seed lives within us, the Holy Spirit will enable us to rise above temptations and circumstances and take authority over Satan. Satan must be unmasked in relationships and business associations. The blood of Jesus Christ will stand in the gap so that Satan cannot overcome us.

Where does mixture exist in the Church? Mixture exists in prayers. James said, "You ask and do not receive, because you ask amiss, that you may spend it on your pleasures" (James 4:3). God never told us to pray for a comfortable house or a new car. He told us to seek first the Kingdom of God and He would provide for our needs. Those who think they have achieved "the ultimate" because they have material things will lose out with God. Our prayers must be like the prayer that Jesus prayed when He reached the culmination of His earthly ministry: "Not My will, but Yours be done." Jesus also prayed, "Father, make them one. Let them be one as We are one so that the world may believe."

Ask God to send revelation to the Church. Intercede for pastors, elders and deacons. Pray against principalities and powers in heavenly places. Isaiah prophesied, "How you are fallen from heaven, O Lucifer, Son of the morning!" (Isaiah 14:12). God wants to take Satan out of the heavenly places. He can be defeated with the prayers of a mature Church who knows how to intercede effectively. Mixture in the prayers of God's people must end.

Mixture exists in our worship. Music and art should exalt the Creator, not personalities. Worship should purposely include the use of God-given creativity that God may receive glory. Singers who call attention to themselves with their personalities, abilities or talents rather than to the Creator cause mixture in worship. Dancers who attract more attention to their physical movements than to the Creator are not in the Spirit of God and should not participate in worship. People who lead in worship should spend quality time with the Lord. Jesus Christ should be seen as they reflect the glory of God.

Mixture in publications and television outreach ministries must not exist. Compromise in what we write and broadcast concerning God's cause will not further the Kingdom of God. Time must be used well because the message of the Kingdom means the difference between life and death in these last days. The written word must be bold, pure and clear.

It is important to understand the difference between the New Breed and the New Age. God gave me a vision of the round rainbow in which I saw the throne of God as surely as John saw his revelation of Jesus Christ. I could not see who sat upon the throne, but I could see the energy emitting from it. I could see Jesus Christ and the elders around the throne of God. As I watched the rainbow around the throne of God, I saw its circular force. People often ask me about the rainbow and want to know if we are a part of the New Age group. No, of course we are not. Satan is not original. He is a master of counterfeit and imitation. A vision of God must not be destroyed because the world attempts to imitate it. Always be ready to give an answer concerning a covenant with God. We must not allow mixture or fear to cause us to compromise.

Learn the difference between love and trust. God is love, but the Kingdom of God is built in trust. Jesus loved the rich young ruler, but he turned away from Jesus because the price of following Him was too great. He didn't trust what Jesus said to him. Trust is the foundation of faith. Trust is the substance of our covenant. Abraham trusted even though he didn't see the promises of God. The Seed came because Abraham believed God's promise and trusted in Him. God produced the Kingdom Seed through trust. We can change the world if we understand and practice this concept of trust.

Satan will not attack God's people in obvious ways or through obvious people. We easily recognize persecution from the outside. Satan achieves his greatest successes when he moves through people who are well-meaning and sincere. Latent within these people is a covetous desire, an ulterior motive, or the need for recognition beyond their contributions. Because of this danger, we must rely upon direction that comes only from the Holy Spirit.

One hundred and twenty people met in the upper room in Jerusalem to receive the promised Holy Spirit. This gathering represented the end of the flesh movement. The Old Testament Law had served its purpose and was dead. God said "Now I must lift you to a new and higher level." Higher ground is a spiritual plane. We cannot fight Satan without the spiritual weapons which are listed carefully in the Word of God. From the day we receive the Holy Spirit, we no longer have the right to follow our own perceptions. Satan tries to pervert and infiltrate the cause of God in a different dimension than we have seen or known before.

For the message of the cross is foolishness to those who are perishing, but to us who are being saved it is the power of God. For it is written: "I will destroy the wisdom of the wise, and bring to nothing the understanding of the prudent." Where is the wise? Where is the scribe? Where is the disputer of this age? Has not God made foolish the wisdom of this world? For since, in the wisdom of God, the world through wisdom did not know God, it pleased God through the foolishness of the message preached to save those who believe. For Jews request a sign, and Greeks seek after wisdom; but we preach Christ crucified, to the Jews a stumbling block and to the Greeks foolishness. (I Corinthians 1:18-23)

It seems very obvious in this scripture that the Apostle Paul, although he was well-educated, put his education aside so that he could follow the Spirit. God gave us the tools in the written Word. He gave us the Holy Spirit and the call to ministries that we may move forward to do what God has called us to do. He also challenges us to know that we are in great warfare today.

What we have commonly called warfare is usually nothing more than physical or bodily distress. Most of what we call warfare is of our own doing. We make poor choices, go in wrong directions and follow the appetites of the flesh. Then we say we are in great warfare. The truth of the matter is that "he that sows to his flesh will of the flesh reap corruption" (Galatians 6:8).

Warfare is described in the book of Revelation. Revelation is a book that has often been kept out of the pulpit because of a lack of understanding or the fear of conflict and controversy. However, John said, "Blessed are those who read, who understand, or who share this revelation." We have tried to make the Revelation into a legalistic document that we can understand by the flesh, but it cannot be understood except by the Holy Spirit.

The Book of Revelation is the Revelation of Jesus Christ, not a book of eschatology. Revelation is a book depicting how God moves according to His desires for the earth and for mankind. In Chapter 12, a great battle is described. Many battles have already been described in the Revelation as well as in the Old Testament. The word Armageddon, as a matter of fact, is not introduced in the Book of Revelation. Armageddon is a word from the Old Testament. When the armies of

God exhausted their strength and could no longer win, God delivered them by divine intervention. That deliverance is the meaning of Armageddon. We talk about "the millenium" as if the world has never experienced peace, yet God speaks of times of peace even among the children of Israel. Revelation does not describe future events as much as the way God relates to the Church today.

John describes three prominent characters in the tremendous drama of Chapter 12. First, he saw "*. . .a woman clothed with the sun, with the moon under her feet, and on her head a garland of twelve stars*" (Revelation 12:1). We quickly understand that this woman clothed with the sun shows her great radiance. The moon under her feet represents her authority. The twelve stars symbolize her interaction with God and the world, the Trinity and the four corners of the earth.

"Then being with child, she cried out in labor and in pain to give birth" (verse 2). She is delivered of a man Child, which undoubtedly refers to Jesus Christ, the Son of God. Reference to Jesus Christ also refers to the Church, who is the seed of Abraham through Christ. *"And another sign appeared in heaven: behold, a great, fiery red dragon having seven heads and ten horns, and seven diadems on his head"* (verse 3).

No number goes beyond ten because ten is a complete number. Numbers that go beyond ten are simply additions to the number ten. For example, ten plus one is eleven. The use of the numbers ten and seven indicate that Satan was complete in his evil authority over the earth. The ultimate in evil authority is depicted by this great red dragon.

"His tail drew a third of the stars of heaven and threw them to the earth. And the dragon stood before the woman (the Church, the people of God) *who was ready to give birth, to devour her Child as soon as it was born"* (verse 4). Satan intended to devour Jesus Christ, and later as we shall see, to devour the Seed. The scene happening here occurs over and over again. Warfare is occurring in a different dimension today, and it will increase until the final battle has been won. This warfare speaks of God's people, the Church, or spiritual Israel which was at one time national Israel. Satan wars whatever fruit comes from the people of God. He stands ready to subtly attack and devour any spiritual accomplishments of God's people.

Satan has attacked the Church in obvious ways throughout history. But Jesus said that a sign in the last days, before the Kingdom comes, is great deception. The antichrist spirit is the epitome of deception. God has not left His people without the equipment and resources to be victorious over Satan in the days in which we live.

"And she bore a male Child who was to rule all nations with a rod of iron. And her Child was caught up to God and to His throne" (verse 5). This is a description of the firstfruit, Jesus Christ, the first among many brethren. Jesus moved to a heavenly dimension after His physical life on earth was over.

"Then the woman fled into the wilderness, where she has a place prepared by God, that they should feed her

238

there one thousand two hundred and sixty days" (verse 6). The time period of 1260 days is three-and-a-half years. The ministry of Jesus Christ upon the earth was three-and-one-half years, or half of God's total ministry to the earth. Jesus's three-and-a-half year ministry will be equaled by the Church which is now in the process of completing God's seven-year ministry to the world. In my judgment in the Spirit, we are now in that three-and-a-half years. The Church is presently in the wilderness place of confusion, frustration and great attack. As we shall see, only God's Spirit can keep us from devastation and defeat.

There was war in heaven (verse 7), but an even greater warfare rages today because spiritual warfare is at an even greater dimension. The scripture states that there was war in heaven in which Michael and his angels fought against the dragon and his angels. The battle began at the throne of God over the issue of "who is in charge." The battle did not begin in the Garden of Eden. Lucifer, the archangel, lifted himself up and said, "I will exalt my authority above the authority of God." The greatest conflict in the Church today revolves around authority. Someone says, "I thought the issue of the Church was love." Oh no, love is the Church's description and identity. The purpose of the Church, however, is to re-assume God's authority over the earth. Jesus said that He had all authority in heaven and earth, and He told His disciples to wait in Jerusalem until they were endued with His authority and power. Spiritual authority is the reason spiritual leadership is so battled from the inside. When God tries to raise up a Kingdom prototype, Satan will war it. God must rule and reign upon the earth and until the Church learns God's intentions, the Kingdom of God can never come to pass. Obedience to called-out spiritual eldership is absolutely necessary.

One who uses God's authority foolishly prostitutes God's ability to rule and reign. If submission to authority is not lived out in the Church, the Kingdom of God cannot be established upon the earth. In the war in heaven, neither Michael nor Satan prevailed. God had the victory. Although Satan was cast down to the earth, he still had access to the throne of God.

I believe the Church now has the authority and the revelation to bind Satan so that he will no longer have access to the throne of God to accuse us. Anyone reading with a natural mind probably will not understand. Because Satan did not prevail, he, with his hellish force, was cast out of heaven. *"So the great dragon was cast out, that serpent of old, called the Devil and Satan, who deceives the whole world; he was cast out to the earth, and his angels were cast out with him"* (verse 9).

The first chapter of Job tells us that the sons of God, spiritual beings, came before God one day. As God looked over them, he saw the devil. God asked him, "Satan, what are you doing here?" The devil said, "I have come back up here to accuse the brethren." When Satan started his attack against Job, God said, "I will allow you to do anything you want with Job, but you cannot take his life."

Satan was still in heavenly places. Even after what

we call Satan's fall, he still dwells in heavenly places of dominion. I believe he will stay there until the Church dethrones him. I do not believe God will dethrone him, because God has given the Church the power to loose and to bind and to war against Satan in heavenly places. When we understand that authority, we will begin to have Kingdom rule.

> *Then I heard a loud voice saying in heaven, "Now salva-tion, and strength, and the kingdom of our God, and the power of His Christ have come, for the accuser of our brethren, who accused them before our God day and night, has been cast down." (Revelation 12:10)*

A time will come in the history of the Church when we will withstand Satan with such authority that he will have no more power to accuse us. How will that take place? We overcome Satan in three dimensions. First, we overcome him by the blood of the Lamb or the preaching of Jesus Christ. That message is the cross of Calvary which declares that the blood of Jesus Christ is the propitiation for our sins. If we confess our sins, He is faithful and just to forgive us.

Secondly, we overcome Satan by the word of our testimony. I believe that this generation began hearing the "faith" proclamation ten to fifteen years ago. Teachers in the Church began to say that the power of life and death is in the tongue. They said that the Word of God created the world, that "what you speak is what you get," and they were a vital part of God's message. However, that is not the final message. I believe the hour has come for the final part of that victorious mes-

241

sage to be heard.

Thirdly, we overcome Satan by loving not our lives unto death. These Christians seek the Kingdom of God with such tenacity, eagerness and total commitment that death holds no more fear for them. They don't care how great the cost is to pursue what God has called them to do. They forsake everything to follow only what God has spoken.

Some patriarchs of the faith made great accomplishments, such as Abraham. Jesus Christ is the ultimate prototype, the first Kingdom man. He exemplifies one who loved not His life unto death. Jesus said, "Whatever it takes, I will not waver." God requires that we reach that same dimension of overcoming faith. When we attain that level, the heavens will be rent and the authority of Satan will be utterly destroyed. *"Therefore, rejoice, O heavens, and you who dwell in them!" (Revelation 12:12)*. By revelation I add, "Not only those in heaven, but those who dwell in heavenly places." I refer to those who have crucified their flesh and walk in heavenly places with God.

The Apostle Paul wrote, "Those who are Christ's have crucified the flesh with its passions and desires" (Galatians 5:24). We are becoming the image of Christ. As the heavens are told to rejoice, notice the next part of the scripture. *"Woe unto the inhabitants of the earth and the sea!"* Woe to those who live by the mind of the flesh. Woe to those who live by the mind of reason and do not comprehend the deep things, the mysteries of God. *"For the devil has come down to you, having great wrath, because he knows that he has a short time."*

242

Satan is now working in earthly dimensions. Very shortly people who know how to intercede before God will begin to loose and bind as God has said we could do. Warfare will be won in heavenly places, but the final "sweeping up" will be done here on the earth. Satan now works through people and demonic forces on the earth. We may bind him over nations, but he still works in humankind.

When Satan was cast to the earth, what did he do? He started persecuting the woman who brought forth the male Child. Satan began to persecute the Church (God's people) and her revelation. The Church must yet go to the cross. Satan will persecute the Church with an intensity never known before. Revelation 12:14 is the key verse. *"But the woman was given two wings of a great eagle, that she might fly into the wilderness to her place, where she is nourished for a time and times and half a time from the presence of the serpent."* That time period is the other three-and-a-half years, the final thrust of God's Church. It is the final move of the Spirit in God's people. I believe the great eagle with two wings represents prayer and praise, intercession and worship.

The Church gathers strength through understanding how to war against the devil. Our power will not come by conversations with one another. Strength does not come by trying to reason things out or through strategy sessions. Our strength comes by humbling ourselves before Almighty God and knowing, with authority, how to seek His throne. Worship in God's house must be pure. The Church must learn to lay aside patterns and plans and enter into the presence of God with such praise and worship that we can find strength to survive in the wilderness. Satan tries to defeat worship with a misplaced announcement, noise, a crying child, thunder, lightning, or perhaps the sound of an airplane flying over.

If Satan can stop intercession, praise and worship, he will defeat us. Those whom God has called to intercede or lead in praise and worship must drink the cup. Can we withstand the mind of reason? Can the Church withstand the talent seekers and those who would prostitute worship to such a degree that it is lifeless and nothing more than entertainment? The ability to intercede and worship God will preserve the Church during great warfare.

The Church is also fed and nourished by manna and water which are God's revelation and the Holy Spirit. Nourishment comes from God's revelation,while God and the water of the Spirit of God quenches our thirst. *"So the serpent spewed water out of his mouth like a flood after the woman, that he might cause her to be carried away by the flood" (Revelation 12:15).* That flood is humanism, the power of man's own mind to rule.

The battle is the same today as in ancient times. The mouth of the serpent spews philosophy, the mind of reason and humanism. Humanism motivated the building of the tower of Babel. The tower of Babel today consists of people who reason that they are going to have a kingdom of their own. They insist on having a good insurance plan and a good retirement program while the world collapses. Only confusion awaits those who go by their own authority and power, seeking their own lives and never listening to God.

"But the earth helped the woman [the Church], *and the earth opened its mouth and swallowed up the flood which the dragon had spewed out of his mouth"* (verse 16). The earth took in the philosophy and the humanism which the dragon cast out of his mouth. *"And the dragon was enraged with the woman, and he went to make war with the rest of her offspring, who keep the commandments of God and have the testimony of Jesus Christ"* (verse 17).

That condition of war now prevails. Satan has found that in heavenly places, he can be defeated by worship and the prayers of intercessors. We have learned how to overcome Satan's accusations. We have learned how to move in the Spirit in a new dimension. In heavenly places where decisions are made, we are beginning to pierce through deception and now Satan is angry as he begins to war our seed. He wars not only our spiritual seed, but also the natural seed of our lives. I believe the Church will experience great warfare in the coming months among our seed, the generation which will do great things for God.

In my judgment we are very near the final battle. Many say, "Why get excited? It's always been this way! You've always had men crying destruction and doom. Things are like they have always been." No generation before us has had the potential of nuclear warfare that we do. No society has had such advanced technology that the whole world can see an event in a matter of seconds. The whole world can know instantly what happened at the Super Bowl. The whole world knows within seconds when a president is assassinated. We are in a new day and a new age.

But now is Christ risen from the dead, and has become the firstfruits of those who have fallen asleep. For since by man came death, by Man also came the resurrection of the dead. For as in Adam all die, even so in Christ all shall be made alive. But each in his own order: Christ the first-fruits, afterward those who are Christ's at His coming. (I Corinthians 15:20-23)

We will literally experience eternal life at His coming. The dead in Christ shall rise. We who are alive and remain will overcome death and be changed. Then the end of the age will come, and we will enter into a new dimension, a new heaven and a new earth where righteousness will dwell. The Kingdom of God will become a reality, as the new Jerusalem comes down from God out of heaven.

Then comes the end, when He delivers the kingdom to God the Father, when He puts an end to all rule and all authority and power. For He must reign till He has put all enemies under His feet. The last enemy that will be destroyed is death. (I Corinthians 15:24-26)

God has done everything that He can do and He will not do anything else. All God will do now is move in our behalf as He moves through us and we loose His power in the world. In the key verse from Corinthians (verse

25), "He" undoubtedly means not only Christ, but also the Church and the people of God. As Jesus Christ confronted, faced and overcame death, we must also do the same. Until the Church reaches that kind of authority, we will never see the Kingdom of God totally and completely manifested.

The last warfare we will wage against Satan will concern life and death. Learn how to speak life instead of jealousy, condemnation, rejection, or fear. Learn how to live life in order to do away with death. Understand by the Spirit of God that when we learn to live this life in the resurrected Christ, we will attain a totally new dimension.

Warfare is not fussing with one's wife over financial difficulties because of foolish purchases. Warfare is knowing how to bind Satan in heavenly places so he cannot accuse us any longer. Satan will then come down to earth where we can move in such authority that we can challenge everything he does. Our goal should be to diligently pursue intercession and worship until Satan becomes so uncomfortable that he can't remain in heavenly places. When Satan is cast down to the earth, we can challenge everything he does and cast out devils with the authority of God.

God is breaking through in many areas that the world can't define. **The Right Stuff** is a movie about an astronaut who became absolutely dedicated to conquering outer space. His whole life was changed as he became passionately consumed with breaking the sound barrier and soaring to the moon. The story was about men who were made of "the right stuff." The astronauts were dedicated men who went through physical torture and torment because they felt compelled to reach the goal which had actually become their reason to live. God also is looking for people made of "the right stuff," a generation that can bring the Kingdom of God to pass.

God is looking for a seed, a people who will understand the Kingdom message, assimilate it, internalize it and live it to its fullest. These people will become a breed and a race unto God. They will be the incorruptible seed, a family who truly understands the Kingdom of God. These people will see the face of God to such a dimension that nothing will distract them. We have seen glimpses of the Kingdom, but God needs a people who will ascend to the level of angelic beings. They will know such authority and power that they can confront the forces of hell and begin to take dominion in the earth.

One day governments and authorities on the earth will begin to fall apart. People will surface who have been with God and understand what is taking place. People who have been building the tower of Babel will become confused. It will be sad when some look back and ask God why He didn't warn them. God will say, "I did."

We who understand the Kingdom of God consume the message as our meat, our manna, and our water. God's Kingdom becomes the center of our lives. We begin to seek after God and hunger and thirst after righteousness. With everything else put aside, we take ourselves out of the center of God's universe and put

God back on His throne in our hearts. We begin earnestly to seek the Kingdom of God. That seeking gives us the description of the seed of God. That desire gives us the ability to become a whole person, absolutely given to God with all our mind, body and strength.

10

LIFE IN THE ETERNAL KINGDOM

Most Christians believe that God fulfilled His entire plan concerning life and death in the resurrection of Jesus Christ. They believe that resurrection life for believers is only available after they physically die. Because they are convinced that the resurrection of Jesus Christ is all the Church needs as a complete message, they sit back and wait for a sovereign God to complete His plan. Most Christians have adopted the mentality of waiting for "the sweet by and by" in which they will "leave this old world of shame and sorrow." They believe that eternity is lived out somewhere other than on earth. They await a place and time to walk on "streets of gold" in a city with "gates of pearl."

Without apology I emphasize that God is a creative God. His nature and character will never change. God will never cease being creative.

If the normal Christian concepts are true, why were God's people not taken at Jesus's ascension? Why did God leave His people here if the ultimate end of God's plan was Jesus's resurrection from the dead? Jesus conquered death, hell and the grave, and the saints could have ascended with Him to heaven. Some saints indeed were raised from the dead along with Jesus and they walked along the streets of Jerusalem. So why didn't all the saints go home with Him? If the Christian concept in most of the Church is true, why would God give revelation in His Word of a victorious, peculiar people, a people called "a royal priesthood," a people who once were not a definable people who have become a definable people?

Why was the New Testament written if Jesus Christ is the end of the story? Are the gospels merely "reports" or do they also offer some plan of action? If Jesus "did it all" for us, why must we do anything? God gave the five-fold ministry to the Church after the death and resurrection of Jesus. Ephesians 4 clearly states that Jesus went into hell and demonstrated how to conquer death, hell and the grave. Then Jesus promised, "I will build My Church" through a five-fold ministry. Why build a Church on the earth if the resurrection is the end of God's plan for mankind?

Why was the gift of the Holy Spirit given on the day of Pentecost? Jesus said after His resurrection, while preaching forty days on the Kingdom, "Now you go and tarry in Jerusalem until you be endued with authority." Why did the Church need authority to simply report the resurrection? Why does the Church need anything other than a notebook that reads: "Jesus lived thirty-three years, and His ministry was contained in the last three years of His life. He went into the grave and conquered death, hell and the grave, and He arose from the dead. That is the report. Now you go out and give this account." We do not need the baptism of the Holy Spirit to say that! Anyone can give that summary. Why did Jesus say, "I want My Church endued with power and authority?" Why did He say to His disciples, "Pray, Thy kingdom come, Thy will be done on earth as it is in heaven?" As it is in the heavenly realm, so let it be on the earth! Why did Jesus pray that prayer if His ministry was the end of the road?

Jesus Christ conquered death and our eternal hope is in His resurrection, but we know that we have not conquered death when we have pain in our bodies or view someone who has died. Jesus made it clear that He was the firstfruit. A "firstfruit" indicates that more fruit is to come. Jesus called Himself "the firstfruit of many brethren."

But now Christ is risen from the dead, and has become the firstfruits of those who have fallen asleep. For since by man came death, by Man also came the resurrection of the dead. For as in Adam all die, even so in Christ all shall be made alive. But each one in his own order: Christ, the firstfruits, afterward those who are Christ's at His coming. Then comes the end, when He delivers the kingdom to God the Father, when He puts an end to all rule and all

253

authority and power. For He must reign till He has put all enemies under His feet. The last enemy that will be destroyed is death. For "He has put all things under His feet." But when He says "all things are put under Him," it is evident that He who put all things under Him is excepted. Now when all things are made subject to Him, then the Son Himself will also be subject to Him who put all things under Him, that God may be all in all. (I Corinthians 15:20-28)

Jesus overcame death. At His coming, a mature Church will be doing everything Jesus did, including overcoming death. "At His coming . . . then comes the end." Don't miss the order of those words. The end comes when Christ returns to receive His mature Bride who has overcome death. At that point He says, "Then comes the end." Jesus is the Head, or the visionary part of the Body, and we are His implementors. Visionary people are never implementors and implementors are never visionaries.

As the firstfruit, Jesus Christ showed us how to accomplish God's plan. When He comes again, He will come because Kingdom people have learned the secrets of the Kingdom and how to move like Jesus moved. When they, with Christ, have put down all rule opposed to God, even death will be destroyed. Death has not been destroyed except in Jesus Christ. The Church of Jesus Christ has not yet conquered death, but this last enemy will be totally conquered before Jesus's return. Then Jesus will present this conquering people to God the Father, saying, "Father, Your plan of redemption worked. With My power and authority, the Church has overcome the last enemy, death. Now we deliver back to You, God, all that has been conquered. All things have become Yours again."

We have not comprehended Christ's power because we have not yet challenged effectively the areas that God calls us to overcome. Several years ago, a few people in Kentucky and on the west coast said they were not going to die, but they totally misunderstood overcoming death. As a result of their error, people believe that the idea of conquering death is heresy. But, in spite of error and misunderstanding, until the mature Body of Christ challenges death as a group of people, the end cannot come. History will continue millennium after millennium until we do what God has said to do.

The Apostle Paul wrote concerning death, the last enemy:

Otherwise, what will they do who are baptized for the dead, if the dead do not rise at all? Why then are they baptized for the dead? And why do we stand in jeopardy every hour? I affirm, by the boasting in you which I have in Christ Jesus our Lord, I die daily. If, in the manner of men, I have fought with beasts at Ephesus, what advantage is it to me? If the dead do not rise, "Let us eat and drink, for tomorrow we die." Do not be deceived: "Evil company corrupts good habits." Awake to righteousness, and do not sin: for some do not have the knowledge of God. I speak this to your shame. (I Corinthians 15:29-34)

Paul concluded that Christians lacked knowledge in

this area. Because of the lack of knowledge, we carry out acts or forms of religion, and we fail to understand what the Church is supposed to be doing, or why we have been given authority in the Holy Spirit. Without understanding the purpose of the Church, we assume the Church just reports the story of the resurrection. If that is our purpose, the world could do that as easily as we could. The Church was given unlimited authority to storm the gates of hell.

But someone will say, "How are the dead raised up? And with what body do they come?" Foolish one, what you sow is not made alive unless it dies. And what you sow, you do not sow that body that shall be, but mere grain—perhaps wheat or some other grain. But God gives it a body as He pleases, and to each seed its own body. All flesh is not the same flesh, but there is one kind of flesh of men, another flesh of beasts, another of fish, and another of birds. There are also celestial bodies and terrestrial bodies; but the glory of the celestial is one, and the glory of the terrestrial is another. There is one glory of the sun, another glory of the moon, and another glory of the stars; for one star differs from another star in glory. So also is the resurrection of the dead. The body is sown in corruption, it is raised in incorruption. It is sown in dishonor, it is raised in glory. It is sown in weakness, it is raised in power. It is sown a natural body, it is raised a spiritual body. There is a natural body, and there is a spiritual body. And so it is written, "The first man Adam became a living being." The last Adam became a life-giving spirit. However, the spiritual is not first, but the natural, and afterward the spiritual. The first man was of the earth, made of dust; the second Man is the Lord from heaven. As was the man of dust, so also are those who are made of dust; and as is the heavenly Man, so also are those who are heavenly. And as we have borne the image of the man of dust, we shall also bear the image of the heavenly Man. Now this I say, brethren, that flesh and blood cannot inherit the kingdom of God; nor does corruption inherit incorruption. (I Corinthians 15: 35-50)

Is it possible to have a spiritual body today? One of the keys to answering that question is knowing the difference between a living being and a life-giving spirit — between the man, Adam, and the God-man, Jesus. Adam represented a living being. Jesus represented a life-giving spirit. The Church becomes confused by the difference between these two. If we cannot sit now in heavenly places with Christ, seek those things that are above, or be risen with Christ, then the Bible is a lie. The call of the Church is to become the image of the heavenly Man. The apostles, prophets, evangelists, pastors and teachers were given so that the Body might grow to the image of Christ, not to the image of Adam. When we have grown to the image of Christ, we will have the same authority and power that Christ had. Flesh and blood cannot inherit the Kingdom of God.

The Kingdom waits because of the mentality of God's people. People say, "Everything is just like it's always been. They've always talked about these things, but nothing ever changes. It's always going to be this way." Christians have been deceived with that thinking.

For whom he foreknew, He also predestined to be con-formed to the image of His Son, that He might be the firstborn among many brethren. (Romans 8:29)

Many interpret this scripture to mean that after we go into the grave, we will experience resurrection as Jesus did. The devil doesn't want us to believe that maturing Christians are growing into the image of Christ, who is the firstborn of many brethren.

Easter resurrection shows how Jesus moved from being an earthly man to being a heavenly man. Jesus Christ stood toe to toe with the devil and overcame the principalities and powers of death, hell and the grave. How are we going to conquer death? We are overcomers through Jesus Christ because we are learning the tools He used. We are learning to move in His authority and power. We implement the concepts of His heart and mind. Jesus, the firstfruit, teaches us the secrets of overcoming the last enemy.

Jesus did not become like God after His resurrection. Jesus was in God's likeness throughout His entire life. Death and resurrection transferred Jesus's life from one form to another, but He was the same Spirit.

What about relationships in the eternal Kingdom?

The same day the Sadducees, who say there is no resurrec-tion, came to Him and asked Him, saying: "Teacher, Moses said that if a man dies, having no children, his brother shall marry his wife and raise up offspring for his brother. Now there were with us seven brothers. The first died after he had married, and having no offspring, left his wife to his brother. Likewise the second also, and the third, even to the seventh. And last of all the woman died also. Therefore, in the resurrection, whose wife of the seven will she be? For they all had her." Jesus answered and said to them, "You are mistaken, not knowing the Scriptures nor the power of God. For in the resurrection they neither marry nor are given in marriage, but are like angels of God in heaven." (Matthew 22:23-30)

In the last days some teachers will forbid marrying (I Timothy 4:3), but that teaching is not of God. However, Jesus said that when the Kingdom of God is established, we will neither marry nor be given in marriage, but we will be like the angels. How do the angels live? We get another insight into eternal relationships in the situation in which Jesus's natural mother and brothers demanded to see Him.

But He answered and said to the one who told Him, "Who is My mother and who are My brothers?" And He stretched out His hand toward His disciples and said, "Here are My mother and My brothers! For whoever does the will of My Father in heaven is My brother and sister and mother." (Matthew 12:48-50)

The natural is symbolic of that which is eternal. We are usually so fixed in natural understanding that we judge eternal truth by natural laws. We do not realize that the natural is only a step that leads toward a far deeper dimension. Someone asks, "In that eternal Kingdom, will there be any children born?" I cannot answer whether children will be born or not, but I know that any birth would not involve pain or suffering. The birth process would be like having children in the Garden of Eden before the curse befell mankind. Pain and suffering didn't exist until after man's fall.

Eternal relationships will be like those in the Garden before the curse. Relationships in the eternal Kingdom will not be like the natural relationships of fallen man. This concept torments some people.

Some women who have henpecked their husbands don't want to go to heaven because they won't have anyone to henpeck. Some men who enjoy being dominated don't look forward to heaven because they won't have anyone to give them orders. Enjoy natural relationships now because they are temporal.

What kind of form or body will we have in the eternal Kingdom? "When He shall appear, we shall be like Him" (I John 3:2). The bodily form that Jesus had after the resurrection is the same form that we will have. He was not limited by space, time or any particular form. The disciples were gathered in a room talking when Jesus appeared among them without entering through the door (Luke 24:36). Two were on their way to Emmaus, and Jesus appeared in their midst and started walking with them. Limitations we know now will no longer hinder us. Everything happening after the curse imposed guidelines upon us. The Law gives guidelines to man, but in that eternal Kingdom, guidelines will be unnecessary.

In two different accounts, the Bible tells us that

Jesus ate in His disciples' presence so they would see that He was flesh and bones.

Now as they said these things, Jesus Himself stood in the midst of them, and said to them, "Peace to you." But they were terrified and frightened, and supposed they had seen a spirit. And He said to them, "Why are you troubled? And why do doubts arise in your hearts? Behold My hands and My feet, that it is I Myself. Handle Me and see, for a spirit does not have flesh and bones as you see I have." When He had said this, He showed them His hands and His feet. But while they still did not believe for joy, and marveled, He said to them, "Have you any food here?" So they gave Him a piece of a broiled fish and some honeycomb, and He took it and ate in their presence. (Luke 24:36-43)

Jesus said to them, "Bring some of the fish which you have just caught." Simon Peter went up and dragged the net to land, full of large fish, one hundred and fifty-three; and although there were so many, the net was not broken. Jesus said to them, "Come and eat breakfast." Yet none of the disciples dared ask Him, "Who are You?" knowing that it was the Lord. (John 21:10-12)

Both of these incidents took place after the resurrection. Because Jesus had access to the throne of God, He could appear in one form to Saul of Tarsus on the road to Damascus, and yet appear as the Lamb of God sitting at God's right hand.

Heavenly beings have that ability. When Satan came to visit one day at a gathering of the sons of God, God asked him what he had been doing. Satan answered, "I've been going to and fro in the earth, and walking back and forth on it" (Job 1:7). Satan had access to both the earth and the heavenlies. When we pass through the veil of death, we will lose all the limitations imposed upon us by this earthly dimension.

How, then, do we go from our existing bodily form to that form exemplified by Jesus Christ? The usual Christian concepts are not evil or false, but they are incomplete. In Jesus Christ and His resurrection, we have hope and we understand the hope for those who have died. We know the dead in Christ will come forth on that glorious day because of Jesus's resurrection. That is part of the truth.

We are dealing with two dimensions. Jesus said that something most significant has been overlooked.

Jesus said to [Martha], "I am the resurrection and the life. He who believes in Me, though he may die, he shall live. And whoever lives and believes in Me shall never die. Do you believe this?" She said to Him, "Yes, Lord, I believe that you are the Christ, the Son of God, who is to come into the world." (John 11:25-27)

We must understand that another dimension of life exists in Jesus Christ, a place of faith and maturity where we will never die. I Thessalonians 4:13 is usually interpreted totally out of context, and doctrines concerning a rapture sound reasonable because we lack the comprehension of two distinct dimensions. Those who are asleep will come forth on the last day in the glorious resurrection. Paul is writing to the church at

Thessalonica, to comfort them concerning Christian brothers and sisters who have died.

> *But I do not want you to be ignorant, brethren, concerning those who have fallen asleep, lest you sorrow as others who have no hope. For if we believe that Jesus died and rose again, even so God will bring with Him those who sleep in Jesus. For this we say to you by the word of the Lord, that we who are alive and remain until the coming of the Lord will by no means precede those who are asleep. For the Lord Himself will descend from heaven with a shout, with the voice of an archangel, and with the trumpet of God. And the dead in Christ will rise first. Then we who are alive and remain shall be caught up together with them in the clouds to meet the Lord in the air. And thus we shall always be with the Lord. Therefore comfort one another with these words. (I Thessalonians 4:13-18)*

When Jesus returns, He will bring with Him those believers who have already died. Why would Jesus bring believers back to earth? Why doesn't He simply take us to be where they are? Jesus is going to bring saints together where we—the New Jerusalem, the people of God—are.

Another scripture that explains this concept further concerns the ten virgins (Matthew 25:1-13). When the virgins heard the cry that the bridegroom was coming, they went out to meet Him. Many Christians assume that going out to meet Him, or being "caught up" as it says in I Thessalonians 4:17, means that we will be caught away to a place we have never been before. But the New Jerusalem, which is the Bride, will come down

263

from God out of heaven (Revelation 21:1-3), and we will
share and partake of the glories of God eternally here
on the earth. Will we be able to visit other planets? We
will have new bodies! I plan to see the whole universe,
everything that God has made! Everything belongs to
the Lord, but this earth will be the place where God's
people will rule and reign. "We who are alive and
remain shall be caught up together with them in the
clouds" (I Thessalonians 4:17). He does not say He will
take us to some other place. The King is coming to join
us where we will rule and reign forever. Then will the
scripture be fulfilled, "The earth is the Lord's, and all
its fullness, the world and those who dwell therein"
(Psalm 24:1).

When my granddaughter, Pennielle Brook, was born
in 1982, the Spirit of the Lord told me that this is the
generation who can be alive and remain until the coming of the Lord. With that promise comes the responsibility to become a mature Church. The Kingdom com-
pletion could have happened thousands of years ago,
had the Church of that day achieved the necessary
maturity. Jesus will come only when the Church has
matured to the place that our lamps are trimmed and
burning and we are looking for the coming of the bridegroom to celebrate the marriage supper.

*Now this I say, brethren, that flesh and blood cannot
inherit the Kingdom of God; nor does corruption inherit
incorruption. Behold, I tell you a mystery: We shall not all
sleep, but we shall all be changed, in a moment, in the
twinkling of an eye, at the last trumpet. For the trumpet
will sound, and the dead will be raised incorruptible, and*

we shall be changed. (I Corinthians 15:50-52)

Paul thought he was going to be alive when Jesus returned. I believe every Christian generation that has ever lived had that same expectation, but they did not have the necessary proof of demonstration. They did not have the evidence of a mature Church. In a moment, in the twinkling of an eye, when the Church is mature and ready for Jesus Christ to come back, we shall be changed. The dead who have died in Christ will rise, and we will experience a glorious reunion with the Bridegroom. Those who are alive and remain are the ones who will make the difference.

Enoch, another firstfruit of the Kingdom, represents those who are alive and remain. The Bible says of Enoch that he did not see death (Hebrews 11:5) because he pleased God. We who are alive and remain are left here for one ultimate purpose: to conquer the last enemy which is death. God has left us here to take dominion over death. Most people exercise dominion over headaches or the common cold, but the Word says that the last enemy to be conquered is death. Sickness is only symbolic of death. The redemption of the Body has not yet taken place except by faith in Jesus Christ. One generation, however, will experience the reality of that redemptive process.

We must solve the mystery of overcoming death, which is the concern of those who are alive and remain. We must conduct ourselves so that we conquer death by the Spirit of Christ within us.

After Jesus's crucifixion and burial, the Bible tells us that when Mary came to the tomb, she found that the stone was rolled away from the entrance. The Spirit of the Lord dropped a thought in my mind. Why was the stone rolled away from the tomb? Surely it was not rolled away to allow Jesus to leave the tomb. If Jesus could pass through locked doors, the stone at the tomb would have been insignificant to Him. Jesus didn't come through the door of the tomb or those who kept watch outside would have seen Him. Therefore, the stone must have been rolled away to let the disciples inside the tomb.

We have walked into Jesus's tomb, but we have never fully understood the mystery. The last enemy controls us because we have not really understood death. We have not opened our hearts to comprehend the mystery. God opens the tomb and says to us, "Go in, look around and see what is there. Take your time and see what the mystery is all about." The age we live in now is a time when God is saying, by revelation, "I want to give you the understanding of the mystery."

I asked God to give me understanding by revelation of what He was saying to my spirit. He took me to I Corinthians 10:11 which says, "Now all these things happened to them [the Israelites] as examples, and they were written for our admonition, on whom the ends of the ages have come."

God said, "Look at that verse again." Israel was given as an example of how to overcome and be victorious. The Lord took me to Exodus to give me the key to overcoming death. God told Paul that if he wanted to understand the mysteries at the end of the age, he should explore what happened to the children of Israel step by step. That study will uncover the way to overcome. Those who are alive and remain to the end will overcome by this method.

Israel was in bondage to Egypt which always represents death. The children of Israel were bound by the fear of death That description of Israel applies to the Church today, for the Church is in bondage to death just as Israel was in bondage to Egypt. Israel had firstfruits of deliverance and the hope of getting away from Egypt through their prophets, but they were still under bondage.

God instructed Moses to tell the Israelites how to get out of Egypt (death). First, they had to understand that God was God. Then the people had to accept Moses as God's prophet. To misunderstand either of those truths would leave the people absolutely hopeless.

God told Moses to gather the elders together and He gave them explicit instructions on how they could be released from Egyptian bondage.

God told Israel to use a lamb for the Passover. The lamb itself was not as significant as the obedience of the people. They were to take the blood of the lamb and put it on the doorpost. The people were fully dressed and ready to go while they ate the roasted lamb. The people could choose whether they would believe the man of God or ignore Him. Finally, the hour came when the death angel passed by. Those who heeded the words of the prophet and were obedient in putting the

lamb's blood on the doorpost, set out for the Promised
land, leaving Egypt, the land of death. They got to the
Red Sea which symbolizes the place the Church fails
over and over again. We arrive at the place where we
acknowledge that the body is corrupt, but we don't
understand how to move from corruption to incorruption.

To move from one form to another, we must cross the
Red Sea. Between the two dimensions is a gulf separat-
ing corruption from incorruption. When the children of
Israel got to the Red Sea, God said to His prophet,
"Throw out the rod across the water." The rod represents the miraculous power of God—the return of the
Elijah ministry. Had the people not walked with
Moses, they would never have passed safely to the
other side. Any Israelites who lagged behind or
watched from a distance were drowned with the Egyptians. As soon as they got to the other side, God told
Moses to stretch out his rod again. When he did, the
waters closed. The Egyptians who followed the Israelites drowned, but those who had followed in obedience
arrived safely on the other side. Paul indicates that
Israel is an example to show us how to get from death to
life. The Exodus shows us how to get from the old land
to the new land. The secret of Israel's escape is the
secret of overcoming death.

God led His people. He told them exactly how to go
and what to do. Unfortunately, by the time they
reached the Promised Land, they were so bogged down
with murmuring, complaining and unbelief that God
kept them from entering the land He had for them.

Israel's passage through the Red Sea represents passing from death unto life. That experience is the mystery of baptism, or circumcision of the heart. The same hindrances that kept the Israelites out of the Promised Land keep God's people today from possessing all that God has for us. Murmuring, complaining and unbelief are stimulated by the love of money. Many people cannot receive God's promises because they serve the god, Mammon. They fail to understand what God is saying because they are so caught up in the desires of their own flesh. We live in an evil day when men often do not understand their own motivations.

The Israelities camped in Rephidim, but there was no water to drink. The murmuring and complaining against Moses grew so bitter that he cried out to God because the people were almost ready to stone him. Then God performed another miracle and gave them water. God gave Israel miracle after miracle and although they had seen the fruit of Moses's ministry, they still did not trust God. Unbelief was also true of the disciples. As far as we know, John was the only one who believed that Jesus was raised from the dead (John 20:8). That percentage is still true among God's people today. However, the Church is about to begin a period of great Elijah ministries. This is the day of anointed apostles and prophets in the Church. The prophetic Word of God is about to be unleashed to move with authority and the beginning of a new Apostolic age.

And they journeyed from Elim, and all the congregation of the children of Israel came to the Wilderness of Sin,

*which is between Elim and Sinai, on the fifteenth day of
the second month after they departed from the land of
Egypt. Then the whole congregation of the children of
Israel murmured against Moses and Aaron in the wilderness. And the children of Israel said to them, "Oh, that we
had died by the hand of the Lord in the land of Egypt,
when we sat by the pots of meat and when we ate bread to
the full! For you have brought us out into this wilderness
to kill this whole assembly with hunger." Then the Lord
said to Moses, "Behold, I will rain bread from heaven for
you. And the people shall go out and gather a certain
quota every day, that I may test them, whether they will
walk in My law or not. And it shall be on the sixth day that
they shall prepare what they bring in, and it shall be twice
as much as they gather daily." Moses and Aaron said to
all the children of Israel, "At evening you shall know that
the Lord has brought you out of the land of Egypt. And in
the morning you shall see the glory of the Lord; for He
hears your murmurings against the Lord. But what are
we, that you murmur against us?" Also Moses said, "This
shall be seen when the Lord gives you meat to eat in the
evening, and in the morning bread to the full; for the Lord
hears your murmurings which you make against Him.
And what are we? Your murmurings are not against us
but against the Lord."... This is the thing which the Lord
has commanded: 'Let every man gather it according to
each one's need, one omer for each person, according to
the number of persons; let every man take for those who
are in his tent.'"... And Moses said, "Let no one leave
any of it till morning." Notwithstanding they did not heed
Moses. But some of them left part of it until morning, and*

it bred worms and stank. And Moses was angry with them. . . . Now it happened that some of the people went out on the seventh day to gather, but they found none. And the Lord said to Moses, "How long do you refuse to keep My commandments and My laws?" (Exodus 16: 1-8, 16, 19-20, 27-28)

Why did the Israelites wander in the wilderness for forty years? They did not heed the Word of the Lord. God's people did not possess the Promised Land because they were disobedient. The great hindrance today in overcoming death is the lack of simple obedience. Malachi said those not giving to God as He commands are robbers and thieves. Instead of honoring God as he directs us, we have followed our own instincts and laws by refusing to listen to what God is saying. We have made idols from the mind of reason. We must remember, however, that God's ways are higher than our ways.

Of the twelve spies who were sent to spy out the Promised Land, only Caleb and Joshua believed that Israel could possess it. The Caleb-Joshua ministry moved by obedience and miracles. They moved by obedience of men and miracles of God. God promised if they obeyed Him, He would perform miracles. "If you will obey Me, I will send you bread." "If you will obey Me, I will part the sea." "If you will obey Me, I will be a God of miracles." The miracle working power of God awaits to find an obedient people.

Israel was obedient by taking the blood of the lamb and smearing it on their doorposts. Symbolically, they left death when they left Egypt. They escaped through the Red Sea by baptism, moving from one kingdom to another. After baptism, they had to live out their faith. The time of wandering was a time of demonstration. The Church is now in the time of demonstration. Like Israel, God requires us to demonstrate. God calls for obedience so He may again perform miracles in these days. All Christians must die to live the Christian life in power. Death does not necessarily mean "natural" death, for most Christians will indeed experience a physical death, I believe that God desires us to learn how to die to our wills and our flesh and to reckon ourselves dead. Paul said:

> *If then you were raised with Christ, seek those things which are above, where Christ is, sitting at the right hand of God. Set your minds on things above, not on things on the earth. For you died, and your life is hidden with Christ in God. (Colossians 3:1-3)*

One reason the Kingdom of God cannot come is that our minds and affections are not set on things above. We are still attached to earthly kingdoms instead of the heavenly Kingdom. We are praying, "God, make Your heaven become as it is on earth," instead of, "God, make Your earth like heaven."

All flesh must die. How do we die? We die when we take our wills to the Garden of Gethsemane; when we obey God; when we refuse to argue with God; when we follow the Spirit instead of our own ideas; when we learn to say, "God, if this is Your way, I want to participate in what You are doing." The Promised Land waits for the Church.

Secondly, we must learn to walk in the Spirit. If we walk in the Spirit we will not fulfill the desires of the flesh (Romans 8:1). Most people think the desires of the flesh are adultery, overeating, etc. Those sins are obvious, but many more subtle sins are at the root of fleshly desires. Desires of the flesh refer to the god, Mammon, or the controls of our lives. How spiritual are our thought patterns? We as God's people must learn to walk in the Spirit so that we can witness to the world as spiritual men and women in spiritual families, and declare that everything we have belongs to the Lord. The Bible says we are not to forsake the assembling of ourselves together. If our flesh directs us away from the Body of Christ, we are in trouble. When the Spirit is in control and our flesh has been put under subjection, we can say, "The Kingdom of God is at hand." We must die to self-will and self-desire. Because the flesh follows the Spirit, the Spirit must always be in control.

Thirdly, we need to abide in Jesus. Flesh and blood cannot inherit the Kingdom of God. Jesus said to seek first the Kingdom of God and His righteousness. We should align all of our desires and ambitions against Kingdom motivations. The "hidden agenda" of every project needs to ask, "How does this project affect the Kingdom of God?" Every relationship we establish should be based on how it affects the Kingdom of God. Does this relationship contribute to our being a man or woman of God? Everything that we do before God's Kingdom can come must demonstrate Kingdom relationships, thought patterns and lifestyles.

Little children, it is the last hour; and as you have heard that the Antichrist is coming, even now many antichrists have come, by which we know that it is the last hour. They went out from us, but they were not of us; for if they had been of us, they would have continued with us; but they went out that they might be made manifest, that none of them were of us. But you have an anointing from the Holy One, and you know all things. I have not written to you because you do not know the truth, but because you know it, and that no lie is of the truth. Who is a liar but he who denies that Jesus is the Christ? He is antichrist who denies the Father and the Son. Whoever denies the Son does not have the Father either; he who acknowledges the Son has the Father also. Therefore let that abide in you which you heard from the beginning. If what you heard from the beginning abides in you, you also will abide in the Son and in the Father. And this is the promise that He has promised us—eternal life. These things I have written to you concerning those who try to deceive you. But the anointing which you have received from Him abides in you, and you do not need that anyone teach you; but as the same anointing teaches you concerning all things, and is true, and is not a lie, and just as it has taught you, you will abide in Him. (I John 2:18-27)

To overcome death and move into the Kingdom, we must first die to ourselves. Secondly, we must walk in the Spirit. Thirdly, we must abide in the branch or the root. Fourthly, we must learn the spirit of obedience. Jesus was obedient even unto death. Obedience means following God, His Word and His provision. When we follow the Lord, God will match our obedience with miracles. God opened the Red Sea. When the Israelites were obedient, He provided manna and water in the desert. He drove out the enemy. He made the walls of Jericho fall. God wants us to know that we are His people as we begin to move in His name in our communities. Now is the time to move with dominion. God is not always going to be where we expect Him to be. God is found where the need is.

Jesus waits to establish His Kingdom. He is waiting for His people to be obedient. God is searching for Caleb and Joshua spirits who will say, "With God's help we can change the circumstances in which we live." Some people will be alive and remain and stand toe to toe with death just as Jesus did. They will declare war against the "valley of death." They will stand confidently awaiting the King of kings and the Lord of lords. The trumpet will sound and Jesus Christ will come again because His Church is mature. I thank God for what Jesus did. His example shows the very real possibility of some generation fully demonstrating God's plan. But we must learn by obedience, following Him in His footsteps. We must learn that even as He moved, we shall move.

The prophet Isaiah had foretold Hezekiah's death, but Hezekiah prayed to God, "Remember now, O Lord, I pray, how I have walked before You in truth and with a loyal heart, and have done what is good in Your sight" (II Kings 20:3). Isaiah then prophesied, "Thus says the Lord . . . I have heard your prayer . . . I will add to your days fifteen years" (II Kings 20:5-6). With a grateful heart, Hezekiah wrote:

"What shall I say? He has both spoken to me, and He Himself has done it. I shall walk carefully all my years in the bitterness of my soul. O Lord, by these things men live; and in all these things is the life of my spirit; so You will restore me and make me live. Indeed it was for my own peace that I had great bitterness; but you have lovingly delivered my soul from the pit of corruption, for you have cast all my sins behind your back. For Sheol cannot thank you, death cannot praise You. Those who go down to the pit cannot hope for Your truth. The living, the living man, he shall praise You, as I do this day; the father shall make known Your truth to the children. The Lord was ready to save me; therefore we will sing my songs with stringed instruments all the days of our life, in the house of the Lord." (Isaiah 38:15-20)

The prophet Isaiah foresaw the possibility of conquering death a long, long time ago. He said that the dead do not praise God, but some generation to come will stand victoriously against death. That generation will be those who are "alive and remain." They will overcome death because they will reach a place of maturity. They are destined for the throne, a peculiar people of God, a people who do things differently. They are not normal, ordinary people, but a people called of God for a special ministry, to sing special songs. God is going to raise up a people, even as Ezekiel saw them, and life is going to come into old bones. That resurrected Body will arise and the Spirit of God will move on the face of the earth.

11

DEVELOPING A
PARADISIACAL MENTALITY

Without a vision, the people perish. The original manuscripts literally say, "Without a prophetic word, the people are in confusion." We are in such a day of controversy in the Church that I feel sometimes like the Apostle Paul when he said, "Need I defend myself?" Chapel Hill Harvester Church in Atlanta exemplifies equality of women, minority groups or any person regardless of his or her life situation.

With the understanding that I am a defender of any suppressed group of people, I will not defend my position on equal rights issues except to say, "Remember the fruit of my ministry." Mature, spiritual understanding of ministry will bring the subject of equal rights into its proper perspective.

Nobody appreciates the ministry of women more than I do. Gloria Copeland, Anne Gimenez and other called women of the Lord are fearlessly moving ahead into areas that proclaim the message of the hour to God's people. I honor the ministry of women who are moving quickly into comprehending what God is saying today. To fully appreciate these women's contributions to the Body of Christ, we must understand what God intended the world to be like and what God wants His Church to be like. This understanding comes with a view of the inner workings of Paradise.

> *Then God said, "Let Us make man in Our image, according to Our likeness; let them have dominion over the fish of the sea, over the birds of the air, and over the cattle, over all the earth and over every creeping thing that creeps on the earth." So God created man in His own image; in the image of God He created him; male and female He created them. Then God blessed them, and God said to them, "Be fruitful and multiply; fill the earth and subdue it; have dominion over the fish of the sea, over the birds of the air, and over every living thing that moves on the earth." And God said, "See, I have given you every herb that yields seed which is on the face of all the earth, and every tree whose fruit yields seed; to you it shall be for food." (Genesis 1:26-29)*

This scripture portrays a working order of a paradisiacal mentality. These few verses tell us exactly what God intended for man. By the spirit, I shall attempt to convey how God sees His Church, what His intentions are for us, and how He hopes to accomplish His will.

First, God said, "Let us make man in Our image." Notice, that when God spoke of the creation of man, He gave us only one description. He gave the specific description of His image as male and female. He gave no other qualifications or description. He simply said, "In Our image," meaning male and female. We must understand by the Spirit that God never varies His purposes from the book of Genesis to the book of Revelation. God always establishes patterns and principles which never vary. God said, "My image requires both male and female. Male or female alone cannot fulfill My purposes."

God is male when He provides for creation as a father. God's masculine nature gives us provisions. In ancient societies when the hunter went out, it was the male who hunted game and brought the provisions to the household. God is male as a God who provides for us and gives us necessary correction. The male image of God personifies the concept of headship. God is male when He injects a seed of the Kingdom of God within the Church and moves aggressively to bring the birth of Kingdom life into the world.

God is female when He gives food with breasts which have already made the food acceptable and digestible to the human body. God is female when He becomes an incubator of truth. In the womb of the Church grows the seed of truth. God is female when in incubation, He brings truth to life. God's female qualities identifies the necessity of women fitting into God's plan. We see the "helpmeet principle," which is a female attribute of God.

279

Some people are offended when we talk about the female aspects of God. If the image of God is both male and female, those who try to make God totally male or totally female do not understand what God has said about His image. I shall share with you as God has led me in that understanding.

And so it is written, "The first man Adam became a living being." The last Adam became a life-giving spirit. However, the spiritual is not first, but the natural, and afterward the spiritual. (I Corinthians 15:45-46)

Paul said, "Does not nature itself teach you?" (I Corinthians 11:14). We learn about spiritual things from the natural. He said, "The first man was of the earth, made of dust. The second man is the Lord from heaven. As was the man of dust, so also are those who are made of dust. And as is the heavenly man, so also are those who are heavenly. As we have borne the image of the man of dust, we shall also bear the image of the heavenly man." Notice, he said, "spiritual is not first, but carnal is first."

We see man and woman as Adam and Eve, the two of them together in physical and spiritual oneness. God said, "Learn from that." This unity is God in the flesh. God in the flesh is male and female in spiritual unity. Adam and Eve were God's demonstration of His own image. God said that it is not good that man should be alone, and He might as well have said, "It is not good that woman should be alone." Likewise a ministry cannot be alone either. A ministry that is alone is in danger of confusion. It is not good for man to be alone, nor for woman to be alone because the image of God is both male and female. God instructs us to learn spiritual truth from the natural.

Then God did something very unique in Paradise that I've never heard anyone preach. After He created man in His image, the Bible says, "Then He blessed them." Notice, He blessed them in their togetherness. He did not bless either man nor woman alone. He blessed them, male and female, in their togetherness. He cannot bless man and woman in an estranged relationship. He cannot bless a church that is totally directed by males, nor can He bless a church that is totally directed by females. God will not bless a church that is totally black or one that is totally white. God blesses what I call the "togetherness principle." God demands unity of faith. God requires that balance in order to bless His image.

God has established a principle of togetherness which He will not violate. I don't think that this concept has been written anywhere except in the Bible. I haven't read this principle in any book. I will take the responsiblity for declaring this truth to the Church, and I will accept whatever blessings go with it. I am so convinced that this balance is God's truth that I would defend it.

First we see God as He defines His image, male and female. In their togetherness He blesses them and then he begins to give what I call "Paradise laws," or laws which historically become Church or Kingdom laws. These laws, which were given to develop a Paradisia-

cal mentality, have never changed since man was in
the Garden of Eden. When He finished, God pronounced "goodness" on His creation of male and
female. His creation functions in togetherness and
oneness. God said, "Everything I need to bless Me is in
the Garden." Anything that Christians do which
detracts them from that Pardisiacal mentality is not of
God. Other motivations become self-serving and are
only portions rather than the total blessing of God.

The first law of Paradise is "Be fruitful and multiply." The mature person understands this principle of
life. Male alone cannot be fruitful and multiply, nor can
female alone be fruitful and multiply. In order to
accomplish this basic law of God's Paradise, He
requires oneness of male and female. Seed comes forth
and only with the fertilization of an egg by the seed can
life ever come forth. Oneness brings multiplication.
That is a natural law. God said through the Apostle
Paul, "Learn from the natural." No multiplication
comes forth in the Spirit unless male and female interact in ministry. This is God's "togetherness principle." Very clearly, the principle that runs like a cord
throughout God's plan is that He said to "reproduce
after your own kind."

The woman reproduces after her kind. She reproduces the attributes of womanhood in her daughters. Man
produces after his kind through his sons. One of the
grave problems of our day is the inability to reproduce
ourselves "after our own kind." The prostitution of that
principle causes the Church today to dangle on the
threshold of confusion. Paul instructed older women

to teach the younger women. No wonder Paul said of himself that there is but one father and that spiritual father led by the Holy Spirit cannot be substituted by naturally-minded teachers. If we miss the principle of spiritual reproduction, we have missed the Paradisiacal mentality and there is no way to birth God's Kingdom on earth today. Understanding this concept will bring liberty and freedom that can only come from truth. Apart from truth, no real freedom exist. False freedom always results in confusion.

How is spiritual multiplication accomplished? God gives some very interesting instructions in the Garden that perhaps we have overlooked. God told Adam and Eve that they would be fruitful and multiply by speaking names. Words of our creation, our thought patterns, our holy desires birth the creative process. Learn the creative processes of the Holy Spirit. We cannot get so set in whatever has already been accomplished that our minds are not open to other creative ideas which God will give to us. Creation began when God said to be fruitful and multiply. He told them to multiply by naming things. After we have spiritual comprehension, and the seed of God in our Spirits, then God instructs us to speak out our desires so that creation can become a reality. So the first principle in the Garden of Paradise is "Be fruitful and multiply."

The second principle that God established in the Garden was "to subdue and have dominion." God formed every beast of the field and every bird of the air out of the ground, and brought them to Adam to see what he would call them. Whatever name Adam called each living creature, God honored. Adam gave names to cattle, birds and beasts, but Adam did not find a helper equal to him.

God entered Adam into the process of creation. God's first creative process was so perfect that the earth didn't need a defense mechanism to protect its creatures. The scripture omits any mention of insects with stingers, venomous creatures or animals that clawed others. The Garden had no need for the shedding of blood because the Garden was perfect. When our thoughts and desires are subdued and in order, life is without confusion and competition.

If we don't overcome our selfish desires in the flesh, we will never overcome them in the spirit. If we cannot control fleshly desires, our spiritual desires will never please God. The two dimensions interact in such a way that they are absolutely inseparable. God gave instructions to Adam and Eve concerning what foods they were to eat. And God said, "Your food has two requirements — it must be an herb that bears seed, or a tree whose fruit yields seed. The herbs and fruits must have seeds because God wants his creation to continue. Eating meat and many other foods began out of our thought processes and our desires for dietary standards that please ourselves. As a matter of fact, in order to have skins for clothing, something had to die.

Animal sacrifice was the built-in redemptive process which God established. Sacrifice for sin is the cross of Paradise, and sacrifice became necessary because of disobedience. Blood was never shed until man disobeyed God. The Paradisiacal mentality was satisfied with herbs and fruit. I know that the Bible says to "call nothing common and unclean." I know that Jesus was standing on the bank broiling fish when the the disciples came from their ships. All that is true, but the Paradisiacal mentality was satisfied with herbs and fruit.

God's redemptive process must include the shedding of blood without which there is no redemption or remission of sin. Now we understand the reason the whole earth groans. The Paradisiacal mentality was, "Adam and Eve were naked and not ashamed." God could bless them in their innocence and freedom. They were totally transparent. Sin forced them to wear skins to cover themselves. Their shame had to be covered because of their disobedience. As we move toward the Garden (the Kingdom of God), we will become more and more transparent and fearless. People who are afraid somebody is going to spiritually discern them have already identified a spirit they don't like in themselves. We need to be vulnerable enough to understand and receive loving correction, especially from those who are over us in the Lord. Sometimes we must obey without totally understanding God's purposes. When we follow the principle of obedience, God will bring about results which will honor Him.

Adam and Eve were naked and not ashamed because they were created in God's image. They were blessed of God. Their productivity and ability to multiply was because they were created in the image of God. The Church must reflect the image of God. Any other image or direction is not of God. In Genesis 3, an interruption in Paradise resulted when an uncovered woman talked with Satan. An uncovered woman tried to fight spiritual warfare. An uncovered woman attempting to fight spiritual conflicts by herself met with inevitable defeat. Adam and Eve together could have defeated Satan, but apart they were powerless against him. Paradise was interrupted when an uncovered woman began making decisions without consulting her spiritual authority. As a result, God pronounced curses for disobedience. First, God said that Satan is going to be totally defeated. The seed of the woman shall defeat Satan.

So the Lord God said to the serpent: "Because you have done this, you are cursed more than all cattle, and more than every beast of the field; on your belly you shall go. And you shall eat dust all the days of your life. And I will put enmity between you and the woman. And between your seed and her Seed; He shall bruise your head. And you shall bruise His heel." To the woman He said: "I will greatly multiply your sorrow and your conception; In pain you shall bring forth children' Your desire shall be for your husband, and he shall rule over you." (Genesis 3:14-16)

The curse ended mutual relationships by making the woman subservient to a man ruling over her. Because an uncovered woman tried to fight the devil alone, God instructed that she would be ruled by her husband. Worldly principles still maintain that the man rules over the woman. Disobedience prostitutes relationships. God told Adam that because he heeded the voice of an uncovered woman, ". . .and have eaten the tree of which I commanded you, saying, 'You shall not eat of it': Cursed is the ground for your sake; in toil you shall eat of it all the days of your life. Both thorns and thistles it shall bring forth for you, and you shall eat the herb of the field. In the sweat of your face you shall eat bread till you return to the ground, for out if it you were taken; for dust you are, and to dust you shall return" (Genesis 3:17-19).

Under the curse, man experiences hardships in his work patterns. Labor becomes very difficult whether a man works in carpentry, insurance, real estate or whatever occupation he chooses. God says that a man's difficulty in his work will become part of the curse in his life. And yet, in spite of the curse, something interesting occurs.

Everything comes from God. Even evil comes out of God's creation. In creating choice, God also created a potential for evil. Now notice, in spite of the curses resulting from disobedience, man still continued to have creative ability. However, now creation is violent. Venomous creatures are common in the world. Warfare erupts among the animals and throughout the human race. We see a new kind of creation: thorns and thistles, claws and stingers.

Fallen man is exemplified in the building of the tower of Babel. God said, "Their creative power is such that I must put them in confusion." Confusion always results when man creates the wrong things. Originally, God was pleased with His creation. He said, "It is good." Though man entered into rebellion and sin, he continues to have creative power and to create new things. Man's creativity produces pornographic movies. Man created illicit drugs. Man created alcohol with its potential of destroying lives. All of those things were created because we are "little gods." We don't cease being "little gods" just because man chose rebellion and lost the Paradisiacal mentality.

Rebellion exists in the Church when great creative forces are used for the wrong purposes. One of the great problems in the Church today is not understanding creative power that is in rebellion, yet seems to be for the good of man. Men and women in total rebellion can still heal the sick and do things that appear to be very spiritual. Some ministries in total rebellion against God in their personal lives are publicly honored for their great works. Because ministries are honored as being successful, that success does not mean that those endeavors are God's best plan. Sometimes those ministries hide their battles, confusion, and wrong directions. Ultimately rebellion always leads to destruction.

We had an interruption in the Paradise plan. The purpose of the Bible is to get man back to Paradise. How do we recapture the order that God intended? How do we restore the proper place of male and female so that God can bless us?

God's plan to overcome the curse is the Church. Men and women should understand that they are no longer cursed in certain areas of their lives and the Church is becoming God's prototype of the Paradise Garden. The Church points the direction back to Paradise. Abraham had great faith and God said, "Abraham, because of your faith principles, I'm going to build a new nation." National Israel becomes spiritual Israel which is Abraham's seed. The Bible says that the one seed of Abraham is Jesus Christ Who is the Head of the Church. God's plan produces a totally new order. Jesus is the firstfruit of the Kingdom of people who will take the world back to Paradise. Understand what God is doing! We can get back to Paradise if we learn how to defeat Satan. When we can say, "I belong to God and am no longer under the curse," we move back toward Paradise.

First, let's look at some facts. Jesus announced that His Church will become the epitome of God in the flesh on the earth or the Kingdom prototype. God did something else. Even before Jesus announced that hell could not stop the Church that He would build, He called apostles, or disciples. Oddly enough, Jesus called men and He made no apologies for His choices. Mark 6:3 says that Jesus not only had brothers, but He also had sisters. Jesus could just as easily have said to His sister, "I'm going to make you one of My disciples," but He did not.

I intend to clarify the place of women in the five-fold ministry. Someone asks, "Were there women apostles in the Bible?" Perhaps Junia was (Romans 16:7). She may well have been. But Jesus called men whom He drew to Himself away from the crowds. He took these men, discipled them, and poured Himself into them. However, Jesus also openly accepted the ministry of women who served Him. Mary, His mother, Mary Magdalene who stood at the cross, Martha who brought food to Him, and Mary who sat at His feet are just a few of the women who loved and ministered to Jesus. A very key verse that has been overlooked is found in Matthew:

And many women who followed Jesus from Galilee, ministering to Him, were there looking on from afar, among whom were Mary Magdalene, Mary the mother of James and Joses, and the mother of Zebedee's sons. (Matthew 27:55-56)

This scripture tells us that many women ministered to Jesus. Do you think Jesus received the ministry of these women? Do you think Jesus approved of what they were doing?

Jesus called His disciples who became apostles among men. But clearly Jesus also accepted the ministry of women. That pattern was followed by Paul because Phebe ministered to Him. Paul writes back and refers to the ministeries that he considered to be co-laborers with him. Two together, male and female, is the relationship that God can bless.

We have dealt with the three laws of what I call the "Paradisiacal mentality." How do these laws work in the Church today? I call the demonstration "Paradise reclaimed." Doesn't that sound great? Paradise reclaimed! Paradise is only reclaimed in the Church. If the Church lives like the world, we are in trouble.

The first law of Paradise was to "Be fruitful and

multiply." Remember the reference which said to learn by observing the natural? It cannot happen without the blessings of God which come only through right relationships. Without right relationships in the ministry, God's blessings are only partial at best. Be fruitful and multiply is the seed principle. It is the seed that Satan wants. As we multiply, we must learn how to tutor, care for and protect our seed. Is the seed adequately cared for? What about our provisions for the seed in the Church? Are we providing proper provisions for the seed when mothers must work? Who ought to take care of those tender boys and girls? Should they learn from some worldly nursery, or the family of God who takes the seed and cares for it?

Discipling demands special care. Jesus poured Himself into twelve men, and God's Word instructs older women, "Pour yourselves into young women." I weep inside when I write this, "Mothers and elder women, teach the younger women how to serve their husbands." God only knows how that teaching has been lost. God only knows how that admonition has failed to be demonstrated. Yes, a wife is the queen of a household and she ought to be respected as a queen, but if she does not learn that her husband is the lord in her life, she will never see the Kingdom. A basic principle in the Kingdom of God is pouring oneself, elder women, into the younger women and saying, "This is how to treat your husband. Here is how to give yourself to him."

Elder men pour themselves into the younger men saying, "Here is how to treat a wife. Love her as Christ loved the Church. Treat her with great courtesy. She is the queen of your life." Some older men try to glory in their strength by competing with younger men. The Bible says to let a young man glory in his strength, but an older man glory in his hoary head which represents experience. Strength and wisdom together produce the Kingdom. If we don't honor the "hoary head" in our churches, God will not bless those churches. Young men are implementors, but wisdom is given through the elders of a church. What a balance God puts in the Paradisiacal mentality! Discipline is necessary to know and respect the abilities in one another.

God has shown me a gray area in spiritual counseling. Many counselors are teaching about healing memories, but sometimes even bringing up those wretched memories becomes counter-productive. God helps us forget those things which are behind by making all things new. New life in Christ includes our emotions.

God can not only give someone healed emotions. He can make them brand-new inside. God can make all things new in His Kingdom. This is the solution for those people who were abused by their fathers and dominated by their mothers. We must open our spirits to a creative God and let Him make us new inside and totally, emotionally whole in the name of the Lord Jesus Christ.

Be fruitful, multiply and care for the children God has given us. If any lack natural fathers, provide a place in the Church to give them spiritual images of fatherhood. If a child does not have a mother, the Church's job is to become that spiritual mother. Her (the Church's) breasts feed and comfort. His (the Church's) protective hand guides and leads. The Paradisiacal mentality brings us into proper relationships in God's Church. Persecutions, stonings, accusations and battles will inevitably come. If the world killed Jesus, they will persecute His Church. But the way back to the Kingdom of God is found in right relationships and fruitful productivity.

Secondly, God said, "Subdue and have dominion." Notice, He didn't say to "take" dominion. Authority does not exist until there is submission. Authority never precedes submission. Submission becomes a condition of having spiritual authority. When I began this ministry, I diligently sought elders to whom I could submit. Before I even came to Atlanta to begin a church, I called an elder and I asked him, "Does this vision agree with your spirit? I have heard from God, but I want to submit it." Had those spiritual elders said, "Don't do it," I promise before God, I would never have begun. An uncovered ministry is never of God. Submission always seeks authority, but true authority never seeks to rule. What a misunderstanding exists throughout the Church in this area!

Dominion means the restoration of oneness. Properly understood, Jesus's prayer in John 17, "Make them one," refers to the Garden concept of male and female. In oneness, God allows man to have dominion. God blesses oneness. The world sees something different when we submit to one another. True spiritual authority is one who has influence with God. We often call "spiritual" what is really "positional" authority.

Spiritual authority and positional authority are totally different. A woman may have spiritual authority who never has had a position in the Church in her life. But she knows how to touch God and has spiritual authority with God. Spiritual authority may produce positional authority, but it does not necessarily indicate positional authority.

The prophets of God were dynamic spiritual authorities, and yet they hid in the woods most of the time. Whenever God spoke, they listened. Whenever God decided to do something, He told them. He said, "Abraham, I have decided to do this." "Elijah, get ready for this confrontation." Spiritual authority is influence with God. Total dominion restored to God's people is found in one simple scripture. God's Word says, "There is neither male nor female, bond nor free, circumcision nor uncircumcision, but we are all one in Christ and we submit one to another." That description is Paradise restored.

A woman's conference can only be blessed by God when it directs women's ministries into the heart, core and central life of God's Church. If any ministry becomes an appendage, that ministry is not of God.

In God there is neither male nor female, Greek nor Jew, bond nor free. The Paradisiacal mentality says, "Yes, a woman who does the work of an apostle is indeed an apostle. A woman who does the work of a prophetess (the Bible has many examples) is a prophet. A woman who does the work of a pastor is a pastor. A woman who does the work of an evangelist is an evangelist. And the woman who does the work of a teacher is a vital part of the five-fold ministry. Each of these spiritual callings applies to both male and female and requires submission one to another in the Body of Christ. When women feel that they are self-sufficient and can function alone, they create a mentality like that in the women's rights movement. Too many groups today are conducting their own movements to assure the rights of specific individuals. God's Church is not black or white, male or female. We are all one in the Lord Jesus Christ. We must get the Paradisiacal mentality in our spirits!

The Bible gives a very key understanding when it says, "Women working with women make a mistake, and men working with men make a mistake." Exclusivism is not God's plan. His goal for His Church is oneness. The most successful conference I have ever conducted in my own local church was when I taught the women for two nights. We sold more tapes from that conference than any other I have conducted because God honored my interaction in their lives. That conference promoted oneness. I needed to say some things that only a man could say to those women. Together a woman and a man make the image of God, but apart God's image is incomplete.

The third Paradisiacal concept in the Garden was food or eating correctly. Learn the difference in spiritual milk and spiritual meat. The breast gives milk that even babies can drink. The meat of revelation provides the food for spiritual maturity. Without that prophetic word of maturity, revelation that takes projectury out of God's Word, the Church cannot grow.

We must learn how to attack Satan. Animals sometimes have spirits that are belligerent. To practice spiritual authority, jog in a community with some mean dogs! If we have to pick up a stick and run to protect ourselves, we don't have authority. Turn and say, "In the name of Jesus Christ, get off me." The newspaper recorded the story of a little woman weighing 110 pounds who was confronted by a man trying to rob the store in which she worked. Alone, at one o'clock in the morning, the little woman looked at him and said, "Why, you goofy man! That spirit in you wants to rob me and kill me. I come against you in the name of Jesus Christ! You get out of here." The man hastily ran the other way.

The Church is God's witness against worldly systems and methods. Here are four things that are absolutely invaluable in understanding how to move in the Paradisiacal mentality.

First of all, recognize and submit to authority. Jesus said, "You have not used My name, but now you may use My name because you understand who you are and how to walk in My authority." We cannot use the name of Christ if we violate His character. We must only use the name of Jesus in the character of His name: love, longsuffering, peace. We must measure our authority by His character.

Secondly, we must always remember our source. Our source is not the intellect. The problem in the Garden was the choice of whether or not to eat of the tree of knowledge of good and evil. We still choose either the fruit of obedience or the fruit of disobedience. Know whether our source is God. Our source in the Holy Spirit is inseparable from the Kingdom. Our source is God in the flesh. We easily sing about "Jesus in me." We love to go to the mountainside or the lake and say, "O God, I honor You! The Lord is great! The earth is the Lord's and the fullness thereof!" But what about verses saying, "Obey those over you in the Lord?" What about God in the flesh? Do we rejoice when a pastor looks us in the eyes and says, "The Lord has given me a word of correction for you?" What about spiritual authority in our households? Spiritual authority does not start in the Church. Authority flows through the Church leadership, but understanding authority starts in the home. Know your source.

Thirdly, know your enemy. God has made me realize that many Christians cannot discern the enemy. Jesus went through the tombs, and the maniac attacked Him because he thought Jesus was his enemy. Some people are going to hear the Kingdom message and say that this teaching is an enemy of what they believe. Search the Spirit! Is this teaching in keeping with God's plan? The Bible reveals who the true enemy of God is. Our enemy is not a saintly mother who prays each night for her children. Our enemy is not a godly wife who tries to keep her husband out of hell. Our enemy is not a father or mother keeping their children away from drugs and alcohol. Our enemy is the one who destroys our virtue.

Jesus says, "I will build My church and the gates of hell shall not prevail against it." God asked me, "Do you understand that?" I was in the middle of a sermon and I answered, "I am not sure, God. What do you mean?" God said to me, "Notice how I said that.'The gates of hell will not prevail against it.' Those gates are not attacking My Church, though that is the way people usually visualize it. 'The gates of hell shall not prevail' means you should begin to attack the gates of hell. You should say, 'In the name of Jesus Christ, you get out of my life!' " We need to walk through the authority of hell and establish the Kingdom of God in our lives. Our enemy is the authority of hell. Satanic forces create rebellion. Our enemy is anything that keeps us away from truth. Know the enemy!

Finally, learn the meaning of co-laborer. Relinquish every tinge of self-centered independence. God will never bless an independent church or an independent ministry. If we don't demonstrate the principle of co-laborers in the flesh, we will never understand the Kingdom. Glory in God's calling. A young person glories in his calling as an example to other youth. Older people glory in their wisdom and experience and learn how to give it without becoming domineering. An older woman must learn how to pour herself into younger women. A young woman must learn how to implement truth.

The theme of this chapter is, "In His likeness, we overcome." God's likeness is male and female. God's image is properly related ministeries following the leading of the Spirit. In that understanding, we become one and we overcome with authority because we have the blessing of God.

12

THE FINAL HOUR

The final hour was drawing near. Jesus had gone through three years of intense ministry and He was physically weary. He had experienced the upsurge of applause and adulation from the crowd, but now on a hill not far away there loomed a cross. Jesus felt the weariness in His body, and His disciples were also tired.

Then they came to a place which was named Gethsemane; and He said to His disciples, "Sit here while I pray." And He took Peter, James, and John with Him, and He began to be troubled and deeply distressed. Then He said to them, "My soul is exceedingly sorrowful, even to death. Stay here and watch." He went a little farther, and fell on the ground, and prayed that if it were possible, the hour

*might pass from Him. And He said, "Abba, Father, all
things are possible for You. Take this cup away from Me;
nevertheless, not what I will, but what You will." Then He
came and found them sleeping, and said to Peter, "Simon,
are you sleeping? Could you not watch one hour? Watch
and pray, lest you enter into temptation. The spirit truly is
ready, but the flesh is weak." (Mark 14:32-38)*

Notice that Jesus told Peter, James and John to stay
behind and watch. These three who were closest to
Jesus were acutely aware that people were trying to kill
Him, but they knew that He needed a moment alone
with His Father. Jesus told them one simple thing to
do: "Stay here and watch." Then He went ahead to be
alone with His Father. People who are not in leadership
positions do not understand that leadership must
always go farther in dedication, prayer and commitment.

The disciples had gone through so much with Jesus
and at the final hour they fell asleep. Peter, who had the
revelation of who Jesus was when he said, "You are the
Christ, the Son of the Living God," was one of those
who fell asleep at that crucial time.

Satan attacks us when we are weary and weak. That
is the time we are most vulnerable to making wrong
decisions. When the disciples became weak, they failed
their Lord. Their flesh began competing with what God
was doing.

People who were closest to Jesus and His vision were
weary. The very ones who should have understood the

importance of not growing weary in well-doing were the ones who succumbed to weariness of the flesh.

There is such a critical need in the Church for the people of God to stand out in front like Aaron and Hur who knew the importance of supporting Moses, God's man for the hour (Exodus 17:11-12). God needs support ministries today more than He needs voices. He has anointed voices to speak His Word. Those prophets of God need people who will support them and say, "I know that this man is speaking for God. I will support and strengthen him so Satan's kingdom will be destroyed." In these last days we cannot afford the luxury of growing weary.

I do not believe any person who has met Jesus Christ and in whom the Spirit of God dwells has not also been called of God to do something for the Kingdom. God is beginning to open the hearts and minds of His people. They are shaking themselves like Samson of old and rising up in this final hour.

Samson thought his life was over. He had been blinded. No longer could he flex his muscles and cause everyone to tremble. A lad had to lead him by the hand. Samson's hair had grown back and he had reestablished his covenant with God. He told the lad who was leading him, "Let me feel the pillars which support the temple, so that I can lean on them." He asked God, "O Lord God, remember me, I pray! Strengthen me, I pray, just this once." Samson took hold of the two middle pillars and pushed with all his might. In his final hour, God honored Samson's request, and the temple collapsed and fell upon the Philistines who were within.

Weariness may come upon us and cause us to feel that the hour is far gone. But we must shake ourselves and say, "This is God's hour and I cannot fall short of what God has called me to do."

When the Israelites wanted a king, God called upon Samuel, His spokesman, to choose a king. God never goes around those whom He calls. God never goes around a vision or uproots that which He has established.

Then Samuel took a flask of oil and poured it on his [Saul's] head, and kissed him and said: "Is it not because the Lord has anointed you commander over his inheritance? . . . Then the Spirit of the Lord will come upon you, and you will prophesy with them and be turned into another man. And let it be, when these signs come to you, that you do as the occasion demands; for God is with you. You shall go down before me to Gilgal; and surely I will come down to you to offer burnt offerings and make sacrifices of peace offerings. Seven days you shall wait, till I come to you and show you what you should do." (I Samuel 10:1,6-8)

Before the seventh day arrived, Saul became restless and began to move where he should not. He began to get out of God's will.

Then [Saul] waited seven days, according to the time set by Samuel. But Samuel did not come to Gilgal; and the people were scattered from him. So Saul said, "Bring a burnt offering and peace offerings here to me." And he offered the burnt offering. Now it happened, as soon as he had finished offering the burnt offering, that Samuel came; and Saul went out to meet him, that he might greet him. And Samuel said, "What have you done?" And Saul said, "When I saw that the people were scattered from me, and that you did not come within the days appointed, and that the Philistines gathered together at Michmash, then I said, 'The Philistines will now come down on me at Gilgal, and I have not made supplication to the Lord.' Therefore I felt compelled, and offered a burnt offering." And Samuel said to Saul, "You have done foolishly. You have not kept the commandment of the Lord your God, which He commanded you. For now the Lord would have established your Kingdom over Israel forever. But now your kingdom shall not continue. The Lord has sought for Himself a man after His own heart, and the Lord has commanded him to be commander over His people, because you have not kept what the Lord commanded you." (I Samuel 13:8-14)

If Saul had been obedient, David's kingdom would not have been established. But when Saul lost his ability to hear God and did things according to his mind of reason, his disobedience marked the end of his kingdom. He refused to wait on the Lord and do exactly as God said to do.

Now the word of the Lord came to Samuel, saying, "I greatly regret that I have set up Saul as king for he has turned back from following Me, and has not performed My commandments." And it grieved Samuel, and he cried out to the Lord all night. (I Samuel 15:10-11)

Samuel was grieved to see that Saul had failed God by getting carried away with his own flesh. He was grieved to see that Saul was no longer listening to God's command.

Then Samuel went to Saul, and Saul said to him, "Blessed are you of the Lord! I have performed the commandment of the Lord." But Samuel said, "What then is this bleating of the sheep in my ears, and the lowing of the oxen which I hear?" And Saul said, "They have brought them from the Amalekites; for the people spared the best of the sheep and the oxen, to sacrifice to the Lord your God; and the rest we have utterly destroyed." Then Samuel said to Saul, "Be quiet! And I will tell you what the Lord said to me last night." And he said to him, "Speak on." So Samuel said, "When you were little in your own eyes, were you not head of the tribes of Israel? And did not the Lord anoint you king over Israel?" (I Samuel 15:13-17)

Saul said, "I did what I was commanded to do." No, he only partially performed the commandments of the Lord. When we are little in our own eyes, God can use us.

My father was raised on a farm. He was taken out of school when he was in about the third grade to work on the farm. When the kids passed him on their way to school, he cried because he couldn't go. At seventeen, God looked down into that boy's heart and called him to preach.

Today my father's eyesight is almost gone because

he read for hours by the fireside. His family couldn't afford candles, so my dad would go into the creeks and get lighter knots. During the dark night hours, he would sit by the open fire and read the Bible. He would plow the fields all day and sometimes run ten or twelve miles to preach at churches in the evenings. The man knew he had heard from God. Years later, he sat before the King and Queen of England. Presidents of the United States knew Earl Paulk by name. Why? He was little in his own eyes, and he was willing to be used by God.

Many people have potential that my father never had, yet they sit around wasting their lives away. They are too lazy to care. God is still searching for people who are willing to stay little in their own sight. To be successful in God, we need to get on our faces and say, "God, if You leave me and Your Spirit is gone, I'm worth nothing." Will we grow weary and fall asleep? Or will we say, "My God, we're almost there"? To miss what God is doing today would be a terrible mistake. God is speaking today with immeasurable force.

God used Samuel to speak to Saul, and He speaks to us through His called-out leadership. Every believer has access to God as a priest of his own household. Those believers who have the baptism of the Holy Spirit can have close communion with the Lord. But God has established the ministries of the apostles, prophets, pastors, evangelists and teachers to determine the direction of His Church. When Samuel asked Saul why he had not obeyed God, Saul tried to make excuses. "I brought back Agag the King," he told

Samuel. God had said to kill everyone. Saul continued,

"But the people took of the plunder, sheep and oxen, the best of things which should have been utterly destroyed, to sacrifice to the Lord your God in Gilgal." Then Samuel said, "Has the Lord as great delight in burnt offerings and sacrifices, as in obeying the voice of the Lord? Behold, to obey is better than sacrifice, and to heed than the fat of rams. For rebellion is as the sin of witchcraft, and stubbornness is as iniquity and idolatry. Because you have rejected the word of the Lord, He also has rejected you from being King." Then Saul said to Samuel, "I have sinned, for I have transgressed the commandment of the Lord and your words, because I feared the people and obeyed their voice." (I Samuel 15:21-24)

Many times I have been warned, "Pay attention to what people are saying. Don't get separated from the people." Does God really want a prophet or pastor to listen to people's opinions? No. God wants His leaders to pray, "God, what are You saying to these sheep? What is happening in the heavenly places? What do You want spoken today?"

Saul became misguided because he feared the people's opinions. When Saul saw that the Spirit of the Lord was leaving him, he reached out and grabbed hold of Samuel and wouldn't turn loose.

So Samuel said to him "The Lord has torn the kingdom of Israel from you today, and has given it to a neighbor of yours, who is better than you. And also the Strength of Israel will not lie nor relent. For He is not a man that He should relent." Then he said, "I have sinned; yet honor me now, please, before the elders of my people and before Israel, and return with me, that I may worship the Lord your God." So Samuel turned back after Saul, and Saul worshiped the Lord. Then Samuel said, "Bring Agag the king of the Amalekites here to me." So Agag came to him cautiously. And Agag said, "Surely the bitterness of death is past." But Samuel said, "As your sword has made women childless, so shall your mother be childless among women." And Samuel hacked Agag in pieces before the Lord in Gilgal. (I Samuel 15:28-33)

God is weary today with adversaries who go about warring what He is saying. We need to say, "God, we do not know it all. Whatever You want to say, You can say it because You are the King of kings and the Lord of lords." Our responsibility is to be sure that we are being led by the Spirit as we hear the voice of the Lord. God has His checkpoints, but they are not our concern. All God has to do is cut off life. Will He do that? Of course He will! Read the story of King Saul. We needn't worry about leaders who won't listen to God for He will deal with them. The people of God need only to be concerned about not missing what God is saying. They need to be sure of knowing the call of God upon their lives and being secure in the place to which He called them.

Jesus spoke the parable of the two sons.

"But what do you think? A man had two sons, and he came to the first and said, 'Son, go, work today in my vineyard.' He answered and said, 'I will not,' but afterward he regretted it and went. Then he came to the second

and said likewise. And he answered and said, 'I go, sir,' but he did not go. Which of the two did the will of his father?" They said to Him, "The first." Jesus said to them, "Assuredly, I say to you that tax collectors and harlots enter the kingdom of God before you. For John came to you in the way of righteousness, and you did not believe him; but tax collectors and harlots believed him; and when you saw it, you did not afterward relent and believe him." (Matthew 21:28-32)

Some have heard the Gospel of the Kingdom. When they first received newness of life and heard the vision God was giving, they were on fire for God. They said, "I used to do lots of other things, but the most exciting thing in the world now is serving Jesus!" But not many days passed until they were back in the garbage from which they had come. Others accepted the Lord and just sat quietly, listening and growing in the Lord. Maybe they weren't leaders, but they kept up their prayer life and study of the Word of God until one day they said, "Yes, count me in! I want to be a part of what God is doing!"

This parable exemplifies two extremes. One says he'll do something but does not obey. Because he became weary, he could not follow through. Others did not commit themselves so boldly, but little by little, they have grown strong. They may have backed away for awhile and become discouraged, but they have finally heard the Word of the Lord and have made up their minds to follow God. The final hour is upon us.

The Spirit of the Lord said to me, "I am beginning to

turn the headship of the Church." When headship is turned, the whole Body will turn. The great Pentecostal movement at the turn of the century was a mighty move of God. Then came the great Charismatic movement when the Holy Spirit leaped over denominational boundary lines. Beyond the great power of the Charismatic and Pentecostal movements, a new move today will establish the Kingdom of God.

We are beginning to see a oneness in God's people that will knit their hearts together. Instead of bickering over unimportant things, we will say, "Jesus Christ is the Lord of our lives." The Church will begin to affect this planet as never before. Some people are still singing about the "sweet bye and bye," but the time has come to sing about the Lion of Judah! Jesus Christ is alive, and the Lion of Judah reigns and prevails on planet earth!

This is no time for us to run from what God wants. Stand up and say, "The Lord God of Israel rules and reigns! Jesus Christ is the Lord of my life! He is the Lord of my business! He is the Lord of my family!" If we leave God out of our lives and plans, we are settling for far less than our best.

God is speaking today to His leaders. Paul was a great man of God, but certain Jews—so-called religious people—so stirred the people up that strong division arose against Paul. Paul was run out of town and he went to Lystra. When he got there, the first thing he did was to heal a crippled man who had never walked (Acts 14:8-11). The people were so aware of the anointing on Paul that they said, "The gods have come down to us in the likeness of men!" But the Jews followed Paul from Iconium to Lystra and again they stirred up persecution. These same people who had wanted to make gods out of Paul and Barnabas now said, "Let's stone them to death!" They stoned Paul, dragged him out of the city and left him for dead.

Some people today say, "Let's talk more about the King and less about the Kingdom." They fail to understand that a kingdom cannot exist without a king and a king cannot exist without a kingdom. The two are totally inseparable. Any attempt to separate the two is a deception from Satan to confuse our minds. The Gospel of the Kingdom and the Gospel of Jesus Christ are the same. But the demonstration of the Gospel of the Kingdom is the Gospel the world waits to see. We can preach the Gospel to the world, but until we live it out, the world will not believe it works. They will not be convinced by simply hearing the Gospel. They will believe it works when they see it demonstrated. Many will say to Jesus, "Lord, Lord, have we not prophesied in Your name, cast out demons in Your name, and done many wonders in Your name?" And Jesus will say, "I never knew you; depart from Me, you who practice lawlessness!" (Matthew 7:22-23)

The people who work with us will know that Jesus Christ is real when we demonstrate Christian principles. Let it be said of God's people, "They live what they preach." It is time for God's people to know who they are in Jesus Christ so they will not be shaken when Satan attacks.

The same crowd who cried, "Hosannah to the King,"

are the ones who put Jesus on the cross. What am I saying? Sheep cannot be trusted to be leaders. Leadership cannot and will not be found among sheep. They are too easily swayed by outside influences. They will go in the wrong direction or into the wrong pastures every time. God is raising up men and women today who have heard from the Lord. Those people have become leaders in these last days: teachers, pastors and preachers.

God will become even more specific in choosing leadership as the return of Christ nears. Before this decade is over, God will bless His leadership to such a degree that the world will know those leaders who have been ordained of God. We cannot follow what the crowds are saying. We must say, "God, whatever it means, whatever the price is, whatever You are saying to us, we will not compromise the truth."

If we have willfully sinned against Him, we must go back to God through the same way we came out. Until we right the wrongs, God cannot reconcile us. What does that mean? If we have said things we should not have said, we must take deliberate steps to undo the damage our words have done. We must say, "I'm sorry. I talked about things I did not understand. I involved myself when I had no business."

For if we sin willfully after we have received the knowledge of the truth, there no longer remains a sacrifice for sins, but a certain fearful expectation of judgment, and fiery indignation which will devour the adversaries. Anyone who has rejected Moses' law dies without mercy on the testimony of two or three witnesses. Of how much worse punishment, do you suppose, will he be thought worthy who has trampled the Son of God underfoot, counted the blood of the covenant by which he was sanctified a common thing, and insulted the Spirit of grace? (Hebrews 10:26-29)

We insult the Spirit of grace if we go back to the old way of life after God so bountifully picks us up out of nothing and restores us.

For we know Him who said, "Vengeance is Mine; I will repay, says the Lord." And again, "The Lord will judge His people." It is a fearful thing to fall into the hands of the living God. But recall the former days in which, after you were illuminated, you endured a great struggle with sufferings: partly while you were made a spectacle both by reproaches and tribulations, and partly while you became companions of those who were so treated. (Hebrews 10:30-33)

Those who first heard the Gospel and those who first heard about Pentecost went through great abuse, but they didn't give up. At their jobs many were bold enough to say, "Yes, I received the baptism of the Holy Spirit. Yes, I believe in speaking in tongues."

I remember the day when we were called children of a "holy roller" preacher. Because my father was the pastor of the Church of God in Anderson, S. C., and the state overseer of South Carolina, we received much abuse. I was once tied to a tree—not because I was wrong—only because I was the son of a holiness preacher. Now the pendulum has swung the other way.

Today congressmen, senators and presidents call on us. It is not going to be long until God's people are going to be a powerful and mighty voice of influence. We must not forget who we are. God forbid that we should compromise the truth. Living free from sin and in the power and anointing of God is still God's plan for mankind.

For you had compassion on me in my chains, and joyfully accepted the plundering of your goods, knowing that you have a better and an enduring possession for yourselves in heaven. Therefore do not cast away your confidence, which has great reward. For you have need of endurance, so that after you have done the will of God, you may receive the promise. (Hebrews 10:34-36)

In this scripture the Apostle Paul is warning those who had been enlightened and were moving with grace through many struggles and sufferings not to get their eyes off God. We must not forget where we have come from as we are given acceptance and respect by governmental and educational leaders. We must remember that everything we have to give them comes from God. We must not take for granted what God is doing.

The time has come for us to endure. Whatever we do, we must do it with twice the intensity. When we pray, we must pray twice as diligently. If our ministries change people's lives, know that we will be attacked by Satan because he is out to defeat us. We must go back to the first time God spoke to us, get on our faces and say,

"God, what did You tell us to do? What were the words You said to us?" In spite of temptations of the flesh, we need to say, "God, we are going to do it Your way."

Some are getting into error now because they have missed what God said. If we miss one small thing that God has said (as Saul did), eventually we will miss the big things that God says. Revelation can become so commonplace that we won't even know when we are hearing a message from God. We will anticipate getting out of church as quickly as possible because we are not listening to God any longer.

The hour has come when God will speak in circumstances. What is our view of death? Are we ready to stand before God? The scripture tells us, "If our heart does not condemn us we have confidence toward God" (I John 3:20). "If our heart does condemn us" means getting things right before God. We can play games only so long. After awhile we are condemned.

An embryo in its mother's womb does not know about another life. It is only vaguely familiar with muffled voices and sounds. Its whole world is the womb. If it were told that people, birds and animals existed outside the womb, it wouldn't believe because it cannot see them. It cannot see the things that God has created. But after awhile, at the moment of birth, with a spank on its behind and a cry, the baby has come into a new world. He learns to identify dogs, cats and relationships that affect his life.

Another dimension of life that we cannot see with our natural eyes exists. It is the spiritual realm of prin-

314

cipalities and powers, a world about which the prophet Elijah said, "Let my servant see." It transcends anything the natural mind can comprehend. God has called us to enter into that third world. The Spirit of God is beginning to prepare His people to enter through intercession, supplication, prophecy and discernment. In this vital hour, we must not miss this new realm. Those who miss what God is doing today will forever cry in eternity, "My God, I missed it!"

How does a man know he is the spiritual head of his family? God is limited as to what He can do in a household which is not in covenant with Him. God cannot bless a household if a man will not assume his rightful place as a priest. A wife with a Vashti spirit in that household brings rebellion because the man has failed to assume his responsibility (Esther 1:12). If a woman fails to be the spiritual helpmeet that God has called her to be, God will close His bowels of mercy. A spiritual wife puts her hands on a loving husband when he is in need and prays for him as an intercessor rather than condemning and accusing him. The basic problem rests in the home today. Many of the problems with children could be solved if parents would do what they know is right to do. Instead of assuming our God-given responsibility, we want someone else to do it for us. We do not want to pay the price.

Are we listening to what God is saying? Are we in the very heartbeat of what God is doing? Are we sure that we have done everything that God has told us to do? If not, we must say, "God, forgive me before it is too late."

Here are three checkpoints to see where we stand

with God today:

First, are we as excited today about God as we were when we first loved Him? Remember when we were first saved? Remember receiving the baptism of the Holy Ghost? Remember when God called individual ministries? Do we take for granted what God has done? God is looking for a people, and if Saul doesn't do it, God has a little David somewhere ready to step in. If we think that we are indispensable, we need to find out who God is.

Secondly, we are judged by our own words. Have we made commitments to the Lord that we are not keeping? We need to ask, "What am I doing with my life? What is the end of this path?" Don't forget — we are judged by our words.

Thirdly, who is big in our eyes? Is God big in our eyes, or have we become big in our own eyes? It is so important that we not forget that if anything happens in ministries, it is because of God's greatness, not our own. Do not look at mortal man. Look at Jesus. God will bring honor to His Church. His Church will be so strong that the gates of hell will not prevail against it. We must have no bitterness or impurity in our hearts. Our spirits must be right before God. Who is big in our eyes—God or ourselves? A leader in God must first be a servant because God's servants will usher in the Kingdom of God in mighty power.

NOTES:

For further information please contact:

Chapel Hill Harvester Church
4650 Flat Shoals Road
Decatur, Georgia 30034
(404) 243-5020

K-Dimension Publications by Earl Paulk
ORDER FORM

Please send me the following items:	Qty.	Amount

BOOKLETS:
Requested Donation $1.05 each.

☐ Form With Power _____ $ _____
☐ Unity of Faith _____ $ _____
☐ The Handwriting On The Wall _____ $ _____
☐ So Close and Yet So Far Away _____ $ _____
☐ The Proper Function of The Church _____ $ _____
☑ The Great Escape Theory _____ $ _____
☐ Laws of the Precious Covenant _____ $ _____
☐ Set For The Defense of The Gospel _____ $ _____
☐ Faith Finished _____ $ _____

BOOKS:

Requested Donation

☐ Divine Runner *$3.25* _____ $ _____
☐ The Wounded Body of Christ *$3.50* _____ $ _____
☐ Ultimate Kingdom *$5.95* _____ $ _____

TOTAL FOR ORDER $ _____

Please allow four to six weeks for delivery
If quicker delivery is desired, add 15% to
the cost of your total order for
FIRST-CLASS POSTAGE & HANDLING.
(For U.S. residents only) $ _____

Residents outside of the U.S.A.
add 6% for postage $ _____

Enclosed is *my gift* to Earl Paulk
Ministries. All gifts are tax deductible $ _____

TOTAL AMOUNT ENCLOSED $ _____

Name_____

Address _____

City _____ State _____ Zip_____

Telephone (_____) _____
Just in case there is a question concerning your order.